*Oracle Press*™

Oracle NT Handbook

Anand Adkoli
Rama Velpuri

Osborne/**McGraw-Hill**

Berkeley New York St. Louis San Francisco
Auckland Bogotá Hamburg London Madrid
Mexico City Milan Montreal New Delhi Panama City
Paris São Paulo Singapore Sydney
Tokyo Toronto

Osborne/**McGraw-Hill**
2600 Tenth Street
Berkeley, California 94710
U.S.A.

For information on translations or book distributors outside the U.S.A., or to arrange bulk purchase discounts for sales promotions, premiums, or fund-raisers, please contact Osborne/**McGraw-Hill** at the above address.

Oracle NT Handbook

1234567890 DOC DOC 90198765432109

ISBN 0-07-211917-9

Publisher
Brandon A. Nordin

Editor-in-Chief
Scott Rogers

Acquisitions Editor
Jeremy Judson

Project Editor
Mark Karmendy

Copy Editor
Dennis Weaver

Proofreader
Pat Mannion

Indexer
Richard Shrout

Computer Designers
Michelle Galicia
Ann Sellers

Illustrator
Lance Ravella

Series Design
Jani Beckwith

To Our Parents

About the Authors...

Anand Adkoli is a development manager at Oracle Corporation in its FrontOffice Applications Division. During the course of his seven-year career at Oracle, he has worked for Worldwide Customer Support, the Products Division, and the Worldwide Alliances and Technology Division. Anand has delivered projects for Oracle Corporation in the United States, Australia, and India. He has published over 40 technical papers and has made numerous presentations at various international conferences on Performance Tuning, Oracle7 and Oracle8 architecture, networking products, and Developer/2000. He has trained Oracle application developers and support staff in Europe and Asia. He is the coauthor of *Oracle Troubleshooting* and *Oracle8 Backup & Recovery Handbook* from Oracle Press.

Rama Velpuri is a director at Oracle's FrontOffice Applications Division. He is the author of Oracle Press' *Oracle Backup & Recovery Handbook* and *Oracle Backup & Recovery Handbook 7.3*, and the coauthor of *Oracle Troubleshooting*. Previously the director of Oracle India Product Engineering Center, Velpuri has worked with Oracle Corporation for almost ten years. He has presented more than 18 technical papers at various IOUW and other Oracle user conferences on disaster recovery, and has trained Oracle support personnel in 17 countries in problem-solving techniques.

Contents At A Glance

Contents

Acknowledgments

s always, this book would not have been possible without the help of others. We would like to thank Louis Selincourt, Vice President of IFAD Operations for his support. Our special thanks to Joe Garcia, Senior Manager, NT Product Management at Oracle Corporation and his team for reviewing this book and providing invaluable suggestions. We want to acknowledge the assistance provided by Kavita Raghunathan in providing us with test cases.

Thanks to the crew at Osborne/McGraw-Hill for helping us complete this book in record time: Jeremy Judson, Mark Karmendy, Michelle Galicia, and Lance Ravella.

A project of this nature could not have been completed without the support of our family and friends. We would like to specially thank Lola, Sunita, Vinu, Anuradha, Akhil, and Sushma for bearing with our long workdays and tight schedules.

Introduction

s an ancient Indian poet once said, *"the worth of a man is known by the effect of his effort"*. As databases have proved to be the nerve centers for many businesses around the world, system and database administrators are under pressure to keep pace with the changes in technology. As we approach a new millennium, Windows NT has become the fastest growing operating system in the world. With version 4.0 of Windows NT, Microsoft Corporation has created an operating system that is scalable and has a widely accepted graphical user interface (GUI). The Oracle8 Server is the accepted leader in relational database technology. Many sites today are attempting to combine the benefits of the Oracle8 Server and the Windows NT operating system.

Oracle NT Handbook is intended to be a one-stop reference for Oracle DBAs on Windows NT. The information in this book will help database administrators manage Oracle8 Servers of all sizes on the Windows NT operating system.

Audience and Scope

Any person who wishes to manage an Oracle8 Server on Windows NT will benefit from this book. It covers all aspects of database administration from installation to performance tuning. The information in this book will allow experienced system and database administrators (DBAs) on other operating systems like UNIX to get a jump-start on administering the Oracle8 Server on Windows NT. In addition, experienced Windows NT administrators can quickly acquire the knowledge required to manage the Oracle8 Server. As we have made no assumptions on current knowledge and skills, this book will prove useful for all levels of users.

How to Use This Book

This book focuses on the Oracle8 Server on Windows NT. We begin with the fundamentals of the Windows NT operating system and cover the tools and utilities available with the operating system. The GUI is explained in sufficient detail for the beginner. After that, we discuss the installation of Oracle8 products on Windows NT. We cover basic installation procedures in client/server and Oracle Corporation's Network Computing Architecture (NCA). We have also included advanced installation topics like database cartridges. We have dedicated a chapter to each of the Oracle tools and utilities that will allow DBAs to perform their tasks using GUI as well as command line interface (CLI).

The book is divided into nine chapters and one appendix.

Chapter 1: An Overview of the Windows NT Operating System

Chapter 1 provides an overview of the Windows NT operating system starting with simple concepts. A detailed coverage of the tools and utilities available with the operating system is provided. We have kept the requirements of Oracle DBAs in mind in this chapter and specific issues related to Oracle software are highlighted.

Chapter 2: Basic Installation of Windows NT

In the first part of this chapter, we provide tips that will allow you to select the hardware resources required for the Oracle8 Server on Windows NT.

We then include information that will benefit individuals attempting a Windows NT installation for the first time.

Chapter 3: Basic Installation of Oracle8 on Windows NT

In Chapter 3, we cover a basic installation of the Oracle8 Server, the Web Application Server, and Net8. The possible configurations from stand-alone to three-tier architecture are discussed. Examples are included for each configuration.

Chapter 4: Advanced Installation of Oracle8

In Chapter 4, we include the advanced options and cartridges available with the Oracle8 Server. The chapter begins with the *objects* and the *partitioning* options. After these, we cover Oracle8 cartridges. Useful information on distributed databases, Parallel Server, and advanced replication is included.

Chapter 5: GUI-Based Approach to Oracle Administration

Oracle8 for Windows NT provides an entire array of tools and utilities that allow DBAs to manage the Oracle8 Server entirely with GUI. In Chapter 5, we cover a majority of these tools including Database Assistant and Oracle Enterprise Manager. Helpful examples and illustrations are included.

Chapter 6: CLI-Based Approach to Oracle Administration

Many experienced DBAs prefer to use CLI for routine DBA tasks as it allows for a high degree of automation through scripts and scheduling. In Chapter 6, we have focused on CLI solutions to routine DBA tasks. A discussion of the CLI tools and utilities is also provided.

Chapter 7: Advanced Oracle Administration

Chapter 7 includes advanced topics like Multithreaded Server and the advanced Net8 features like checksumming and encryption. We have also covered the diagnostic tools and utilities available with the Oracle8 Server. A section on performance tuning issues with focus on Windows NT is also provided.

Chapter 8: Database Upgrades and Migration

Many sites require that you upgrade from earlier versions of the Oracle
Server to Oracle8. Many others need to migrate their databases from other
operating systems such as UNIX and Novell Netware. Chapter 8 is
dedicated to database upgrades and migration. Oracle Data Migration
Assistant has been detailed.

Chapter 9: Windows NT for UNIX and Netware Administrators

This chapter is dedicated to experienced Oracle DBAs on UNIX and Novell
Netware. It is designed to be a quick reference to those who are familiar
with Oracle database administration on UNIX and Novell Netware. Chapter
9 provides Windows NT solutions to common tasks on UNIX and Novell
Netware.

Appendix A: Frequently Asked Questions

Appendix A provides short answers to some frequently asked questions on
Oracle8 for Windows NT.

CHAPTER

1

An Overview of the Windows NT Operating System

icrosoft Windows NT has fast become one of the most widely used operating systems in the world. It has evolved considerably since its first release in the summer of 1993. With version 4.0 of Windows NT, Microsoft has created an operating system that is scalable and has the familiar look and feel of Windows 95. The graphical user interface (GUI) of Windows 95 has been embraced by the computer industry. Today, Windows NT is accepted as a premier operating system for the Intel-based x86 machines. In fact, it has become so popular that it is being made available on other platforms such as Digital Alpha. Many sites that had standardized on other operating systems such as UNIX are now beginning to realize the value of Windows NT as a server. The client/server architecture adopted by Windows NT has made it a viable alternative in cooperative computing. In this chapter we will provide a quick introduction to Windows NT for the novice user. Our goal is to introduce Windows NT features that are useful to Oracle database administrators (DBAs). Individuals who are familiar with Windows NT administration can browse this chapter for information on specific tasks that apply to Oracle software. Throughout this book we will use Windows NT 4.0 and the Oracle8 Server in all our discussions.

We will begin the chapter with a brief introduction to the Windows NT architecture and then look at some useful tools, commands, and utilities for Oracle DBAs. We will also provide a quick look at some administrative tasks in Windows NT. If you are an experienced administrator on any other operating system and Windows NT is new to you, this section will be useful for you. In Chapter 2, we will take a quick look at a Windows NT installation.

Windows NT Architecture

The Windows NT architecture consists of a set of core routines—known as the *kernel*—and a number of subsystems that extend the capabilities of the kernel. Each of the subsystems provides support for a distinct function. For example, the Windows on Windows (WOW) subsystem is used to run all 16-bit Windows applications. The operating system has two distinct modes: the *kernel mode* and the *user mode*. All programs must run in one of the two modes. The kernel mode is used to execute low-level routines such as those that access physical devices on the machine. Devices like the motherboard, the CPU, and the drives are only accessible from kernel routines. Device drivers to control such devices are also run in the kernel mode. It is also important to note that the memory space is completely managed by the kernel. The user mode is used to execute the subsystems and user applications. A key difference between the two modes is that programs in the user mode never directly access a physical device. User-mode applications also need to be validated from the standpoint of system security. On the other hand, programs in the kernel mode have direct access to physical devices and have a somewhat loose concept of security.

The two modes ensure that there is a distinct boundary between programs. User-mode applications cannot crash the system or compromise system security by accessing kernel areas. Similarly, a poorly written user-mode program cannot take control of a physical device, because these devices can only be accessed by the kernel. In general, user-mode programs and subsystems package their requests to use resources on the system using kernel routines.

Win32 Subsystem

The largest and most important subsystem in Windows NT is the Win32 subsystem. This subsystem also provides the 32-bit interface that is used by most Windows NT applications.

An application program interface (API) provides access to all the functions necessary for 32-bit applications. The API includes graphical device interface (GDI), functions for multimedia capabilities, remote procedure calls (RPC), and other system services. The GDI provides all the graphics functionality. The Windows NT multimedia layer provides support for audio and video while RPCs provide the ability for distributed computing. System services are required to access the memory, file systems, threads, and processes. Applications can also create windows, pop-ups, and dialog boxes using the Win32 API. Windows NT also provides some standard extensions with Win32. A good example of a Win32 extension is Dynamic Data Exchange (DDE), which is a form of interprocess communication (IPC) that allows Windows applications to share data.

Support for Multithreaded Applications and Multitasking

The idea behind multithreading is to allow the main program to continue execution while other threads execute subsidiary routines simultaneously. Windows NT enables applications to use more than one "thread" of execution. Threads allow portions of the same program to run asynchronously.

Windows NT is a preemptive multitasking system. It allows many programs to run simultaneously through time-sharing. Each program is allowed to use a resource for a time interval that is decided by the operating system. Critical resources like the CPU are shared by programs at the discretion of the operating system. The preemptive nature is critical to ensure that a program does not take control of a resource. It is possible to interrupt a program from the operating system at any point during execution. The Windows Task Manager is used for this purpose. In contrast, earlier versions, including Windows 3.1, could crash as a result of a malfunctioning application. Such occurrences are unlikely on Windows NT.

Networking Support

In today's world, most computers need the ability to access other computers using networks. Windows NT provides support for popular protocols including the Transmission Control Protocol/Internet Protocol (TCP/IP), NWLink (IPX/SPX) from Novell, and the NetBIOS Extended User Interface (NetBEUI). TCP/IP is available on almost all commercial operating systems and is necessary to access public networks such as the Internet. IPX is Novell Corporation's proprietary network layer, and is still dominant around the world. NetBEUI allows Windows NT to support networks using Microsoft LAN Manager and Windows for Workgroups. It can also be used to network computers using Windows NT.

Oracle provides a layer of software called Net8 that allows clients to connect to the Oracle Server over the network. Net8 is required to support Oracle's client/server architecture. The Net8 layer uses the underlying network for data transfer. You must install the Net8 Server software on the database server and the Net8 Client software on the client's. Net8 provides protocol adapters for all popular network protocols. You must install protocol adapters for all network protocols you wish to use for Oracle client/server connections. Details on Net8 are provided in Chapters 5 and 7.

Security

Security is always a big concern on any operating system. Windows NT 4.0 provides C2 security as defined by the National Computer Security Center (NCSC). Security is controlled at various levels using rights and privileges. A *right* typically applies to an object—for example, access to a file—while *privileges* apply to operations on the system. The privilege to load a device driver is a good example. System-level security ensures that the Windows NT registry is protected from malicious users. Application-level security is easily implemented on Windows NT. Windows NT also provides support for domains and groups. These features allow administrators to control security for a large group of users.

Oracle provides a facility that allows for external authentication of users via the operating system. You can use Windows NT user authentication to manage logins to the Oracle server. External authentication is discussed in Chapter 5.

Compatibility for 16-Bit Applications

Windows NT provides full support for 16-bit applications for MS-DOS and Windows 3.1. This allows for backward compatibility and ensures that older applications can run under Windows NT. The Windows on Windows (WOW) subsystem is used to run 16-bit Windows applications.

You can run most Oracle 16-bit applications on Windows NT. If you are using client/server applications, you must install the proper 16-bit version of SQL*Net in order to use a 16-bit application against an Oracle server. Chapter 7 provides more information on this subject.

File Systems

Windows NT 4.0 supports three file systems: File Allocation Table (FAT), New Technology File System (NTFS), and CD-ROM File System (CDFS). Earlier versions of Windows NT also supported the High Performance File System (HPFS) for OS/2 support. Brief discussions of the three file systems are provided to help you choose a file system based on your needs.

Raw partitions can also be used for Oracle8 Server on Windows NT. The Oracle Parallel Server requires you to use raw partitions.

File Allocation Table (FAT)

FAT is a commonly used file system. It is supported by all versions of DOS, Windows 3.1, and Windows 95. If you want to access partitions from a combination of these operating systems (for example, to configure dual-boot), FAT is the best choice since partitions are visible from either DOS, Windows 3.1, Windows 95, or Windows NT. However, the FAT file system does not provide full C2 security. You must also consider using FAT to avoid backward-compatibility issues. For example, if you are migrating an Oracle database from Windows 95 to Windows NT, continue to use FAT. The impact of the 8.3 filename restriction must be considered before choosing FAT. Oracle 16-bit software also requires FAT since it only supports the 8.3 filenaming convention. So, if you are planning to use any 16-bit Oracle applications, you will need a FAT partition.

New Technology File System (NTFS)

NTFS was developed especially for the Windows NT operating system. It provides support for large-capacity media, long filenames, and security attributes. NTFS also provides support for hard links and case-sensitive naming. If you are planning to use Windows NT exclusively and have no need to share data on the partition with other 16-bit operating systems like DOS and Windows 95, use NTFS. If you are planning to use the Portable Operating System Interface (POSIX) subsystem on Windows NT, you must have at least one NTFS partition. All Oracle8 software supports NTFS.

CD-ROM File System (CDFS)

As the name suggests, CDFS supports read-only media such as CD-ROMs. Most of the systems today have an internal CD-ROM drive, which is visible as CDFS.

The Oracle DBA is normally not required to make a choice of a file system for Windows NT. If you do need to make a choice, we recommend NTFS for its support of long filenames and for better security. Of course, you must use FAT if you want to make the file system visible to 16-bit operating systems like DOS and Windows 95. In addition, a CD-ROM under CDFS is almost always necessary, as most Oracle software is available on CD-ROM only.

Windows NT Tools, Commands, and User Interface

Windows NT provides several commands, tools, and utilities that allow for easy administration. Users can interact easily with the operating system because of the GUI. Following are brief descriptions of some of these facilities that will be useful to Oracle DBAs. If you are an experienced Windows NT user, browse these sections for any Oracle-specific information that we have included in our discussion. We must caution you that there are several methods to accomplish a task on Windows NT. The method we use to perform a task may not be the one that you prefer.

Disk Administrator

The Windows NT Disk Administrator is a GUI tool that allows you to manage disks on Windows NT systems. It is typically used in situations where you want to perform certain disk operations after installing Windows NT.

Some important tasks that can be accomplished using the Disk Administrator are as follows:

■   Creating and Deleting Partitions

■   Managing Volumes

■   Creating and Deleting Logical Drives

■   Assigning Drive Letters to disks and CD-ROM drives

■   Format partitions for FAT or NTFS

To access Disk Administrator, select Start | Programs | Administrative Tools (Common) | Disk Administrator or run **windisk.exe** from the **winnt\system32** folder. You must be a member of the Administrators group in order to use Disk Administrator. Figure 1-1 shows the main screen of the Disk Administrator.

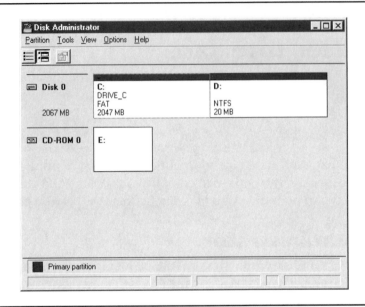

FIGURE 1-1. *Windows NT Disk Administrator*

Oracle administrators typically use Disk Administrator to format a partition for FAT or NTFS before installing the Oracle Server. Occasionally, you might want to change the drive letter of the CD-ROM drive. We strongly recommend that you do not change the drive letter of a partition after installing Oracle products. Oracle software uses entries in the Windows registry that will become invalid if you change the drive letter. You will also need to update the database control file if you choose to alter the drive letter of a drive containing database and log files.

User Manager

Windows NT provides C2-level security as defined by the National Computer Security Center. The Windows NT User Manager is a GUI tool that allows you to manage security and user accounts on Windows NT.

Some important tasks that can be accomplished using the User Manager are as follows:

- Create and manage users and groups

- Manage rights and policies for users and accounts

- Audit policies

- Reset passwords

To access User Manager, select Start | Programs | Administrative Tools (Common) | User Manager or run **musrmgr.exe** from the **winnt\system32** folder. Figure 1-2 shows the main screen of the User Manager.

You can view detailed information for a user account by selecting the Properties item under the File menu. Figure 1-3 shows the properties of a user account named *SYSAD*.

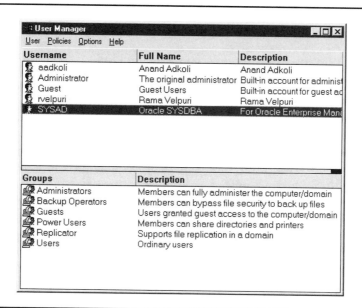

FIGURE 1-2. *Windows NT User Manager*

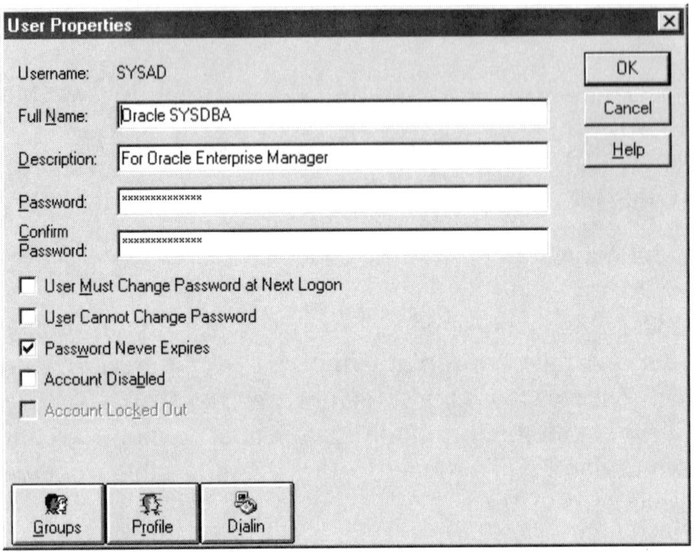

FIGURE 1-3. *User Properties screen in User Manager*

You can control group memberships by clicking on the Groups button. Figure 1-4 shows group information for the user *SYSAD*.

User Manager can also be used to reset passwords for a user. Windows NT administrators can reset the password for any user on the system using the User Properties screen of User Manager. Figure 1-5 shows the User Properties screen for a user called *aadkoli*.

Most Oracle software does not require any special privileges for execution on Windows NT. Oracle Enterprise Manager is one exception. A special privilege is required for a user to execute jobs in Oracle Enterprise Manager. Refer to Chapter 5 for more information on this subject.

If you are using NTFS, we highly recommend that you create a special Windows NT user (or a group of administrators) for Oracle administrative tasks.

Event Viewer

Event Viewer is a tool used to monitor events under Windows NT. Windows NT creates logs for three classes of events: System events, Security events, and Application events. All event logs can be viewed from the Event Viewer if you have the required privileges. A typical System event is when Windows

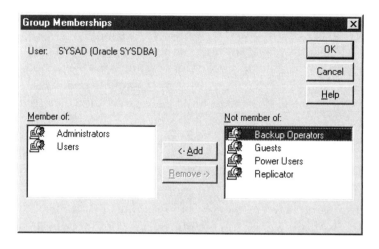

FIGURE 1-4.   *Group Memberships screen in User Manager*

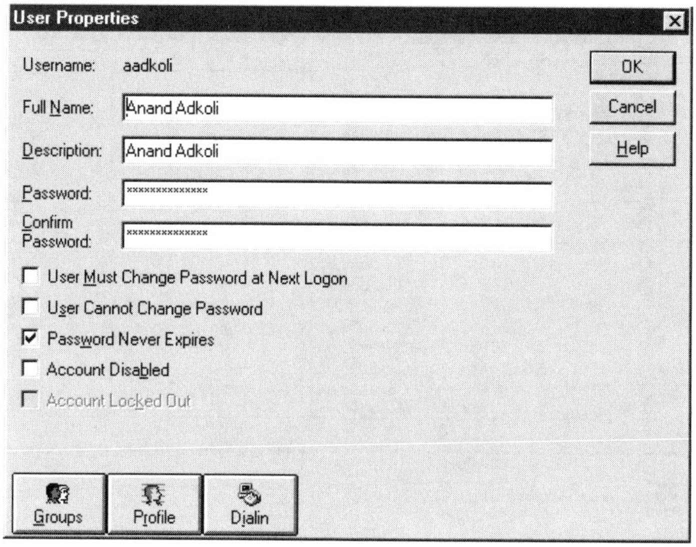

FIGURE 1-5.   *User Properties screen in User Manager*

NT is unable to load a device driver. Security event logs can be viewed by administrators to determine if security has been violated on the system. Application events are recorded by Windows NT applications. For example, when you start up or shut down an Oracle instance, corresponding entries are recorded in the application event log. Figure 1-6 shows the Event Viewer and Figure 1-7 shows a typical entry for the Oracle8 server. Pay special attention to the icons in the first column of the event log. These icons have special meaning. For example, the Stop sign indicates a warning and the *i* indicates the successful execution of some event.

The *Eventlog* service creates the event logs. You can control this service by using the Services applet in the Windows NT Control Panel. If you are not interested in event logs, you can shut down this service.

To access Event Viewer, select Start | Programs | Administrative Tools (Common) | Event Viewer or run **eventvwr.exe** from the **winnt\system32** folder.

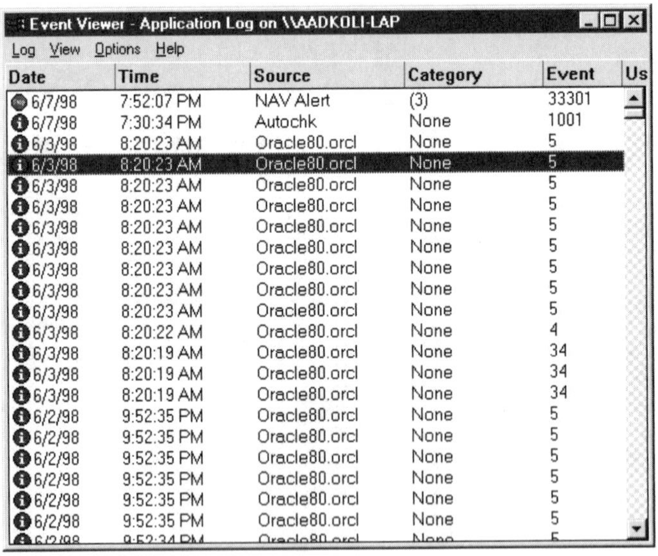

FIGURE 1-6. *Windows NT Event Viewer screen*

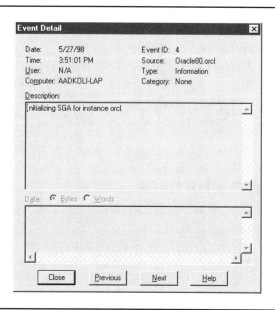

FIGURE 1-7. *An application event for the Oracle8 Server*

As an Oracle administrator, you can use Event Viewer in situations when an Oracle-related service fails to start. If a Windows NT service is unable to start, you will see a warning dialog box similar to this one:

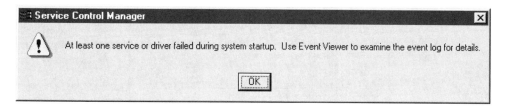

The Event Viewer has a built-in search capability that can be used to search for events based on Type, Source, Category, Computer, or User. In addition, you should regularly monitor the **alert.log** file, which provides information on database errors.

TIP
You can sort and filter events displayed in the event log. We suggest that you create a filter that provides a view of Oracle events. You can accomplish this by choosing Filter Events from the View menu and entering appropriate information in the Filter dialog box as shown in Figure 1-8.

Performance Monitor

Performance Monitor is a GUI tool that allows you to monitor the performance of Windows NT systems across a network. The performance of the CPUs, memory, caches, and processes can be viewed through charts and reports. Alerts can also be generated based on user-specified threshold values. Figure 1-9 shows a chart that displays the processor usage on a Windows NT system.

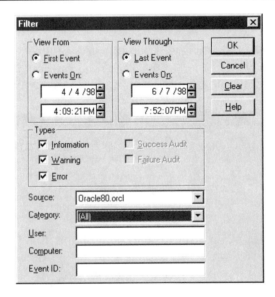

FIGURE 1-8. *Filter dialog box in Event Viewer*

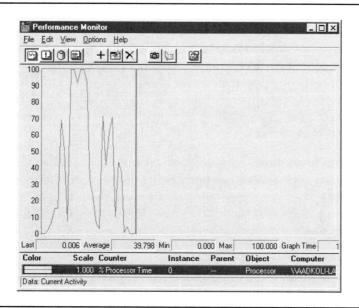

FIGURE 1-9.   *Chart displaying processor usage on Windows NT*

To access Performance Monitor, select Start | Programs | Administrative Tools (Common) | Performance Monitor or run **perfmon.exe** from the **winnt\system32** folder.

As an Oracle administrator, it is critical to ensure that adequate system resources are available to ensure good performance. Resources like processor usage, paging file, and physical memory should be monitored on a regular basis. You can use the information from Performance Monitor to tune your system. For example, if the paging file size is consistently 20MB, you should consider adding physical memory to compensate for this paging activity.

Windows NT Diagnostics

The Windows NT Diagnostics tool provides system information, including system memory, the Windows NT environment, the ports, and interrupts used by devices. You can also get consolidated information on the services running on the system. This utility is typically used to diagnose some fault on the system.

To access Windows NT Diagnostics tool, select Start | Programs | Administrative Tools (Common) | Windows NT Diagnostics or run **winmsd.exe** from the **winnt\system32** folder. You can also access a remote computer on the network by specifying the computer name on the network. To access a computer named **ntserver1**, you can use the following command:

```
C:\> winmsd \\ntserver1
```

As an Oracle administrator, you can ensure that the Oracle environment such as PATH variable is set properly using this tool. Additionally, you can monitor the Oracle services running on the system and the memory usage from this utility. Figure 1-10 shows a sample screen from the Diagnostics utility that shows the current environment on the system.

FIGURE 1-10.   *Environment viewed from the Windows NT Diagnostics tool*

Remote Access Admin

The Remote Access Admin utility allows you to configure your system for remote access (RAS) over telephone or leased lines like ISDN. You can control the level of access to a network, callbacks, and send messages to active users using RAS.

To access the utility, select Start | Programs | Administrative Tools (Common) | Remote Access Admin or run **rasadmin.exe** from the **winnt\system32** folder. One restriction to be aware of is that on the Windows NT Server, RAS supports up to 255 simultaneous client connections, whereas on the Windows NT Workstation, RAS supports only one client. Oracle software has no special RAS configuration requirements.

Repair Disk

Windows NT provides a utility called Repair Disk that allows you to save your current system settings to an emergency repair disk. This emergency disk can be used to restore your Windows NT setup if the system files get damaged. Most importantly, the repair disk allows you to repair the Windows registry. You should use the Repair Disk utility to update the emergency disk every time you change your hardware or software configuration.

To start the Repair Disk utility, select Start | Programs | Administrative Tools (Common) | Repair Disk or run **rdisk.exe** from the **winnt\system32** folder. We recommend that you update the emergency repair disk after an Oracle installation or upgrade.

Task Manager

Windows NT Task Manager is a utility that allows you to monitor and control all the programs and processes running on your system. This utility allows you to get a quick preview of the CPU and Memory usage on your system. Figure 1-11 shows the Task Manager screen with a list of applications running on the system.

FIGURE 1-11. *Sample screen of the applications running on Windows NT*

Figure 1-12 shows a screen that provides performance statistics on the system. The performance statistics can be used to gauge the load on the Windows NT system.

Windows NT Task Manager is especially useful in shutting down malfunctioning Windows applications. Occasionally, an application might hang or stop responding to user input. In such situations, you can start Task Manager and terminate the offending program.

You can also view the amount of CPU and memory used by an individual process, along with the process ID (PID) of that process, using Task Manager. Figure 1-13 shows a sample screen that provides a listing of the processes running on the system. Note the **oracle80.exe** process for the Oracle8 server.

Task Manager can be accessed in different ways. The method you choose will depend on what is convenient in a given situation. You can access Task Manager by running **taskmgr.exe** from the **\winnt\system32** folder. Alternatively, you can use the CTRL-ALT-DELETE keys to bring up a dialog box from which you can invoke the Task Manager. This method is

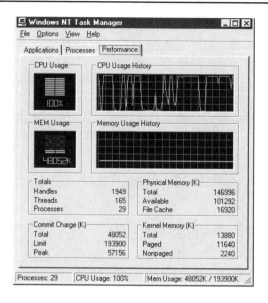

FIGURE 1-12. *Sample screen of the performance statistics on Windows NT*

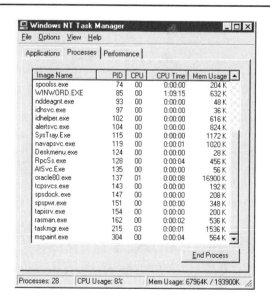

FIGURE 1-13. *Sample screen of process listing on Windows NT*

especially useful when you are in an application that has stopped responding and the desktop does not respond to any other keys or mouse clicks. Finally, you can access Task Manager by clicking the right mouse button in the taskbar.

Under normal conditions, you should not need to use Task Manager to shut down Oracle applications. However, you can use Task Manager to force an Oracle application to shut down. We do not recommend shutting down the database using Task Manager at any time. If there is an urgent need to force the database to shut down, you should use Oracle Instance Manager or Oracle Server Manager to shut down the database with the Abort option.

Windows NT Scheduler

The Windows NT Scheduler can be used to schedule the execution of batch or command jobs on Windows NT. A Windows NT service named Schedule must be running in order to use this facility. The Windows NT Scheduler can be accessed by running **at.exe** from the **\winnt\system32** folder. Jobs can be scheduled at a specified time and date, and you can choose to run a job on a recurring basis. Jobs can be targeted on any machine available on the network if you have proper permissions.

NOTE
Do not confuse the term "Windows NT Scheduler" with the mechanism used to prioritize threads for execution and the concept of time slicing.

Oracle administrators can use the Windows NT **at** command to schedule startups and shutdowns. In addition, this command provides a convenient method to schedule backup jobs for the database. Refer to Chapter 7 for more information on this subject.

Windows NT Network Monitor

If you have installed the Windows NT Server, you can monitor network data and performance across the network. You can get statistics on any Windows NT machine on your network that is running the Network Agent service. Click on Start | Programs | Administrative Tools menu to start NT Network Monitor.

Windows NT Backup

Windows NT Backup is a GUI tool that allows you to create backups of designated FAT and NTFS volumes to tape. Additionally, the utility allows you to create backups on an incremental basis. You can schedule backups and obtain logs of backups using this utility, and create multiple backup sets on one tape. The same utility is also used to restore data from a tape. You must configure a tape drive on the system using the Tape Devices applet under the Windows NT Control Panel.

To access the utility, select Start | Programs | Administrative Tools (Common) | Backup or run **ntbackup.exe** from the **winnt\system32** folder. Figure 1-14 shows the startup screen of the Backup utility.

The Windows NT Backup utility is useful to backup Oracle applications such as Oracle Developer/2000 files to a tape. It is not very useful to backup a database unless you ensure that the database is shut down normally. We recommend that you write a command job for Oracle database backups or schedule backup jobs using Oracle Enterprise Manager. If you are backing up the hard disk of a Windows NT machine to a tape using the Backup utility, we suggest you do not include the Oracle database files in the

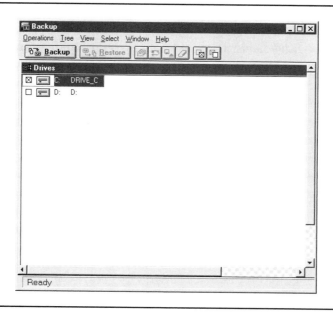

FIGURE 1-14. *Sample screen of the Windows NT Backup utility*

backup unless the database is shut down. If the database is running when the backup is taken, the resulting backup is not useful for recovery. See the section on backups in Chapter 5 for information on database backups. You can also save some time and space on the tape by not including the database files in the backup in such cases.

Windows NT Explorer

The Windows NT Explorer is a GUI tool that can be used to view the folders (directories) and files on a system. The Windows NT Explorer has replaced the File Manager from earlier versions of Windows. You can view the folders belonging to the local machine or those on the network if you have an access path and the appropriate permissions. You can map drive letters to network drives for your convenience. Folders can be designated for sharing across the network. If you are using the NTFS, you can set file permissions using the Explorer. If you are using the FAT system, security is not guaranteed because file permissions do not work under FAT.

To access the Windows NT Explorer, select Start | Programs | Windows NT Explorer. Alternatively, you can run **explorer.exe** from the **\winnt** folder. Some users prefer the old File Manager. You can access the File Manager by running **winfile.exe** from the **\winnt\system32** folder.

Oracle administrators use the Windows NT Explorer to manage files. The Explorer can be used to create a cold backup by using the **copy** function of the Explorer.

CAUTION
*Moving or renaming database files, log files, and control files requires special procedures. Refer to Chapter 8 for examples of moving data files and log files. Oracle software is installed by default in the **\orant** folder.*

Windows Taskbar

The Windows Taskbar appears normally at the bottom of the screen on Windows NT. It contains the START menu that can be used to launch other programs, access the help system, and find files. The taskbar also shows the date and time along with icons for some devices, such as audio devices. When a program is running, a button is created for that program in the

Taskbar. You can navigate between programs by clicking on the appropriate button in the Taskbar. You can customize the Taskbar by right-clicking the mouse on the Taskbar and setting the appropriate properties. You can also access Windows Task Manager by right-clicking the mouse on the Taskbar.

Windows Desktop

The screen that is seen when you start Windows NT is known as the desktop. You can customize the desktop by right-clicking the mouse on any free portion of the desktop and editing the property sheet. Among other properties, you can set the background screen and change the screen saver settings by modifying the desktop properties. The desktop can be customized for individual users under Windows NT. You can customize the desktop quickly by opening the **\winnt\Profiles** folder and editing the appropriate shortcuts. Separate folders contain shortcuts for All users, Administrator, Default user, etc.

   If you choose to install Oracle Enterprise Manager, you can optionally display the Administrator Toolbar on the desktop. This will allow you to launch Oracle Enterprise Manager (OEM) Tools like Instance Manager and Storage Manager quickly. We recommend that you create shortcuts to your favorite applications, such as Oracle Forms Builder and SQL*Plus.

Shortcuts

Windows NT allows you to create shortcuts on the desktop. Shortcuts can be created for programs and even folders. We recommend that you create shortcuts for frequently accessed Oracle applications. Some especially useful ones include the Services applet, Oracle Server Manager, Oracle Enterprise Manager, and utilities such as the Net8 Listener control utility named **lsnrctl80.exe**.

   When you create shortcuts, choose the starting folder carefully. For your application shortcuts, it is useful to set this to the folder containing the application executables or binaries. For some shortcuts like Server Manager, you may set the starting folder as the one containing your SQL scripts. To set the starting folder, right-click the mouse on the shortcut and select the Properties item. A tab named Shortcut is available on the property sheet. You can set the starting folder in the field named Start in. We also suggest that you set a startup key sequence for quick access to your favorite shortcuts.

Control Panel

The Windows NT Control Panel can be used to configure system accessories such as modems and tape drives, configure printers, set the system date and time, and configure the network. The Control Panel can be accessed by selecting Start | Settings | Control Panel. Alternatively, you could access the Control Panel from the Windows NT Explorer. Figure 1-15 shows a typical Windows NT Control Panel.

Oracle administrators use the Control Panel for a variety of tasks. The network interface card and the network protocol, along with other network settings, must be configured using the Network applet in the Control Panel. Printers can be configured using the Printers applet in the Control Panel. If you plan to use open database connectivity (ODBC), you must use the

FIGURE 1-15. *Windows NT Control Panel*

ODBC Administrator applet in the Control Panel. Virtual memory settings can be changed by using the System applet. The Windows NT environment can also be set by using the System applet. If you are planning to use a tape device for a backup, an applet is available for this purpose in the Control Panel. The Services applet is necessary to start up and shut down services on your Windows NT machine. We recommend that you set Oracle services to start up automatically.

One setting that can impact application performance is the performance boost setting. You can access this setting by selecting the Performance tab in the System applet. For best performance, set maximum boost for applications running in the foreground. However, if you run several applications simultaneously on your Windows NT machine, you might want to choose a setting that is more appropriate for your needs.

Windows NT Services

Windows NT and applications under Windows NT use a variety of services that are necessary for specific tasks. Services are controlled using the Services applet from the Control Panel. You can start, stop, and disable individual services. Some system services like the Scheduler and Eventlog are installed when you install Windows NT. Other services are installed when you install application software such as Oracle or networking software. You can designate a service to start up automatically when the system starts up or you can choose to start up a service manually. Most services are owned by the built-in user named *System*. Under certain conditions, you can specify a user to own a service. We recommend that you create a shortcut to the Services applet on the desktop since it is accessed frequently.

Installation of Oracle software creates many services on your Windows NT machine. Services for the database, Oracle Web Application Server, and Net8 are examples of Oracle services. Table 1-1 provides a listing of some common Oracle services.

Table 1-1 is by no means a comprehensive listing of Oracle services. Other Oracle services are installed for Web Request Brokers (WRBs) and Oracle cartridges like Oracle ConText. Figure 1-16 shows a list of Oracle services on our test machine.

Name of Service	Description	Recommended Startup	Comments
OracleServiceORCL	Oracle RDBMS service	Automatic	Must be running in order for the database to be started
OracleStartORCL	Startup Oracle instance	Automatic	You can use Server Manager or Instance Manager to start up the database as an alternative
OracleTNSListener80	Oracle Net8 listener	Automatic	Only required if you need Oracle clients to connect to database services on the machine
OracleAgent80	Oracle Intelligent Agent	Automatic	Only required if you plan to schedule jobs and configure events using Oracle Enterprise Manager
OracleWWWListener 30Admin	Oracle Web Application Server 3.0 Admin service	Manual	Only required if you plan to administer Oracle Web Application Server

TABLE I-I. *Common Oracle Services on Windows NT*

Name of Service	Description	Recommended Startup	Comments
OracleWWWListener 30xxxx	Oracle Web Application Server, typically on port 80	Manual	Set it to Automatic if you plan to run Oracle Web Application Server on the machine
OraclWebAssistant	Oracle Web Assistant	Manual	Required if you want to create HTML pages dynamically based on SQL queries using the Web Assistant

TABLE 1-1.   *Common Oracle Services on Windows NT* (continued)

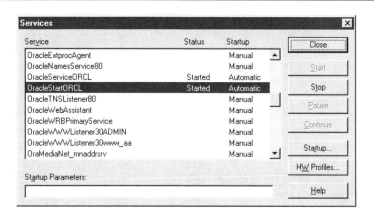

FIGURE 1-16.   *Sample list of services*

NOTE
Our test machine was running Windows NT Workstation 4.0 and had the Oracle8 Server and Oracle Web Application Server installed on it.

Windows Registry

Windows NT maintains a database that contains information about a system's configuration. In Microsoft Windows 3.1, such information was stored in individual **.ini** files. The database is maintained in a specific hierarchy made up of trees, subtrees, keys, and values, which are maintained in sections known as *hives.* Most applications modify the Windows registry during their installation process. It is highly unlikely that you will need to edit the Windows registry manually. In the rare event that you need to edit the registry, we suggest you create a backup by using the **Export Registry** function in the Registry Editor. The Windows registry also can be viewed and edited using the Registry Editor. The editor can be invoked by executing **regedit.exe** from the **\winnt** folder or **regedt32.exe** from the **\winnt\system32** folder. You will get slightly different views of the registry depending on whether you use **regedit.exe** or **regedt32.exe**. Table 1-2 provides a summary of the *root keys* in the registry.

Oracle software creates several entries in the Windows NT registry. Most of the entries can be viewed by expanding the Software node under the hive

Root Key	Description
HKEY_CLASSES_ROOT	Includes entries for OLE and file associations. These entries are used by applications to associate file extensions with an application. For example, the **.doc** file extension can be associated with Microsoft Word.
HKEY_CURRENT_USER	Includes user settings and the profile for the current user.

TABLE 1-2. *Description of Root Keys in the Windows NT Registry*

Root Key	Description
HKEY_LOCAL_MACHINE	Includes settings and information about the local computer, such as installed hardware. Settings pertaining to device drivers and system services are also maintained here.
HKEY_USERS	Data for individual user profiles on the machine.
HKEY_CURRENT_CONFIG	Current configuration settings for software.
HKEY_DYN_DATA	Internal to Windows NT, not configurable by the user.

TABLE 1-2.   *Description of Root Keys in the Windows NT Registry* (continued)

HKEY_LOCAL_MACHINE. Figure 1-17 shows the Oracle entries in the registry of our test machine.

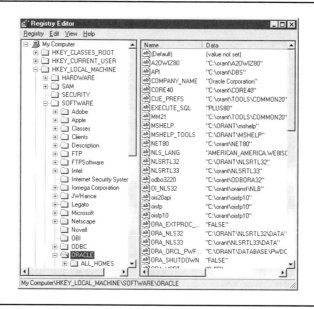

FIGURE 1-17.   *Sample Oracle entries in the Windows NT registry*

Windows NT Help

Windows NT has a fairly comprehensive online help facility. Most Windows NT programs provide a Help menu item on the application window. Search and find facilities are also available. In many situations, you can access context-sensitive help by pressing the F1 key on your keyboard. Many applications also provide an answer wizard in addition to the standard search function.

All Oracle software is available with a help system that is integrated into the Windows NT operating system. Help can be accessed from the Help menu or from the F1 key on the keyboard. Oracle also provides online documentation in HTML format. Some Oracle software also provide online documentation in Adobe's Acrobat format (**.pdf** files). Older Oracle software provided online help in Oracle Corporation's Oracle Book format.

Common Administrative Tasks

As mentioned earlier, Windows NT 4.x has a widely accepted GUI based on Windows 95. As we have seen throughout this chapter, many tools and utilities are provided with a GUI that allow for easy administration. In this section, we will highlight some common administrative tasks that will get you started as a Windows NT administrator. If appropriate, we will also mention the equivalent command(s) in the UNIX operating system.

Creating Groups and Users

Use User Manager to manage groups and users in Windows NT. If you are an authorized user, you can create and manage groups and users. Start User Manager by clicking on Start | Programs | Administrative Tools | User Manager. Menu items for creating new users and groups are available in the User menu. You can set appropriate properties for your group or user. Note that Windows NT has some built-in groups such as Administrators, Users, and Guests. For most sites, the predefined groups are sufficient for all practical purposes. You might want to create a group for Oracle DBAs, which will allow you to control access rights to Oracle files.

When you create a user, pay special attention to the password properties that you set for the user. You can force users to change their password and even set up the account so that the user cannot change his/her password.

You can also disable a user from logging in by setting the Account Disabled property.

Windows NT does not have files such as **/etc/passwd** and **/etc/group**.

Setting and Resetting Passwords

If you are an authorized user, you can set and reset passwords for users on the system. Typically, you must belong to the Windows NT Administrators group to be able to do so. In order to set or reset the password for a user, start User Manager by clicking on Start | Programs | Administrative Tools | User Manager. Select the user for whom you want to set the password and select the Properties item from the User menu. Type and confirm the password. Click the OK button and exit User Manager. Note that Windows NT places an asterisk for every character that you type in the password, for security reasons. However, once the password is typed and stored, the number of asterisks shown may not correspond to the actual length of the password.

If you want to change your own password and you do not have access to the User Manager, you can do so from the Windows NT Security dialog screen that can be accessed by pressing the CTRL-ALT-DELETE keys. Click the Change Password button to change your own password. Note that you will be asked to provide the old password when you attempt to change your password. If you have forgotten your password, you must reset it using the User Manager, using an authorized administrator account.

The Windows NT User Manager is the equivalent of the **passwd** command in UNIX.

Exploring the File System

The Windows NT Explorer provides you with a GUI to explore the file system on your system and the network. To access the NT Explorer, click on Start | Programs | Windows NT Explorer. You can also access the Explorer by right-clicking the mouse on the Start menu and choosing the Explore option. You can also use the shortcut labeled My Computer on your desktop.

Of course, if you are an experienced MS-DOS user, you can use DOS commands to explore the file system from the MS-DOS command prompt. Standard MS-DOS commands such as **dir** and **cd** can be used.

If you are an experienced UNIX user and you are comfortable with the **ls** command with all its available options, you can get similar functionality by setting options under the View menu of the Windows NT Explorer. You can also type **dir /?** at the command prompt to get all the options for this command.

Searching for Files and Computers

Windows NT has an advanced Find utility with a GUI. You can search for files by name or by content. Standard wildcards like an '*' and a '?' are supported. You can also search for computers on your network. To access the Find utility, click on Start | Find. If you select the Files and Folders option, you will see a dialog box similar to the one shown here:

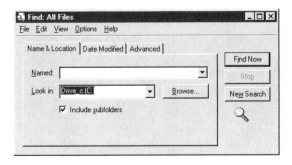

Windows NT also allows you to search for files by date properties and content. You must select the Date Modified or the Advanced tab in the Find utility. The **find** command is also available under the Tools menu of the Windows NT Explorer.

If you are an experienced MS-DOS user, you can search for files containing a certain string by using the **find** command at the command prompt. Type **find /?** to get help on this command at the command prompt. You can also search for a file by using the **dir /s** command as shown below:

```
C:\> dir oracle80.* /s
  Volume in drive C is DRIVE_C
  Volume Serial Number is 3127-16CF
  Directory of C:\orant\BIN
12/22/97  06:37p              8,625,664 ORACLE80.EXE
          1 File(s)           8,625,664 bytes
```

```
Directory of C:\orant\DBS
08/14/96  10:57a                    1,578 ORACLE80.PMW
               1 File(s)              1,578 bytes
```

The Windows NT Find utility is equivalent to the **find** command on UNIX.

Accessing and Sharing Network Resources

If you have configured your machine to run on a network, you can access other resources such as printers and file systems on the network if you have the proper permissions. Windows NT provides a GUI utility to browse the network. Click on the shortcut named Network Neighborhood on your desktop to get quick access to the network resources. You can also access the Network Neighborhood from the Windows NT Explorer. Once you access a computer on the network, you can see all the available resources on the machine. You can map logical drive letters to any remote folder on the network using the Map Network Drive function in Windows NT Explorer.

You can also share resources on your computer by setting the appropriate properties using the Windows NT Explorer. Select File | Properties and provide sharing information under the tab named Sharing. You could also use the **net share** command to share resources on the network. Type **net share /?** at the command line to see details on this command.

Printing

Windows NT enables you to configure local or networked printers using a GUI tool with a wizard interface. To configure a printer, click on Start | Settings | Printers and select Add Printer. Follow instructions in the ensuing wizard interface to configure the printer.

You can also obtain the status of a printer or print queue by selecting a printer in the list of printers available. Tasks such as canceling print jobs and holding print jobs can be performed by using the appropriate commands in the File menu. You can also designate an available printer as the *default printer*. If you designate a default printer, all programs will use this printer by default when you print.

The equivalent functionality is provided in UNIX by commands such as **lpr** and **lpq**.

Setting Permissions

If you are an experienced UNIX or VAX/VMS user, you are most likely
familiar with setting permissions for resources such as files, folders, and
printers. In Windows NT, you can perform such tasks by using the Windows
NT Explorer. Start Windows NT Explorer and select the resource for which
you want to set permissions. Select File | Properties to access the properties
dialog box for the resource. You can set properties such as *read-only* by
selecting the General tab. Figure 1-18 shows a sample screen for setting file
properties.

Permissions for sharing resources can be set as a property by selecting
the Sharing tab. Figure 1-19 shows a sample screen for setting permissions.
You must assign a logical *share name* when you set permissions to a
resource.

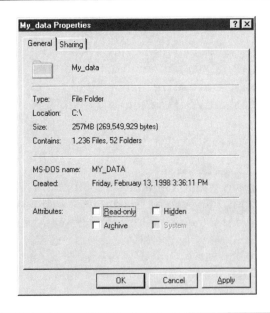

FIGURE 1-18. *Setting file properties*

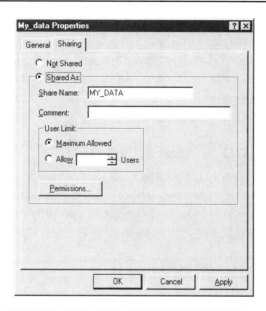

FIGURE 1-19. *Setting file permissions*

Remember that Windows NT file security is only supported by the NTFS file system.

For the experienced UNIX user, the above functionality is equivalent to the **chmod** and **chown** commands.

Compressing Files

Windows NT provides a command named **compress** which can be used to compress files. In addition, many third-party utilities are available to perform tasks similar to the **compress** command on UNIX. One popular such utility that allows you to zip files and create self-extracting executables is the WinZip utility. You can get information on this utility at http://www.winzip.com on the Web.

String Search

Functionality provided by commands such as **grep** and **egrep** in UNIX is available in Windows NT in the Find utility and the **find** command. In addition to this functionality, most Windows applications provide *search* and *search and replace* function under the Edit menu. The context of the search function is application dependent.

Archives and Tape Dumps

Windows NT provides a utility called Backup Manager that allows you to back up files and folders to tapes. There is no direct equivalent of the **tar** or **ufsdump** command on UNIX. You can use a combination of **WinZip utility** and tape backup to get a similar result.

Performance Monitoring

Windows NT provides graphical utilities to view performance statistics. If you are an experienced user, you can get information similar to that obtained by the UNIX **sar** and **iostat** commands in a graphical display on Windows NT. You can use the Windows NT Performance Monitor to measure the performance of Windows NT. Click on Start | Programs | Administrative Tools | Performance Monitor to start the Performance Monitor. You must decide the statistics you want to view in the graphical view.

Useful statistics on memory and CPU usage can also be obtained via the Task Manager. Start the Task Manager and click on the Performance tab to view this information.

In addition, Oracle8 provides a utility called Oracle8 Performance Monitor that can be accessed by clicking on Start | Programs | Oracle for Windows NT | Oracle8 Performance Monitor v8.0. This utility uses a prebuilt chart configuration file named **oracle80.pmw**, which resides in the **orant\dbs** folder, by default to provide performance statistics on the Oracle database using the Windows NT Performance Monitor.

Set your system properties for optimal performance. One key system property is the size of virtual memory on your machine. You can access the system Properties dialog box by selecting the System applet in the Control Panel. Click on the Performance tab to view the settings for virtual memory. We suggest that you let Windows NT maintain the paging file.

Process Management

Windows NT has a concept of processes and threads analogous to UNIX. It provides a GUI to processes in the Task Manager. Start the Task Manager and click on the Applications tab to view the current applications on your machine. You can get a listing of the processes running on your machine along with their process id (pid), and for the CPU and memory usage for each process by selecting the Processes tab in the Task Manager. A button labeled End Process is available if you want to end a process. Similarly, a button labeled End Task is available if you want to terminate an application forcefully. This functionality is similar to the **kill** and **ps** commands on UNIX. Figure 1-20 shows a sample screen that lists some of the Oracle processes on our test Windows NT machine. Note the Oracle process named **oracle80.exe**. In this example, it is consuming a little over 17MB of memory, which includes the memory for the executable and the SGA.

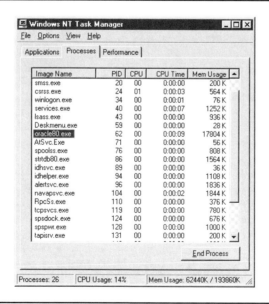

FIGURE 1-20.   *Managing processes on Windows NT*

NOTE
*Windows NT does not have shared memory and semaphores like UNIX. There is no command equivalent to **ipcs** on Windows NT. This is because Windows NT does not require you to configure and build a kernel, as UNIX does.*

Network Utilities

Windows NT 4.x supports many network protocols. If you have installed TCP/IP, standard utilities like **telnet**, **ftp**, and **ping** are available. You can also use the **tracert** utility to determine the route taken to a destination.

Windows NT networking commands begin with the word **net**. If you type **net /?** from the command prompt, you will see all the options for the command. For example, the **net config** command can be used to determine configuration information:

```
C:\>net config server
Server Name                      \\AADKOLI-LAP
Server Comment
Software version                 Windows NT 4.0
Server is active on              NetBT_NdisWan4 (000000000000)
                                 NetBT_NdisWan4 (000000000000)
Server hidden                    No
Maximum Logged On Users          10
Maximum open files per session   2048
Idle session time (min)          15
The command completed successfully.
```

You can get help on any **net** command by typing **net help** and then the command:

```
C:\>net help config
The syntax of this command is:
NET CONFIG [SERVER | WORKSTATION]
NET CONFIG displays configuration information of the Workstation or
Server service. When used without the SERVER or WORKSTATION switch,
it displays a list of configurable services. To get help with
configuring a service, type NET HELP CONFIG service.
SERVER        Displays information about the configuration of
              the Server service.
```

```
WORKSTATION   Displays information about the configuration of
              the Workstation service.
NET HELP command | MORE displays Help one screen at a time.
C:\>net help
The syntax of this command is:
NET HELP command
     -or-
NET command /HELP
  Commands available are:
  NET ACCOUNTS           NET HELP            NET SHARE
  NET COMPUTER           NET HELPMSG         NET START
  NET CONFIG             NET LOCALGROUP      NET STATISTICS
  NET CONFIG SERVER      NET NAME            NET STOP
  NET CONFIG WORKSTATION NET PAUSE           NET TIME
  NET CONTINUE           NET PRINT           NET USE
  NET FILE               NET SEND            NET USER
  NET GROUP              NET SESSION         NET VIEW
  NET HELP SERVICES lists the network services you can start.
  NET HELP SYNTAX explains how to read NET HELP syntax lines.
  NET HELP command | MORE displays Help one screen at a time.
```

Configuring Network Properties

Windows NT provides an applet named Network in the Control Panel that enables you to configure network adapters, network protocols, and network services. You can configure your computer name and also the network domain information using this applet. Figures 1-21 and 1-22 show screens from the Network Configuration utility.

Text Editors

Windows NT 4.x provides two editors: Notepad and Wordpad. You can start these editors by clicking on Start | Programs | Accessories | Notepad and Start | Programs | Accessories | Wordpad. Alternately, you can use **notepad.exe** to start Notepad and **write.exe** to start Wordpad.

Deinstalling Software

You can use the applet named Add/Remove Programs under the Control Panel to deinstall most software on Windows NT. However, the Oracle Installer must be used to deinstall Oracle software. Click on Start | Programs | Oracle for Windows NT | Oracle Installer to access the Oracle Installer.

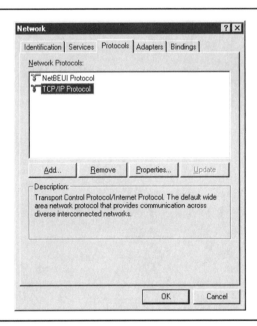

FIGURE 1-21. *Configuring network protocol information*

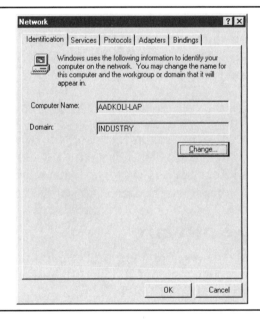

FIGURE 1-22. *Configuring the computer name and domain*

CHAPTER
2

Basic Installation of
Windows NT

he Windows NT operating system has become very popular in the last few years because it takes advantage of the 32-bit PCs. Features like multithreading and preemptive multitasking that were previously available on more expensive computers running operating systems such as UNIX and VAX/VMS are now available on computers under US $2,000. Many sites have been attracted enough to migrate from other operating systems to Windows NT. In this chapter, we will discuss the process of installing Windows NT 4.x on a personal computer based on the x86 architecture. While other platforms such as DEC Alpha and the PowerPC also support Windows NT, we will base our discussion on the x86 architecture since a majority of NT installations are based on this architecture. We will first offer some tips on purchasing the right hardware and then perform an installation. After that, we will provide some tips and techniques to ease your administration tasks.

How to Select Hardware

There are hundreds of manufacturers of PCs worldwide. An incredible choice of peripherals is also available in today's market. Choosing the proper hardware has become a daunting task. Today, PCs prices range from a few hundred dollars to a few thousand dollars, depending on the manufacturer and configuration of the PC. While it is likely that your budget will in many cases determine the PC you buy, we will provide a few tips that might help you buy a PC that meets your requirements. Keep in mind that we are planning the hardware for an Oracle Server on Windows NT.

Buy a Brand Name

If your budget allows for it, you should spend a few extra dollars to buy a brand name. There are several brands available worldwide. A branded machine usually guarantees good customer support and also ensures that you encounter minimal compatibility issues. If you choose to buy components from a variety of manufacturers and add them to your PC, you could end up spending several hours to get everything working just right. Avoiding such situations might very well be worth the extra dollars that you spent on a branded machine. We encourage you to pay special attention to the network card and the Small Computer System Interface (SCSI) devices. You should also factor in your geographical location before you choose your brand. Look for a manufacturer that has a strong presence in your geographic area. This can make a significant difference in some parts of Europe and Asia. Large branded manufacturers also have fairly comprehensive Web sites with useful information such as software updates and device drivers.

Buy Hardware with an Adequate Warranty

Most computer manufacturers today provide comprehensive warranties ranging from one to four years. We advise you to read the fine print to determine the scope of the warranty. You should look for a warranty that covers basic hardware for two years. Anything above that is likely overkill because PCs today are getting obsolete in less than two years!

Shop Around for Bargains

The prices of today's PCs range from a few hundred dollars to a few thousand dollars. Most manufacturers today have special deals on select models. PC technology is changing so rapidly that new models are coming out every few weeks. You should be able to get a great bargain on a PC that has a configuration that is about two to three months old. If you have access to the Internet, you should spend a few hours scouting for a bargain on the Web. Some manufacturers have a separate link on their Web sites that lists all the special deals. A few others even allow you to configure your own machine on the Web. You will be surprised by the range of prices that you see on the Web. You can also get great deals on refurbished hardware. One disadvantage of buying hardware on the Web is that you have to put the machine together when it arrives at your door. If you are not comfortable doing this, you might be better off going to your local computer store. Of course, if you are a corporate customer and you have to adhere to your company's purchasing standards, you might not be in a position to hunt for bargains. You should fight the temptation to buy excessive hardware. Many accessories turn out to be superfluous once the initial euphoria wanes.

Choosing a Motherboard and CPU

You should purchase hardware that includes a motherboard with the Extended Industry Standard Architecture (EISA) or Peripheral Component Interface (PCI) slots. Many PCs today are adopting PCI. Your motherboard should have at least four slots on the motherboard. A simple rule of thumb is to ensure that you have one extra slot after allocating slots to all your cards. You should consider allocating slots for a network interface card, a sound card, a graphics card (accelerator), and a modem. If your motherboard has some of these functions built-in, you might be able to get by with three slots on your motherboard. You must also try and select a motherboard that can accommodate CPU upgrades and additional CPUs.

While Windows NT can run perfectly fine on 486 or better machines, we recommend that you invest in a Pentium 166MHz or better. The cost benefit of buying a lesser CPU is not much. If you are planning to put many users on your machine, you should consider investing in a second CPU.

Random Access Memory (RAM)

The amount of RAM you have on your machine almost always impacts performance directly. While Windows NT runs perfectly well on a machine with 16Mb of RAM, the performance is far superior on a machine with 24Mb of RAM. You must also consider the RAM needs of your Oracle software. You should not run an Oracle8 Server on a machine with less than 32Mb. For most production sites with several users, you should invest in 64Mb or even 128Mb of RAM. Again, the performance benefits that you get for a few hundred dollars can be significant. If you are planning to use the Oracle Web Application Server along with a product such as Developer/2000 2.x, you should invest in at least 128Mb of RAM.

If you have insufficient memory to run your software, you will see a lot of disk activity where Windows NT is attempting to page data in and out of physical memory. Performance is severely impacted in this situation. If you notice high levels of disk activity, you should investigate the use of memory and paging activity with the Performance Monitor.

The amount of memory required by Oracle depends on an area of memory called the System Global Area (SGA). The SGA is allocated when an Oracle instance is created. The amount of memory allocated for the SGA can be controlled by setting parameters in the Oracle parameter file. This file is referred to as the INIT.ORA file in Oracle documentation. This file is

named **initorcl.ora** by default on Windows NT and resides in the
\orant\database folder. Parameters in the INIT.ORA such as **db_block_size**
and **shared_pool_size** directly impact the size of the SGA. You should
attempt to keep the SGA in physical memory as much as possible. We will
discuss this in great detail when we talk about performance tuning in
Chapter 7.

Hard Disk

The amount of hard disk space that you plan to purchase is obviously very
dependent on the software that you wish to install. For a dedicated Oracle
server, you should plan on having a minimum of 2Gb of space on your hard
disk. Again, the prices of hard disks have dropped considerably, and you
should be able to invest in larger amounts of hard disk space for a few extra
dollars. If your budget permits, we recommend that you invest in SCSI hard
disks. Otherwise, Enhanced Integrated Drive Electronics (EIDE) disks are
sufficient. Of course, if you are considering a redundant array of
independent disks (RAID) implementation, you might need to invest in
additional storage devices and software.

In addition to the amount of hard disk space and type of storage you plan
to purchase, there are some simple guidelines for you to manage your hard
disks. We recommend that you have at least two hard disks on your system.
This will allow you to mirror critical Oracle files such as online redo log
files and control files. We will discuss mirroring in Chapter 7.

NOTE
*Having two separate hard disks is better
than partitioning a single hard disk into two
partitions from the redundancy point of view. If
you have a hard disk crash, you could end up
losing all partitions on the hard disk. Mirroring
across partitions will not provide benefits in
such situations.*

You should install Windows NT along with all software (executables),
including Oracle, on one hard disk and create the Oracle database on the
second disk. This helps you to plan your backups better and also reduce the

time taken to perform backups. If you are planning to run a mission-critical application, then you must plan for redundancy. You should plan for at least a software implementation of RAID. If you can spend a few thousand dollars more for a hardware implementation of RAID, that might prove to be useful in minimizing downtimes.

Database performance is directly impacted by the amount of I/O on your disks. If you are planning to run a database that is in the several hundred megabytes to the gigabyte or higher range, consider buying several hard disks so that you can stripe your database. More information on tuning is provided in our discussion on performance tuning in Chapter 7.

Depending on the number of disks that you are planning to purchase, you should also investigate the possibility of having more than one disk controller for redundancy.

CD-ROM Drive

PCs today almost always have a built-in CD-ROM drive. You should certainly invest in a CD-ROM drive if you don't have one built-in. CD-ROM drives are available in many speeds. You should plan for a 16x or better CD-ROM drive. Almost all software today is exclusively available on CD-ROMs. Oracle software on Windows NT is exclusively distributed on CD-ROMs.

Floppy Drive

Most PCs today include at least one 3.5-inch floppy drive. Since all Oracle media for Windows NT is available on CD-ROMs, the floppy drive is not required. Floppy drives also increase the risk of computer viruses being transferred to your machine from floppies. These days, the floppy drive is only required while installing special device drivers that are usually made available only on floppy disks. If you can connect to the World Wide Web, you can probably get your device driver from the Net and not need a floppy disk ever!

However, floppy drives can be useful in times of emergencies. You might, for example, face a situation where you are forced to boot from a floppy disk. Since a floppy drive adds a very small cost to the computer, you should get one just in case.

TIP
The BIOS on almost all PCs provides the option of disabling floppy disks. If you want to minimize the risks of transferring viruses via floppies, you should disable the floppy disk in the BIOS using the BIOS Setup utility.

Backup Devices

If you are running an Oracle server, you should plan for proper backup devices. In a networked environment, you might already have access to a central backup device. If you don't, you should consider investing in a tape drive or a digital audio tape (DAT). Windows NT supports a variety of tape drives. Tape drives are available starting at 250Mb and up to a few gigabytes. DATs can give you larger capacity at a lower cost with some speed benefits. You can use the NT Backup Manager to perform backups to tape. The size of your drive depends on the size of the data you want to back up. At the very least, you must plan on backing up your database on one tape. Changing tapes during a backup can be very inconvenient.

There are other forms of backup storage, such as zip drives, available in the market. The size of your data and your budget should be the overriding factors if you plan to invest in a zip drive. Floppy disks are not very convenient for backups, because one floppy disk is usually insufficient storage for a database backup and it is not practical to change floppy disks during a backup.

Multimedia Kits

Most of the PCs today include multimedia kits. While Oracle software does not require any multimedia capability, you might want to invest in one if your budget allows for it. Of course, if your applications require multimedia capabilities, you should ensure that your hardware supports multimedia. If you do not have a CD-ROM drive, then you should buy a multimedia kit that includes a CD-ROM drive rather than invest in a CD-ROM drive, speakers, and a sound card separately. You can save a few dollars by buying a complete kit rather than separate components.

Graphics Cards

There are several kinds of graphics cards available in today's market. While some of these cards can considerably enhance graphics, this is not a requirement in most database applications. Most of today's PCs typically include 2Mb or more of video ram (VRAM). If you are not running any special graphics software or video, we suggest that you do not invest money in additional graphics capabilities.

Input Devices

All PCs today include a standard keyboard and mouse. Oracle has no special requirements for the keyboard or the mouse. A two-button mouse is sufficient for most applications. Other input devices such as joysticks are not required by Oracle, either.

Output Devices

Standard output devices include monitors and printers. There are several kinds of monitors available in different sizes supporting a range of resolutions. Monitor prices can vary significantly, depending on the size and resolution. If you are planning to create a dedicated Windows NT server and you need a monitor for the console, you should purchase a low-cost 14-inch monitor. If you are planning to do application development on the machine and run graphics, you should consider purchasing a 17-inch or larger monitor. Keep in mind that the dollars you invest in your monitor should reflect the amount of time you spend looking at it!

There are scores of printers available in the market. You should consider the speed, size, and features while selecting a printer. Again, the cost of printers can vary significantly. Oracle software supports all standard printers. We recommend that you purchase a printer that is supported directly by Windows NT. To obtain this list, click on Start | Settings | Printers and select the Add Printer option. Enter appropriate information in the Printer Wizard (including port information) and you should see a list of printers similar to the one shown in Figure 2-1.

You should also consider any special needs for your applications while choosing a printer. For example, if your applications include reports, the size and format of your reports will impact the printer you choose to purchase.

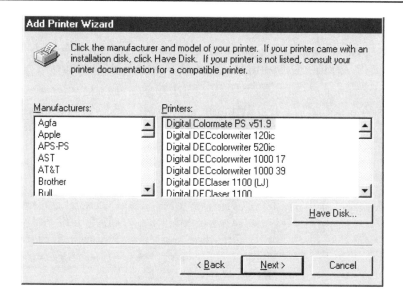

FIGURE 2-1. *Add Printer Wizard*

Windows NT Server vs. Workstation

Windows NT is available commercially in two different packages called the Windows NT Workstation and the Windows NT Server. While the core operating system (the kernel) is the same, they differ substantially in the tools and services they provide. Windows NT Server includes tools for networking, Remote Access Service (RAS), and server administration while the Windows NT Workstation allows basic peer-to-peer networking. By and large, Server provides more fault tolerance and a much wider range of networking options. If you are using Windows NT for printing and file services, Server is a better option. Server can also be tuned for optimal throughput and a larger number of users. Both Workstation and Server provide similar performance for up to ten simultaneous connections. Table 2-1 provides a listing of special capabilities of Windows NT. You can use this table to help make a decision on what package you choose to use.

Windows NT Feature	Description	Comments
Dynamic Host Configuration Protocol (DHCP)	For automatic configuration of Internet Protocol (IP) hosts	Available on both Workstation and Server.
Windows Internet Naming Service (WINS)	For dynamic computer name to IP address mappings in a routed networked environment	Server is required to configure WINS server, but Workstation can use WINS to resolve names.
Remote Access Service (RAS)	To provide remote access over telephone and dedicated lines like Integrated Services Digital Network (ISDN)	Workstation provides one client connection whereas Server provides up to 255 connections.
Gateway Services for Novell NetWare and Macintosh servers	To share Novell NetWare and Apple Macintosh services on the Microsoft network	Available on Server.
Disk striping, mirroring, and RAID5	To create fault-tolerant disk systems	Available on Server.
Microsoft BackOffice	Systems Management Server, Exchange server, Internet Information Server, and SQL Server	Mostly require Server—check individual documentation for restrictions.
Domain administration tools	Server Manager and User Manager for domains	Available on Server only.

TABLE 2-1. *Server vs. Workstation*

The Oracle8 Server has no special requirements on the Windows NT version except for the Oracle Parallel Server option, which requires Windows NT Server. In general, if you plan to have less than ten simultaneous Oracle connections, it is sufficient to install the Windows NT Workstation. You can have multiple client connections to the Oracle server using Net8, even on the Windows NT Workstation. If you want to ensure better scalability, you should procure Windows NT Server. Of course, you must factor in your other requirements before you decide on the version of Windows NT to license.

Preinstallation Tasks

Before you start your installation, you should ensure that you understand the procedure for the installation. You must have a plan for assigning disk storage. You must know how many disk partitions you will create and the storage that you will allocate to each partition. You must decide the primary partition and the extended partitions. You must also have a plan for how you will assign logical drives. You must know if you are creating mirrored sets and if you are using a RAID implementation.

TIP

You should avoid using utilities for disk compression and defragmentation on the Windows NT machine if you are creating an Oracle database on the machine. Disk compression utilities have been known to corrupt databases. We have also experienced situations where data has been corrupted in the process of defragmenting a disk.

Next, you must write down the hardware settings for the network card, the sound card, the graphics card, the modem, and any other cards that you might have. Specifically, you need to write down the I/O port, the interrupt (IRQ) setting, and the memory address. This information is available from the documentation for the card in question. The card manufacturer provides a software utility to change the settings for these cards. If such a utility is not provided, you should be able to modify settings by adjusting switches on the card. Most cards today have a *P-N-P* setting for Plug and Play. We must warn you that Windows NT is not as successful as Windows 95 in detecting hardware settings. The *Plug-and-Play* abilities of Windows NT are yet to mature.

You must choose a file system for your NT installation. If you are planning to use Windows NT with other operating systems like MS-DOS, you should use the FAT file system. If you are planning a dedicated Windows NT server, we recommend that you use NTFS. Features like security and long filenames are available with NTFS. If you choose to use the FAT file system, NT allows you to convert FAT to NTFS even after the installation. However, the reverse is not possible.

CAUTION
You must avoid changing the file system format after installing Oracle software. This can adversely affect the Oracle database, as Oracle maintains pointers to files in the data dictionary and the control files that might be impacted.

Choose a password for a special user named *Administrator*. Windows NT will request that you set the password for this user during the installation. The Administrator user is similar to the user *root* on UNIX systems.

Next, determine the method of installation that you will use. Windows NT can be installed on PCs that have other operating systems installed, like MS-DOS, Windows 95, and Linux. You must decide if you want to maintain more than one operating system on your PC. If you want to do this, then you must install the other operating systems before installing Windows NT. Windows NT will add a boot menu automatically if you have other operating systems on your PC. If you are installing Windows NT 4.x on top of an existing but older version of Windows NT, your old settings will remain intact.

If you are planning to install a printer, write down the printer model. You will need this information during the installation. Also, if the printer is attached to the machine on which you are installing Windows NT, note the port information (LPT1 or LPT2) to which the printer is connected. Most PCs today have one parallel port, termed LPT1. If a printer driver disk was provided with your disk, keep that handy.

Choose a name for the Windows NT machine. If you are installing the Windows NT Server edition, you will also need to determine if this machine will be the primary or secondary domain controller for your network. If you are planning to include the machine in any existing workgroup, you must know the name of the workgroup. The name of the NT machine and the workgroup cannot exceed 15 characters.

You also need to decide on the network protocols that you will install. The configuration information for the network depends on the network protocol. Most Windows NT machines are configured to run on Microsoft networks using NetBEUI in addition to TCP/IP. You might need to consult your network administrator for this information.

Finally, have a 3.5-inch high-density floppy disk ready before you begin the installation. This disk will become the NT repair disk. If you are installing from CD-ROM media, you might need three additional 3.5-inch high-density floppy disks, depending on your installation method.

Installation of Windows NT

The installation steps vary a little depending on the media and the operating system from which you are starting the solution. Table 2-2 provides the initial steps for the installation.

Once you have decided on the installation method that suits you, the installation itself is smooth. You will be required to answer precise questions in special dialog boxes during the installation. The answers are fairly obvious. If you have trouble, you can get assistance by clicking on the Help button in any one of these dialog boxes. We will spare you the details on the installation, but provide you with information that will help you answer these questions.

One of the first tasks during the installation of Windows NT is detection of the permanent media on which the operating system will install. The NT 4.0 Setup program can detect SCSI adapters, CD-ROM drives, and other disk controllers, for the most part. If Windows NT is unable to detect your storage device, you will be given a chance to supply a floppy disk with the

Source of Installation and Media	Operating System from which Windows NT Installation Is Started	Comments	Steps for Installation
Windows NT boot floppies and CD-ROM media	A brand new PC with no installed operating system or a PC with a formatted hard disk	Ensure that you have all floppy disks that contain device drivers for hardware on your machine.	1. Insert the disk labeled "NT Boot Disk" and switch on the PC. 2. Insert Setup Disk #2 and Setup Disk #3 when asked for it.
Windows NT on CD-ROM	MS-DOS	Ensure that the CD-ROM drive is visible from MS-DOS. Also, keep three 3.5-inch high-density floppy disks, which NT will use to create the setup floppy disks.	1. Change drive to the CD-ROM drive from MS-DOS. 2. Change to the **i386** folder. 3. Execute **winnt.exe**. 4. Create the setup floppy disks by following instructions on the screen. 5. Follow the procedure for a brand new PC as detailed above.

TABLE 2-2. *Starting a Windows NT Installation*

Source of Installation and Media	Operating System from which Windows NT Installation Is Started	Comments	Steps for Installation
Windows NT on CD-ROM	Windows 95	Keep three 3.5-inch high-density floppy disks handy. NT will use these floppies to create the setup floppy desks.	1. Insert the Windows NT CD-ROM. If the Auto-run feature is enabled, you should see the introduction screen and you can follow instructions on the screen. 2. If the Auto-run feature is not enabled, execute **winnt.exe** from the **i386** folder.
Windows NT on CD-ROM	Any version of Windows NT		1. Execute **winnt32.exe** from the **i386** folder.
Windows NT CD-ROM available on the network	MS-DOS	You must have MS-DOS network software installed. Keep three 3.5-inch floppy disks ready.	1. Switch to the logical network drive containing the Windows NT media on CD-ROM. 2. Execute **winnt.exe** from the **i386** folder.

TABLE 2-2.   *Starting a Windows NT Installation* (continued)

Source of Installation and Media	Operating System from which Windows NT Installation Is Started	Comments	Steps for Installation
Windows NT CD-ROM available on the network	Windows 95	You must have appropriate network software installed. Keep three 3.5-inch floppy disks ready.	1. Switch to the logical network drive containing the Windows NT media on CD-ROM. 2. Execute **winnt.exe** from the **i386** folder.
Windows NT CD-ROM available on the network	Any version of Windows NT	You must have appropriate network software installed. Keep three 3.5-inch floppy disks ready.	1. Switch to the logical network drive containing the Windows NT media on CD-ROM. 2. Execute **winnt32.exe** from the **i386** folder.

TABLE 2-2. *Starting a Windows NT Installation* (continued)

appropriate driver for your storage device. This floppy disk is made available by the manufacturer of the storage device. If you are unsure, allow the NT 4.0 Setup program to make an attempt to detect your storage device. If it fails to do so, you can supply your own floppy disk.

You will be asked to provide information on the disk partition and the folder where you want to install Window NT files. We recommend that you take the default, which is a folder named **winnt**.

During the installation, you will be asked to provide identification information, including your name and the name of your company. This information cannot be changed once Windows NT is installed. You can use the System applet under the Control Panel to display this information by selecting the General tab.

If you have nonstandard input and output devices such as keyboards and special video adapters, you will be allowed to provide a separate disk for drivers pertaining to these devices.

During the installation, you will be required to select the components of Windows NT that you wish to install. You should avoid components such as games if you are installing a production server.

During the installation, you will be required to provide the CD key that authenticates your license. This information is available on a certificate that is shipped with your Windows NT media.

You will also be allowed to set the time and date based on your geographic region. Windows NT 4.x can automatically adjust for daylight savings time if it applies to your region. Finally, you will be given an opportunity to set the screen resolution and provide the color settings for your display.

After you have completed the installation, Windows NT will reboot and you should see the Windows NT login screen and be able to login as the user Administrator.

If Windows NT has any trouble starting all the services, you will see an alert similar to the one shown here:

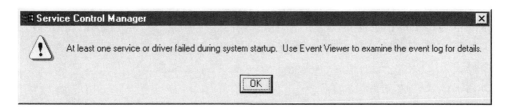

If you see no errors, you are well on your way to using Windows NT 4.x!

Tips and Techniques for Windows NT 4.x Administration

The GUI look and feel of Windows 95 provided by Windows NT makes it a very easy operating system to administer. If you are new to Windows NT, there are many ways to accomplish the same task. In fact, you could be overwhelmed by the number of ways you can accomplish a task in Windows NT. We will provide some tips and techniques in the remainder of this chapter to make your life as an NT administrator easier.

Create Shortcuts

As a Windows NT administrator or user, there are some tasks that you perform on a regular basis. For example, you might go to a folder frequently. Another task you will probably perform a lot is to start an editor. Windows NT provides a feature that allows you to create shortcuts on your desktop. You can create a shortcut to almost anything. We will illustrate three different methods to create shortcuts conveniently.

Creating Shortcuts Using NT Explorer

Start Windows NT Explorer and select a file or folder for which you want to create a shortcut. Select the Create Shortcut option from the File menu to create the shortcut. Alternatively, select the object and right-click the mouse to access available options and choose the Create Shortcut option. You can even drag the object or shortcut on to the desktop directly.

Creating Shortcuts Using the Wizard

Right-click the mouse in a vacant area on your desktop. Select the Shortcut option under the New menu, as shown here, to access the wizard.

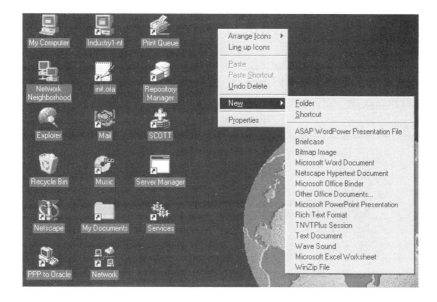

Follow instructions in the wizard to create the shortcut. Figure 2-2 shows a sample screen from the wizard.

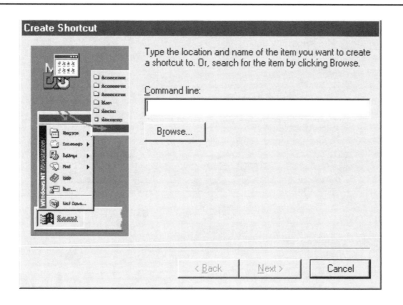

FIGURE 2-2. *Sample screen in the Create Shortcut Wizard*

Creating Shortcuts from the Taskbar

In some cases it is difficult to know the exact command or program name for the shortcut. In such situations, you can create a shortcut for a program from the taskbar. We will illustrate the method by creating a shortcut to Oracle Enterprise Manager.

I. Click on Start | Settings | Taskbar to access the Taskbar Properties screen shown next. Alternatively, take the mouse pointer on to the taskbar, right-click the mouse, and select Properties.

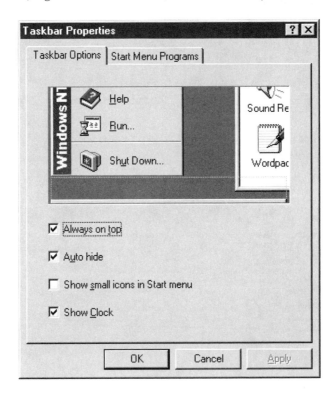

2. Click on the Start Menu Programs tab to see a screen similar to the one shown here:

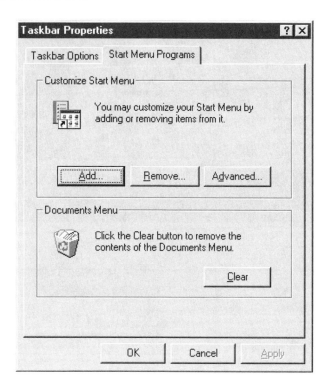

3. Click on the Advanced button to access the Start Menu in the Explorer, as shown in Figure 2-3.

4. Expand the Programs node and drill-down to see the program of your choice. We will pick Oracle Enterprise Manager, as shown in Figure 2-4.

5. Drag the shortcut for Oracle Enterprise Manager (OEM) onto the desktop to create an icon, as shown here:

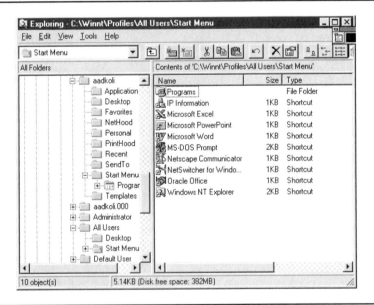

FIGURE 2-3. *Exploring Start Menu programs*

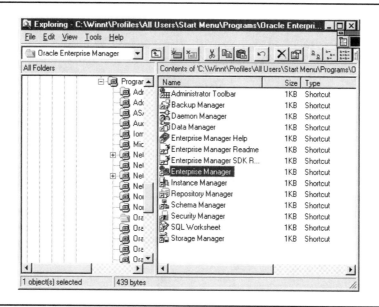

FIGURE 2-4. *Exploring Oracle Enterprise Manager*

Of course, you can navigate to the node *winnt\Profiles\All Users\Start Menu\Programs\Oracle Enterprise Manager* directly in the Windows NT Explorer and create the shortcut directly instead of going through the Taskbar Properties screen.

You can also set key combinations to get quick access to shortcuts by setting a property for the shortcut. This can be very useful to get quick access to some heavily used shortcuts such as the one to start an editor.

Schedule Tasks

One of the disadvantages of Windows NT GUI is that administrative tasks need to be completed interactively. Some tasks, like a database backup, can be scheduled by using the Windows NT Scheduler or the **at** command. The NT Scheduler allows you to schedule tasks at a given time or frequency. Type **at /?** to get more information on all the options provided by the command. We will illustrate the use of the NT Scheduler for database backups in Chapter 7.

Use Drag-and-Drop

Windows NT 4.x has a very advanced drag-and-drop feature.
This can be a convenient method to perform simple tasks like moving
files between folders. You can even move a file to the Recycle bin using
drag-and-drop. If you are using a right-handed mouse, you must hold the
left button of the mouse down while dragging an object.

Use the Clipboard

Windows NT allows you to cut and paste almost anything between programs
using the advanced clipboard feature. Most programs in Windows NT have
and Edit menu with Copy and Paste menu items. Alternatively, you can use
the CTRL-C key combination to copy and the CTRL-V key combination to paste
almost anything in the desktop. This can avoid typos and reduce typing while
transferring information between programs.

Many Windows NT applications also provide icons in the Application
toolbar that allow you quick access to the cut-and-paste feature.

Capture Errors

Windows-based programs are designed to provide detailed error messages
to users via dialog boxes. These errors can provide meaningful information
that allows you to diagnose the issue at hand. Sometimes, you might need
to call customer service to get assistance. You will be required to provide
the exact error message in such situations. You can capture the dialog box
by selecting the window containing the dialog box and pressing the
ALT-PRINTSCREEN keys. This key sequence captures the highlighted window in
the clipboard, which can be pasted into a graphics editor like Paint. In fact,
you can capture the entire desktop to the clipboard by pressing the
PRINTSCREEN key.

NOTE
*The PRINTSCREEN key might be labeled
differently on your keyboard.*

Manage Event Logs

Windows NT 4.x provides three types of logging that detail a variety of events on your system. System logs provide information on system components. For example, an entry is created in the system log if a device driver fails to start. An entry is placed in the security log if there is a breach in security, depending on the audit setting for the user. Similarly, applications can log events to the application log. While these logs provide critical information, they can get fairly large over time and can consume unnecessary disk space. You should set options to control the size of these logs. You can do so by selecting the Log Settings option in the Log menu of the Event Viewer. Below is a sample screen for the log settings on our machine:

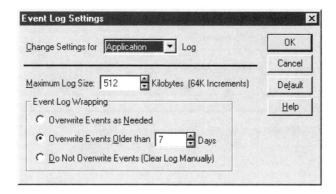

Optimize Startup/Shutdown

Windows NT stores information on the boot options during startup in a file named **boot.ini** in the system partition. This file is stored as a read-only file. If you have many operating systems on your machine, you will be allowed to select the operating system that you wish to start in the Boot menu. The default time for startup of Windows NT is 30 seconds. You should set this to five or even zero seconds, depending on your needs, to allow for a faster boot process. This can be useful in situations where you are depending on an automated boot procedure. In the case where Windows NT crashes, you can also enable automatic reboot after appropriate logging. These options can be set by using the System applet in the Control Panel. Click on Start | Settings | Control Panel | System to start the System applet. Click on the Startup/Shutdown tab to see a screen similar to the one shown in Figure 2-5.

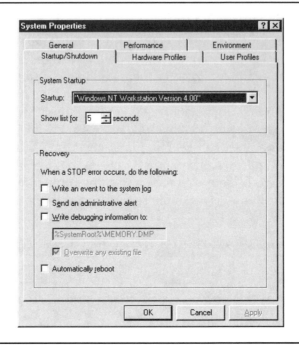

FIGURE 2-5. *Setting options for Startup and Shutdown*

You can also configure alerts for certain events using Oracle Enterprise Manager. Please refer to the section on Oracle Enterprise Manager in Chapter 5.

> **NOTE**
> *In addition to boot.ini, Windows NT creates other files such as **bootsect.dos**, **ntldr**, and **ntdetect.com** in the system partition. You should not delete or move these files at any time.*

Disable Unnecessary Services

Windows NT allows you to exercise control over services running on your system. When you install software, a variety of services get added on your system. These services can be configured to start automatically when the system starts up or they can be started manually as needed. You should take a close look at the services that start up to see if they are configured for automatic startup. Your startup time can be impacted severely by the number of services being started automatically.

To access the Services applet, click on Start | Settings | Control Panel | Services.

Optimize Your Hard Disks

You should keep a close watch on your hard disks. Windows NT provides built-in utilities that allow you to identify and fix disk errors. You should perform checks for disk errors at least every two weeks. To access the disk utilities, select the Properties item under the File menu of Windows NT Explorer and click on the Tools tab. Figure 2-6 shows the disk properties screen from the Explorer.

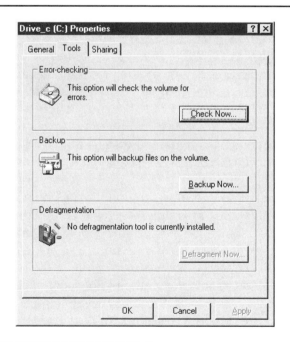

FIGURE 2-6. *Disk Properties screen*

Protect Against Viruses

Viruses can be very damaging on any computer. PC-based operating systems are popular targets for viruses. With a little discipline, you can minimize the risks of a virus attack on your computer. Most viruses are transferred via floppy disks. Avoid using floppy disks as much as possible. If you have to use one, use an antivirus software program to check it out before using it. Another common source of viruses is the Internet. Take the few extra seconds to run an antivirus program to check out all software of unknown origin. There are many antivirus programs available in the market today. We recommend that you test drive antivirus software by downloading it from the Web before choosing to buy one that works for you. We are satisfied with the performance of Norton AntiVirus 4.0 from Symantec Corporation (www.symantec.com). This program also automatically checks software downloaded from the Web.

You should make it a habit to get regular updates for virus definitions. Updates are provided regularly by most vendors of antivirus software.

Use the Mouse and Keyboard Efficiently

Windows NT provides you with the much-accepted Windows 95 GUI. While the GUI is simple to use, with a little practice you can learn to use the lesser known features available with the mouse and the keyboard.

Most Windows NT programs provide hot spots where the left-click and the right-click on a mouse provide you with instant access to relevant commands and functions. While many users are adept at the use of the left-click, the right-click is underused. Make a habit of trying out the right-click wherever possible for easy access to some program features.

In many Windows-based programs, a double-click on a word selects the entire word and a triple-click on a line selects the entire line. You can use the mouse to great advantage to select text in popular programs such as editors. A double-click can also be used to open a selected command or file, depending on the context.

You should get used to some key combinations that provide you with quick access to certain commands. Some key combinations are very generic and work in almost any Windows program. Table 2-3 below provides some useful key combinations.

Key Combination	Description
ALT-F4	Exit from the program/close the window
CTRL-W	Close the current document/window
ALT-TAB	Switch between active windows/applications
CTRL-C	Copy current selection into the clipboard
CTRL-V	Paste clipboard into active window
CTRL-Z	Undo
CTRL-X	Cut selected text
CTRL-A	Select all
CTRL-S	Save
F1	Context-sensitive Help
HOME, END, PGUP, PGDN, CTRL-HOME, and CTRL-END	For quick navigation in your program; the exact function of each key depends on the application
START	Enhanced keyboards that support Windows 95 and NT have a special key that provides quick access to the Start menu
CTRL-ALT-DELETE	Windows NT security screen that provides access to the Task Manager, allows you to log out of your current session, change your password, lock your machine, or shut down your machine

TABLE 2-3.   *Useful Key Commands in Windows NT*

We have already discussed shortcuts earlier in this chapter. You should create hot-key combinations to get quick access to your favorite shortcuts. This can save a considerable amount of time while accessing frequently used functions.

Many users who are experienced in MS-DOS prefer to use the command-line interface of Windows NT. You can get help on any of these commands by typing a question mark following the command name. Figure 2-7 shows a screen that displays help on the **del** command along with all available options.

Several users of Windows 3.1 prefer the old File Manager to the Windows NT Explorer. The File Manager is still available on Windows NT. You must execute **winfile.exe** to start File Manager. You might want to create a shortcut to the File Manager if you are more comfortable with that interface.

Oracle software on Windows NT adheres to Windows standards and provides support for standard key commands. Some Oracle software like

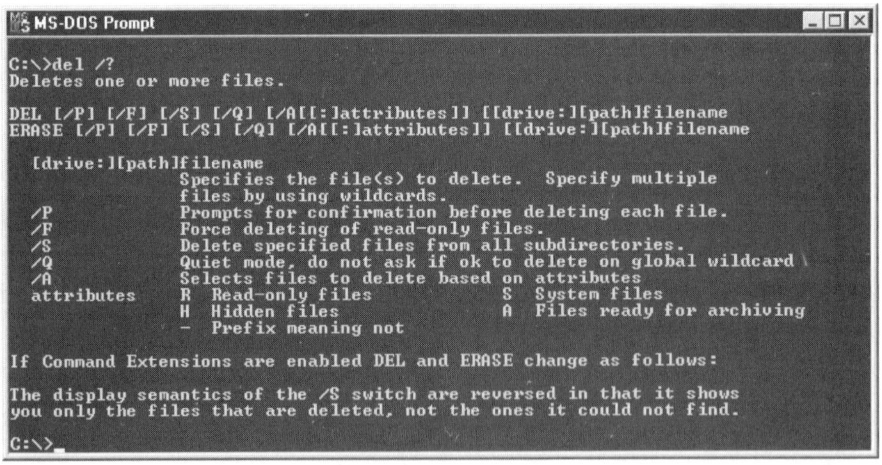

```
MS-DOS Prompt                                           _ □ ×

C:\>del /?
Deletes one or more files.

DEL [/P] [/F] [/S] [/Q] [/A[[:]attributes]] [[drive:][path]filename
ERASE [/P] [/F] [/S] [/Q] [/A[[:]attributes]] [[drive:][path]filename

  [drive:][path]filename
                Specifies the file(s) to delete.  Specify multiple
                files by using wildcards.
  /P            Prompts for confirmation before deleting each file.
  /F            Force deleting of read-only files.
  /S            Delete specified files from all subdirectories.
  /Q            Quiet mode, do not ask if ok to delete on global wildcard \
  /A            Selects files to delete based on attributes
  attributes    R  Read-only files          S  System files
                H  Hidden files             A  Files ready for archiving
                -  Prefix meaning not

If Command Extensions are enabled DEL and ERASE change as follows:

The display semantics of the /S switch are reversed in that it shows
you only the files that are deleted, not the ones it could not find.

C:\>_
```

FIGURE 2-7. *Accessing help on the command line*

Developer/2000 also provides additional support for application functions using key combinations. You can even tailor these key combinations to your convenience using the Oracle Terminal product. Consult your Oracle documentation for more information.

Use a Single Login

Windows NT has a smart login concept that facilitates a single login on the network. If you have accounts on several machines on the network, you should maintain the same login name and password for a given user on all the machines. When you connect to network resources, you will not be asked for a username and password each time you connect to a resource, provided you have the same username and password on each machine. This can be very convenient for restoring existing network connections when you begin a new login session. Of course, this can compromise security rather easily, too. If someone finds out your password, you are potentially exposing all your data on the network! You can reduce the risk by choosing a password that is difficult to guess.

Configure Start Menu for Quick Access

You can configure your Start menu to obtain quick access to programs that are frequently used. Click on Start | Settings | Taskbar and select the Start Menu Programs tab. Click on the Add button and add your program to the Start menu.

Hide the Task Bar

The Windows NT Taskbar consumes a little bit of the screen. We recommend that you enable the Auto-hide property of the taskbar to make better use of your desktop. Similarly, you can set the Auto-hide property for other toolbars, such as the ones for Microsoft Office and the Oracle Administrator Toolbar, if you have Microsoft Office and the Oracle Enterprise Manager installed.

Starting Applications from the Command Prompt

If you are used to the command-line interface, you can choose to start applications from the command prompt. Executables, including batch files, can be executed by typing the name of the file. The following examples run a batch file named **install.bat** and an executable named **setup.exe**:

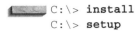

```
C:\> install
C:\> setup
```

Note that it is not necessary to type the file extensions.

CAUTION
*Do not attempt to execute **oracle80.exe**. You must use Instance Manager, Server Manager, or the Services applet to start up and shut down Oracle.*

Dealing with Long Filenames

Experienced MS-DOS users might have difficulties using long filenames from the command prompt. If you have trouble with file or folder names that do not conform to the 8.3 file naming convention, you must enclose the file or folder name within quotes. For example, to navigate to a folder named **Program Files**, use the **cd** command as shown below:

```
C:\>cd "Program Files"
C:\Program Files>
```

If you are using NTFS, it is not necessary to provide the quotes:

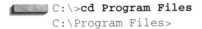

```
C:\>cd Program Files
C:\Program Files>
```

Use Wildcards

Wildcards are supported by Windows NT. You can use asterisks and question marks as wildcards, as shown here:

```
C:\> cd Prog*
C:\temp> del aa*.*
C:\temp> del aa?tst.*
```

Use Doskey

The Doskey program allows you to recall and edit Windows NT commands issued from the command prompt. This functionality is very similar to the **history** command available in **csh** or the command-line editing functionality in **ksh** on UNIX. You can use the **/history** option (it can be abbreviated to **/h**) to recall a listing of commands. On most keyboards, the F7 key will recall the history. You can step through the commands in the reverse order using the UP ARROW key. In the example below, three commands are retrieved from the history. The **dir** command is the oldest command in the history list and the **doskey /h** command is the newest in the history list.

```
C:\> doskey /h
dir
type aa.txt
doskey /h
```

You could also type the first character of the command in the history list and use the UP ARROW key to retrieve the command directly. Continuing with the example above, if you type **d** and press the UP ARROW key, you will retrieve the **dir** command from the history. On some keyboards, the F8 key provides the same functionality as the UP ARROW key for the Doskey program.

Use Toolbars

Almost all applications on Windows NT provide toolbars that contain icons for frequently used commands. You should spend a few minutes familiarizing yourself with the toolbar(s) and icons provided by the application. You can move your mouse over the icon to get a *tip*, or *bubble help*, for that icon. This habit can save you considerable time and effort, as using menus and menu items can be painful at times.

Get Familiar with the Windows NT Commands

If you are an experienced MS-DOS or UNIX user, you are probably more comfortable with using the command line than GUI commands. In this case, you should take the time to get familiar with Windows NT commands. Start the Windows NT Help facility and browse through the available commands. In the Contents tab, open the Windows NT Commands book and double-click Windows NT Commands to access the commands index. You should see a screen similar to the one shown in Figure 2-8.

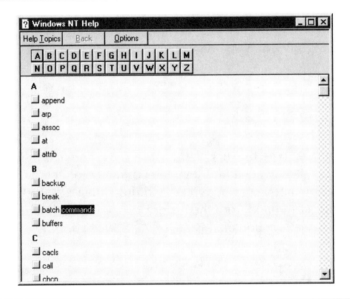

FIGURE 2-8. *Windows NT Commands Index*

Create Batch Files

Like MS-DOS, Windows NT allows you to write batch files to run a set of commands. This is similar to writing shell scripts in UNIX. You should write batch files for routine tasks to make your life easier.

DBAs frequently write SQL scripts for routine administrative tasks. You can use batch files to execute such SQL scripts and even schedule these batch files to run at a certain time. Refer to the section on scheduling database backups in Chapter 7 for an example of creating and scheduling batch files for execution.

CHAPTER
3

Basic Installation of Oracle8 on Windows NT

racle8 for Windows NT provides the full functionality of the world's leading database on the fast-growing Windows NT operating system. Oracle8 for Windows NT brings the full power of the Oracle8 database technology on the easy-to-use Windows NT platform. All major features of Oracle8, including improved performance, scalability, availability, and reliability are available to the user with the intuitive GUI of Windows NT. The huge advances made in today's computer hardware ensure that this combination of Oracle8 and the Windows NT operating system work to address the needs of a wide range of database applications. Small- and medium-sized businesses are especially tailor-made for the Windows NT platform.

Oracle8 for Windows NT is tightly integrated with Windows NT. It takes advantage of the multithreading, multitasking, and I/O capabilities of Windows NT 4.0. Oracle8 utilizes Windows NT features, including services, registry, Performance Monitor, and Event Viewer. Most of the administrative tasks, including creating a custom database, can be performed using wizards. The experienced Windows NT administrator can install the Oracle server within a few hours. A wide variety of GUI tools are available to help administer the Oracle Server. On the other hand, an experienced Oracle database administrator on other platforms can install a Windows NT Server in a few hours and acquire Windows NT administration skills in a short period of time by using GUI administration tools. In this chapter, we will first introduce some key concepts of the Oracle technology. This will be useful for the experienced Windows NT administrator who is getting a first look at Oracle. If you are an experienced Oracle DBA, you can skip this section. Next, we will step through a typical installation of the Oracle8 Web Application Server, along with an Oracle8 database. We will then illustrate the installation of Oracle's application development technology by installing the Oracle Developer 2000 R2.1 product. We will also illustrate the configuration of both the client/server and the three-tier architecture based on Oracle's Network Computing Architecture (NCA). Throughout this chapter and the remainder of the book, we will refer in all our discussions to a sample installation that includes the products listed in Table 3-1.

Product	Version
Oracle8 Server Enterprise Edition for Windows NT	8.0.4.0.0
Oracle Web Application Server for Windows NT	3.0.0.1
Oracle Developer 2000 for Windows NT	2.1 with Forms Builder 5.0.6.8.0 and Report Builder 3.0.5.8.0

TABLE 3-1.   *Oracle Product Versions of Sample Installation*

Table 3-2 provides a listing of the hardware used in a majority of our tests and illustrations throughout this book.

In the remainder of the book we will also assume that Oracle products are installed in the **c:\orant** folder and that Windows NT 4.0 is installed in the **c:\winnt** folder, unless mentioned otherwise.

Hardware	Details & Specification
Windows NT	Workstation 4.0
CPU	Intel Pentium 166 MHz
Physical memory	144Mb
Storage devices	2Gb SCSI Hard disk drive , 3.5-inch floppy disk drive, 20x CD-ROM drive, IOMEGA Zip drive 100Mb

TABLE 3-2.   *Hardware and Operating System Specifications for Sample Installation*

An Introduction to Oracle

Today, Oracle Corporation is the undisputed leader in software for information management. Its products include the industry's leading Relational Database Management System (RDBMS), the Oracle8 Server, and a set of application development tools. Its products allow customers to deploy enterprise-level applications in a host of different environments, ranging from the desktop to mainframes. Customers can deploy applications ranging from stand-alone to client/server, and from client/server to the Web. Applications can be deployed on large networks such as the Internet using Oracle's Network Computing Architecture (NCA). Oracle takes pride in building software that is completely open and scalable. Oracle software runs in over a hundred countries on almost all operating systems and on all standard networks.

If you are new to relational database technology, you can think of an RDBMS as a black box that manages a bunch of data, as shown in Figure 3-1.

The data itself is organized into a set of simple tables that are created with some logical relationships. For example, a table named CAPITALS

CAPITALS

Country	State
USA	Washington
U.K.	London
...	...
...	...
...	...
...	...
India	New Delhi

MAX_TEMP

State	Celsius
Washington	28
London	35
...	...
...	...
...	...
...	...
New Delhi	15

FIGURE 3-1. *Data in a black box*

might contain a listing of all countries along with their capitals and a table named MAX_TEMP might have a list of all the capitals with their recorded maximum temperatures for a given day. By scanning both the tables, it is obvious that we could determine the country that has the hottest capital in the world on a given day. Now imagine hundreds and thousands of tables in this black box, each containing numbers, characters, bitmaps, and even audio and video streams. Every one of these tables has a unique name, rows, and columns.

So, relational databases are black boxes that manage data securely and efficiently and are stored under some rigid rules and guidelines. A database application is software that allows you to access and manipulate data in the black box. In that sense, imagine a bunch of keyholes or peepholes provided in the black box. These would be database applications. Today, Oracle Corporation is the leading vendor of software that allows you to build such black boxes of data, as well as peepholes. Figure 3-2 provides a high-level view of Oracle product technology. The Oracle8 Server is Oracle Corporation's core competence as represented by the innermost box. The company also provides a set of tools like Designer/2000 and Developer

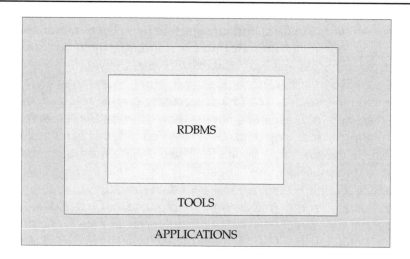

FIGURE 3-2. *Oracle product technology*

2000 that allow application developers to build database applications. The outer box represents the application set that Oracle builds using its technology. Oracle applications can be categorized broadly into the horizontal and vertical segments. Horizontal applications like Oracle Financials and Oracle Manufacturing and are not built for a specific industry segment. In contrast, vertical applications are built for specific industry segments. Oracle Energy and Consumer Packaged Goods (CPG) are good examples of vertical applications.

Oracle applications can be deployed in a variety of different environments. Oracle has been the leading vendor in client/server technology. In the last couple of years, Oracle has concentrated on technology that is suited for large networks such as the Internet. Oracle is a pioneer of the Network Computing Architecture (NCA) that specifically targets applications on the Internet and intranets using three-tier architecture. We will provide a quick introduction to key Oracle products and concepts in the remainder of this section. We strongly recommend that you read the Oracle documentation before you attempt to deploy a production application. The *Oracle8 Concepts* manual provides an excellent starting point for any aspiring DBA.

Oracle8 Server

The Oracle8 Server is the core component in Oracle-based solutions. The Oracle8 database includes support for object technology and is designed for very large databases (VLDBs) and for sites that have large transactions. It is designed to be open and supports industry standards, including Structured Query Language (SQL) and open database connectivity (ODBC).

The Oracle8 Server consists of two main components, namely, the database and the instance. The Oracle database consists of datafiles, online redo log files, control files, and a parameter file. These files provide a physical platform for storing data. Data is stored in terms of database objects such as tables, indexes, and synonyms. The database must be *open* before it can be used. When a database is open, it is associated with one or more instances. The Oracle instance consists of data structures in memory and processes that are used to manage and manipulate an Oracle database. A standard set of data structures is created in a reserved area of memory called the System Global Area (SGA). A set of Oracle processes is used to manage the instance and the database. In addition, user processes are used to interface between user applications and the database.

The Oracle database has a physical and a logical structure. The physical database consists of datafiles, control files, a parameter file, and online redo logs. One or more datafiles are used to store database objects on the file system. Control files are used to track the physical structure of the database. Online redo logs are used if recovery is required in case of media failures. Data that is yet to be written to a datafile is stored in the redo log files. A parameter file (called the INIT.ORA in Oracle documentation) is used to manage a variety of settings for Oracle. Parameters in this file can be used to configure and tune an Oracle database.

Oracle databases also have a logical structure that is quite different from the physical structure. All database objects are stored in a logical set of *tablespaces*. A tablespace physically maps to one or more datafiles. Every Oracle database has at least one tablespace named the SYSTEM tablespace. In most real-world situations, the SYSTEM tablespace is used to store objects that Oracle itself requires for its housekeeping. Other tablespaces are created for user objects. Database objects are also divided into *schemas*. A schema allows for easy management and better control of security. Oracle manages security through a variety of *grants* and *privileges*. An authorized user or DBA on Oracle can create users and groups of users (called *roles*). Normally, one user is associated with one schema.

Oracle creates a *segment* for each database object. The segment allocates physical storage for objects in terms of *extents*. An extent is a contiguous set of *database blocks* on physical storage.

An Oracle DBA is assigned the task of managing a database. Security issues, including managing users and auditing the use of a database, are to be dealt with on a regular basis. Space management, backup and recovery issues, and performance tuning are other critical tasks for DBAs.

Oracle Web Application Server (WAS)

The Oracle Web Application Server (WAS) provides the foundation for database applications in the three-tier architecture. Oracle Corporation is a leading proponent of the Network Computing Architecture (NCA). The simple fact is that today's businesses many times span large geographic areas and the information management solutions need to cater to these needs seamlessly. The Oracle WAS provides a complete solution to deploy enterprise-level applications on the Web. These applications can be tightly integrated with the database.

The WAS consists of Web listeners (similar to HTTP daemons like *httpd*) that allow you access to services such as the database. The terms Web listener and Web Server can be used analogously. Web listeners are configured to poll for service requests on specific ports. You can configure a variety of Web Request Brokers (WRB) and agents to enhance the functionality. For example, an agent named *owa* is used to provide access to PL/SQL procedures. Built-in database packages allow you to create dynamic Web pages. Such applications can be deployed in thin clients as they run in a standard browser.

NOTE

Many applications today are Java-enabled and are dependent on a particular version of Java. For example, Developer 2000 R2.1 needs a browser that supports Java version 1.1.1 or higher.

Other cartridges and listeners are available for a variety of applications. The Oracle Developer 2000 product allows you to deploy forms and reports based applications on the Web. The Oracle Video Server and the Payment Server are available as standard cartridges. Unfortunately, the discussion of specific cartridges is beyond the scope of this book.

NOTE

You can refer to Oracle Troubleshooting, Second Edition *in the Oracle Press series from Osborne McGraw-Hill also written by us for more information on the Video and Payment Servers. It is due to be published in November 1998.*

Oracle Development Tools

Oracle Corporation has a variety of application development tools. Oracle Designer/2000 and Developer 2000 allow you to create applications containing forms and reports with integrated graphics. Applications can be deployed in a standard client/server environment or on the Web. A variety of precompilers allow you to develop applications in standard 3GL with embedded SQL. Other products such as Discoverer/2000 include simple GUI query tools. Oracle development tools can be used to develop applications against non-Oracle databases also.

Net8

The Net8 software allows for connectivity between client applications and Oracle databases. Net8 software is mandatory in client/server applications. A Net8 *listener* process is required on the database server. The Net8 listener has knowledge of all database services available on the server. When a client attempts to connect to a remote database, the Net8 listener validates the connection request and then attaches the client to a process on the server. The process is either dedicated or shared. A dedicated process called the *dedicated server* is spawned on demand while a shared process called the *shared server* is prespawned using the Multi Threaded Server (MTS). We will look at MTS in more detail in Chapter 7, with focus on Windows NT. The server process (dedicated or shared) represents every client request for data. All data and messages back to the client are also routed through the server process.

NOTE
Previous versions of Oracle's networking software were called SQL*Net. Oracle7 products supported the client/server architecture using SQL*Net 2.x.

For a detailed discussion on Net8, refer to *Net8 Getting Started for Windows NT and Windows 95* and the *Oracle Net8 Administrator's Guide*. We will also take a look at Net8 configuration later in this chapter.

Open Database Connectivity

There are several vendors of application development tools. If you wish to use a non-Oracle development tool for your database application but still wish to use an Oracle server in the back end, then you must use open database connectivity (ODBC). Prominent non-Oracle development tools like PowerBuilder and Microsoft Visual Basic can be used to build database applications against Oracle using ODBC technology. You can also use Oracle development tools to build applications against non-Oracle databases using ODBC technology. We will provide configuration tips for ODBC later in this chapter.

Now that we have introduced some key concepts of database technology for the new user, we will take a look at the installation of an Oracle server along with Developer 2000. We will then illustrate the configuration of Net8 and the WAS.

Preinstallation Tasks

The Oracle8 installation on Windows NT is performed by using the Oracle Installer. While the installation is simpler than the installation procedure on other operating systems, we would like to go over some preinstallation tasks that can help you complete the installation successfully on the first attempt.

Choose an Appropriate Oracle8 Server

Oracle8 Server is available on Windows NT in three different packages. This is to cover the entire range of stand-alone to enterprise-level users. Be sure to choose the Oracle8 Server that meets your requirements. We will introduce the three packages here for your benefit.

The entry-level package is *Oracle8 Personal Edition*. This package is useful for stand-alone Windows NT machines. Since Windows NT is rarely used in a non-networked environment, this package is mainly useful for application development, testing, and training. Developers can maintain their own images of Oracle8 software and maintain their own database. Computer-based training (CBT) tools can also be used conveniently in this environment. This package was formerly marketed as Personal Oracle8 (or Personal Oracle7 in the earlier version).

The *Oracle8* package (also called *Standard* edition in some documentation) provides the complete functionality of Oracle8 Server minus the add-on options and cartridges. This package can be used for sites that want to run client/server applications because Net8 Server and Client software is included. However, some management tools are not available with this package. In earlier versions, this product was marketed by Oracle Corporation as Oracle Workgroup Server.

The *Oracle8 Enterprise Edition* is a comprehensive product bundle that includes all add-ons and cartridges. Additional management tools are also available with this edition. This package was formerly sold as the Oracle Server.

Ensure Availability of Resources

Determine the hardware and software requirements of the products you wish to install from the installation guide. Some general recommendations for the installation of the Oracle8 Server are listed here for your reference:

- A PC based on a Pentium processor or better
- Microsoft Windows NT 4.0
- 48Mb of RAM or better
- 500Mb of free space on the hard disk
- CD-ROM drive

Compile a List of Products for Installation

Oracle provides a variety of product bundles for Windows NT. Be sure that you compile a list of products that you want to install and that you have all the necessary media. We suggest that you first install the Oracle8 Server and then the Web Application Server. After this, you can install the development tools you want in any order. The Oracle Installer will automatically perform a check on the prerequisites for the product you are attempting to install and copy all the necessary files automatically.

There should be an insert in every Oracle media that gives you information on the products available on the media and the resources required for the installation. We suggest that you take a few moments to review this insert. If an insert is not available, you can get a listing of products available on the media by viewing a file named **nt.prd** on the media in a text editor.

TIP

*Use the Find utility on Windows NT to search for **nt.prd** files. There could be more than one of these files on the media.*

Choose Among Stand-Alone, Client/Server, and NCA

You should have a strategy for how you will deploy applications on your site. Stand-alone applications are very rare in today's world of networked computers. However, they can be useful for testing and development. If you are deploying client/server applications, you will need to install Net8 Server software on the server and Net8 Client software on all the clients. If you are planning to use the three-tier architecture, you must plan on installing a Web server. Net8 Client Software is not required on clients.

List the Software Required for Connectivity

If you are planning to deploy Oracle applications in the client/server architecture, you must install Net8 software on the server and the clients for connectivity. If you are planning to use non-Oracle front ends like PowerBuilder and Visual Basic against an Oracle Server, you must use ODBC. If you want to deploy an Oracle application against a non-Oracle database, you will need to install the Oracle Open Client Adapter. You can configure ODBC by using the ODBC Configuration applet under the Control Panel. You can also access the ODBC administrator by clicking on Start | Programs | Oracle for Windows NT | Microsoft ODBC Administrator.

Verify the Integrity of Your File System

You should take the few minutes required to verify the integrity of your file system. You can do this using Windows NT Explorer or a third-party tool such as Norton Disk Doctor. Start Windows NT Explorer and select the logical drive that you wish to check. Select File | Properties and click on the Tools tab. You should see a screen similar to Figure 3-3. Click on the Check Now button and follow instructions on the screen until the check is performed.

If you have a disk compression utility installed, we suggest you disable it on the drive where you are installing the Oracle database. Oracle tracks space usage with internal algorithms. If you don't disable the disk compression utility, you can corrupt your database since these algorithms can fail with disk compression. If you are installing Oracle software on a separate disk from the one on which you are creating the database, you can

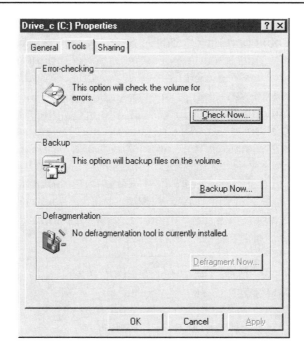

FIGURE 3-3.   *File properties in the NT Explorer*

have compression enabled on the disk where the software is installed. However, you should not compress the disk on which the database will be created.

Understand the Oracle Installation Process

Oracle Installer is used to install all Oracle products. The installer performs the following three tasks:

- Checks dependencies
- Copies necessary files
- Configures the system for use

The first task for the installer is to ensure that sufficient disk space is available to install the desired products. After this, it does dependency checks. A substantial portion of code is written as shareable code for Oracle products, and this code is made available under components such as the *Required Support Files* and *GUI Common Files*. The Installer will automatically upgrade any components that need upgrading. After these checks, the required files are copied over into appropriate directories in the designated destination folder. All Oracle executables and dynamic link libraries (DLLs) are placed in the **\orant\bin** folder, while other product files are placed in corresponding product folders. Finally, the installer creates the program groups and shortcuts required. Required modifications to the registry are also made at this time. A listing of the Oracle components on a machine is maintained in a file named **nt.rgs** in the **\orant\orainst** folder.

TIP
*If you are unsure about the products available on any Oracle media on Windows NT, locate a file named **nt.prd** on the media and view it in any text editor. A listing of products available on the media along with complete version information is provided in this file.*

Installation

Now that you have completed the preinstallation tasks, you are ready for installation. As per Windows NT standards, if you have *Auto-run* enabled on your PC, the Oracle installation program should start as soon as you insert the CD-ROM media into the drive and close the drive. If not, you can execute **setup.exe** from the CD-ROM media to start the installation. There are five types of installation that you could perform, as listed below:

- Stand-alone installation
- Client/server installation
- Three-tier installation (based on NCA)
- Third party products
- Non-Oracle RDBMS

We will provide an overview of each of the above installations and perform a quick installation for your benefit. We will avoid repetition of material as we go through each installation. The guidelines provided in one type of installation can apply equally well to another type of installation.

Stand-Alone installation

A stand-alone installation is one in which all Oracle software, including the database, tools, and applications, are installed on one single Windows NT machine. This is a very rare kind of installation since Windows NT machines are usually networked. However, a stand-alone installation can be useful for testing. The steps to perform a stand-alone installation are as follows.

Step 1   Install the Oracle8 Server.

We recommend that you complete the installation of the Oracle8 Server first. Depending on your media and the license that you have, you can install either the *Enterprise* edition or the *Standard* edition. You will need to perform a custom installation or choose the default installation. The default installation will allow you to install the server or client software and will ask you minimal questions. If you are an advanced user, we recommend that you use a custom installation. You can avoid loading unnecessary software and save some disk space if you choose to perform a custom installation.

We will now illustrate an installation. Insert the Oracle8 for Windows NT media into the CD-ROM drive and close the drive. You should see a screen similar to the one shown in Figure 3-4.

If you do not have *Auto-run* enabled, you can use the Windows NT Explorer to start **setup.exe** from the media. Figure 3-5 shows the contents of the CD-ROM media that we used for our test installation.

Begin the installation by clicking on the Begin Installation icon. You should see a screen similar to the one shown in Figure 3-6 that allows you to specify installation settings such as identification information, the target folder, and the language for your installation.

If you have more than one version of Oracle installed on your machine, we suggest that you choose separate *Oracle Homes* and destination folders. If this is your first and only installation, we suggest that you take the default values for the Oracle Home and the destination folder. You should see a dialog box that allows you to select the type of installation you want. This

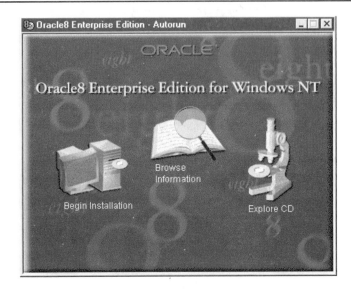

FIGURE 3-4. *First installation screen for Oracle8 Enterprise Edition*

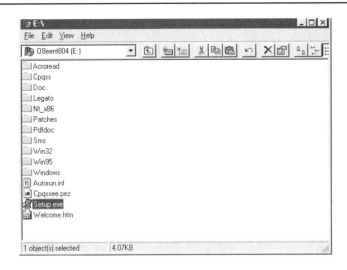

FIGURE 3-5. *Exploring the Oracle8 Enterprise Edition for Window NT media*

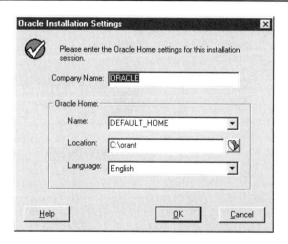

FIGURE 3-6. *Oracle Installation Settings screen*

dialog box will change based on the product you install. For the Oracle8 Server, you should see a screen similar to the one shown here:

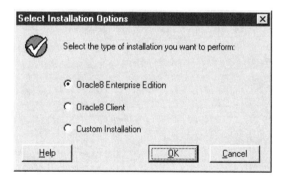

TIP
You can install Oracle8 in the same folder as Oracle7. No files will be overwritten as the names are unique between the two versions. If you choose to install more than one version of Oracle8, install each of these in a separate Oracle home.

We will choose to take the default installation of the Oracle8 Enterprise Edition. You should see a screen similar to the one shown here that allows you to select the cartridges that you wish to install:

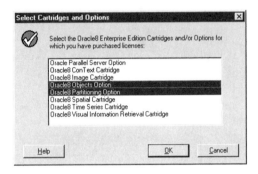

NOTE

If you choose to perform a custom installation, you can choose the product components that you wish to install. In this case, you will see a screen similar to the one shown in Figure 3-7.

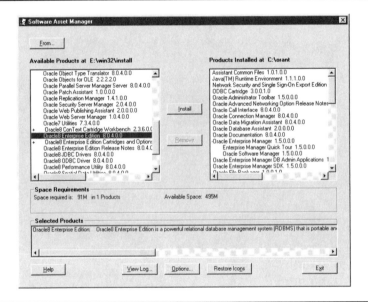

FIGURE 3-7. *Custom Installation screen*

We will choose to install the *Objects* and the *Partitioning* options. You will see another dialog box that allows you to select the type of database that you want to create. We will select the default *starter* database.

CAUTION

If you have a database created in the **\orant\database** *folder, it will get overwritten if you choose to create a starter database. You will see a warning dialog box if you attempt to do so. If you do not want the existing database to be overwritten, you should take the option to create a customized database or to not create a database. You can always use the Database Assistant to create a customized database at a later point in time. More information on this is available in Chapter 5.*

Next, you should see a dialog box that pertains to the installation of third-party media management tools:

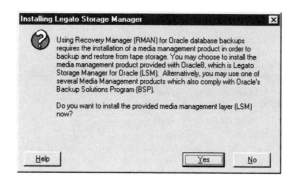

We will not install a media manager at this time. You should see another dialog box similar to the one shown below that allows you to pick the destination for the Oracle documentation (on-line documentation is available in both HTML and Adobe Acrobat format). Depending on your disk space, you can choose to install the documentation on to your hard disk or leave it on the CD-ROM drive. We will choose to install the documentation on to the hard disk.

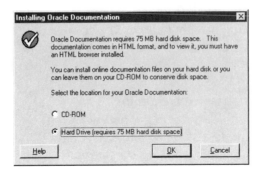

TIP

Visit http://www.oracle.com/st/products /features/backup.html for more information on media managers and features of Recovery Manager.

After this, the Oracle Installer will install the components that you have chosen to install. The process should take 10–30 minutes, depending on the components that you have selected and the speed of your CD-ROM drive and your hard disk. Finally, you will see a dialog box similar to the one shown here to confirm that installation is complete:

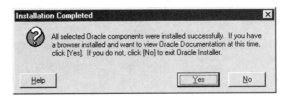

Step 2   Verify installation of Server.

It is best to ensure that the installation of the server was performed correctly. Oftentimes, the tendency is to install a lot of software and hope that everything is installed properly. If there is a problem with the installation, it is best to detect it early! Take a few minutes to ensure that the Oracle services are running. Click on Start | Settings | Control Panel and start the Services applet. Ensure that the appropriate Oracle services are running. If you took the default installation, you should see services similar to the ones shown here running:

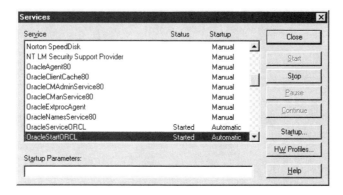

Note the services named *OracleServiceORCL* and *OracleStartORCL*. These are the services for the default Oracle database named *ORCL*. If you chose to install the default Oracle database, you should see database files named **sys1orcl.ora**, **usr1orcl.ora**, **rbs1orcl.ora**, and **tmp1orcl.ora** created in the **\orant\database** folder. You should also see log files named **log1orcl.ora** and **log2orcl.ora** created in the same folder. In addition, there will be control files and a parameter file named **initorcl.ora** created in the same folder.

Step 3   Install the application development software.

Now that you have verified that Oracle8 Server is installed properly, you can use the Oracle Installer to install all the client software, including application development software. Refer to the section on three-tier installation later in this chapter for an explanation of the installation of the Developer 2000 product.

Step 4   Verify connectivity.

After you have installed Oracle client software, you should verify connectivity to the database. Start a client tool and connect to the database using a valid username. If you chose to install the default database, a user account called *SYSTEM* with a password of *MANAGER* should have been created. For example, if you start SQL Worksheet by clicking on Start | Programs | Oracle Enterprise Manager | SQL Worksheet, you should see a Login screen similar to the one shown next.

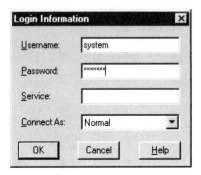

Type in the user and password information and leave the field labeled Service blank and the Connect As field set to Normal. If you are able to connect successfully, you should see a SQL Worksheet window similar to Figure 3-8.

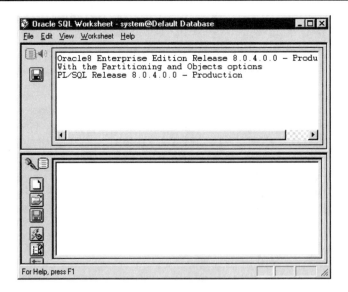

FIGURE 3-8. *SQL Worksheet with default connection*

In Figure 3-8, note that the title bar shows that you are connected to the default database. This is because you left the service field blank and you are automatically connected to an Oracle database with a system identifier (SID) of *ORCL*.

Step 5   Do post-installation tasks.

We recommend that you back up the Windows NT registry after you complete the installation. Start **regedit.exe** and select *Registry -> Export Registry File* to back up the registry to a file. You can use this file to recover a damaged registry at a later point in time.

Some Oracle products require the creation of database tables and/or repositories. You should create these tables and repositories at this time. If you are using Oracle Enterprise Manager, you can create a repository for this using the Repository Manager. We will discuss this further in Chapter 5. Similarly, if you are using Designer/2000 and Developer 2000, you need to create repositories and database tables for these products. Refer to the product documentation for information on creating these database objects.

Client/Server Installation

A client/server installation is probably the most-used environment for database applications. In this section, we will describe the procedure to use Oracle client applications against a remote Oracle8 Server. Oracle clients can connect to an Oracle8 Server using Net8 (previously known as SQL*Net) technology.

Step 1   Verify network connectivity.

As mentioned previously, you need to install Net8 software for Oracle client/server applications. Net8 requires that the underlying network be functional. After you have installed your networking software, you must ensure that the network is functional. The method used to test the network depends on the networking protocol. If you are using TCP/IP on a Windows NT machine, you can use the **ping** or **tracert** command to ensure that the network is functional. Similarly, you can use the **net** command to test the network connectivity if you are using Microsoft networking. The idea is to ensure that you can use the network to use a remote network resource. We have illustrated some of these commands below.

```
C:\> net view /domain:industry
Server Name              Remark
-------------------------------------
\\AADKOLI-LAP
\\RVELPURI-LAP
\\INDUSTRY-NT
The command completed successfully.
C:\> ping industry-nt
Pinging industry-nt.us.oracle.com [130.35.16.200] with 32 bytes of
data:
Reply from 130.35.16.200: bytes=32 time<10ms TTL=128
Reply from 130.35.16.200: bytes=32 time<10ms TTL=128
Reply from 130.35.16.200: bytes=32 time<10ms TTL=128
Reply from 130.35.16.200: bytes=32 time<10ms TTL=128
```

Step 2 Install Oracle8 and Net8 on the Server.

We suggest that you install the server-side software first. Install the Oracle8 server using the same procedure as the stand-alone installation described in the previous section. After this, you should install the Net8 Server software along with the appropriate protocol adapters. Most Windows NT machines today use TCP/IP and Microsoft networking with NetBEUI. You should install at least one matching protocol on the client and the server. We also recommend that you install Net8 Client software on the server, because this will allow for easier troubleshooting.

This Oracle8 Server installation is very similar to the procedure described in the stand-alone installation section earlier in this chapter. We will use a custom installation to illustrate the installation of the Net8 Server and appropriate protocol adapters.

If you choose to perform a custom installation, you will see a screen similar to the one shown in Figure 3-7.

We will expand the listing of products available on the media and choose to install Net8 products, as shown in Figure 3-9. You will see a dialog box that confirms a successful installation.

Step 3 Test a loopback connection.

If you have installed Net8 Client software on the server, we suggest you spend a few minutes testing a loopback connection. The idea is to use Net8 software to connect a client to the server on the same machine.

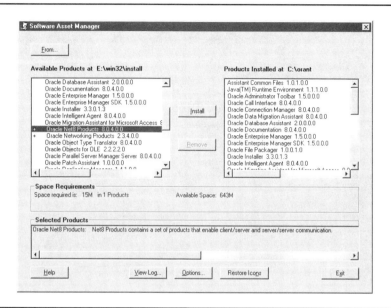

FIGURE 3-9. *Custom installation of Net8 products*

Ensure that the Net8 listener is running. You can do so by using the Services applet in the Control Panel. The illustration below shows the status of services on our test machine. Note the service named *OracleTNSListener80*.

Use the SQL*Net Easy Configuration utility to create an appropriate Net8 alias. Click on Start | Programs | Oracle for Windows NT | Oracle Net8 Easy Config to start the utility. Figure 3-10 shows the first screen of the wizard.

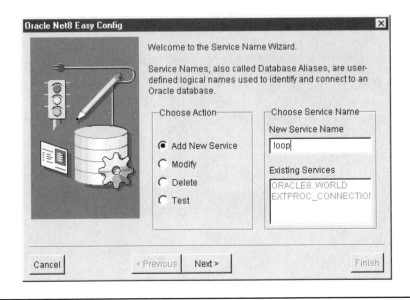

FIGURE 3-10. *Creating a Net8 service*

Choose to add a new service and the wizard will guide you through the configuration. Create an alias for a loopback connection named *loop*.

You can choose to test the Net8 service created within the Net8 configuration utility. You could even start a tool such as SQL Worksheet and use Net8 to connect to the server. Use a valid Oracle username and password and enter the service name of *loop*, created above. The illustration below shows a Login screen for SQL Worksheet on our test machine:

If your connection is successful, you should see a SQL Worksheet screen similar to the one shown in Figure 3-11. Note that the service name used for the connection is displayed in the title bar.

NOTE

*A Net8 utility called **tnsping80** can also be used to test a Net8 connection. This utility is available with the Net8 installation. It can be especially useful to test a connection when you are planning to use a third-party application and you do not have access to an Oracle client product. Type **tnsping80** at the command prompt for usage. The <address> argument is the Net8 service name.*

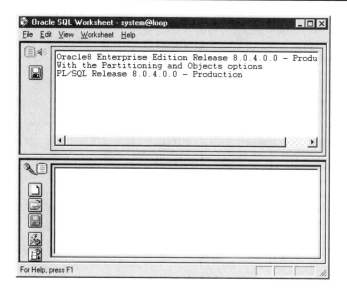

FIGURE 3-11. *SQL Worksheet with Net8 connection*

```
C:\>tnsping80
TNS Ping Utility for 32-bit Windows: Version 8.0.4.0.0
 - Production on 2 12:39:01
(c) Copyright 1997 Oracle Corporation.  All rights reserved.
TNS-03502: Insufficient arguments.
Usage:  tnsping <address> [<count>]
C:\> tnsping80 aa_web 1
TNS Ping Utility for 32-bit Windows: Version 8.0.4.0.0
 - Production on 23-AUG-98 13:04:59
(c) Copyright 1997 Oracle Corporation.  All rights reserved.
Attempting to contact (ADDRESS=(PROTOCOL=TCP)(HOST=aadkoli-
lap.us.oracle.com)(PORT=1521))
OK (210 msec)
```

Step 4   Install Client software and test connection.

Now that you have installed the server-side software and tested it, you can install the Net8 Client software on your client along with the appropriate network protocol adapters. Create appropriate Net8 aliases on your clients using the Net8 Easy Configuration utility and test the connectivity for the service that you have created. After this, you should install your application software and test a connection from the client. You can also use the **tnsping80.exe** utility on the client.

Three-Tier Installation

The three-tier architecture is gaining popularity in today's corporate world. Large public networks such as the Internet have allowed businesses to deploy applications globally on the Web. Thin clients are coming of age. Oracle Corporation proposed the Network Computing Architecture (NCA) about three years ago. The NCA proposes a three-tier architecture consisting of a database server, an application server, and a client. The Oracle8 Server can provide database services. The Oracle Web Application Server (WAS) is a Hypertext Transfer Protocol (HTTP) server that is integrated tightly with the database. The Web Server can take a Uniform Resource Locator (URL) from a browser and can gather information from the database or the file system. The file system can provide static Hypertext Markup Language (HTML) pages or Common Gateway Interface (CGI) scripts that do not need access to the database. Dynamic pages can be created by using built-in database procedures. Live queries can be used to embed data into the dynamic pages. Other software like the Forms Listener can run on the application server and allow applications built with Oracle Forms Builder to run in a browser.

We will perform a default installation of the Oracle WAS and then deploy a form application built with Oracle Forms Builder on the Web. More details on deploying cartridge based applications on the Web are provided in Chapter 4.

Start **setup.exe** from the WAS media. You will see a dialog box where you can select the language for your installation, as shown here:

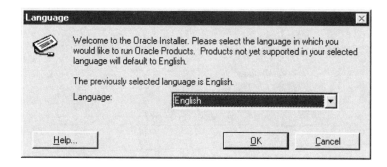

TIP
Install the Oracle8 Server, followed by the WAS 3.0, and, finally, Developer 2000 version 2.1. If you install Developer 2000 prior to WAS, you will need to install the Required Support Files component for Developer 2000 again.

After this, you can optionally add components and cartridges using the dialog box shown here:

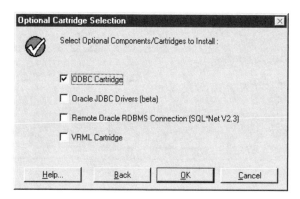

Next, you need to provide information for your Web, such as the name of the site and the host, using a dialog box similar to the one shown below. We recommend that you take the suggested User Datagram Protocol (UDP) port.

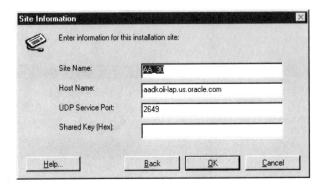

You can set the ports for the listeners that will be used for administration purposes using the next dialog box, as shown below. You will be asked to provide the username and the password every time you attempt to access the Admin pages.

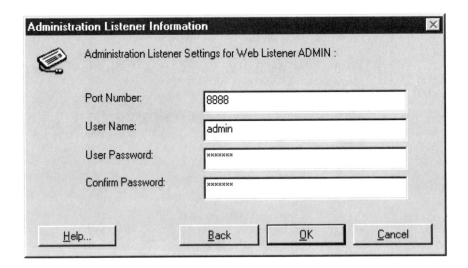

On our sample installation, we do not have any other HTTP servers installed. If we did, these would be displayed in a dialog box provided during the installation. We recommend that you use port 80, which is the default port, for the listener. If you use any other port, you will need to include the port information in the URL. For example, if you use port 6666 for the listener, your URL will be of the format:

 `http://www.company.com:6666`

Similarly you can configure the listener for user requests using dialog boxes similar to the ones shown here:

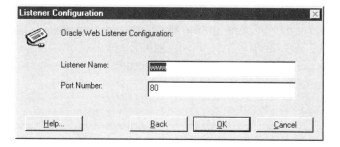

NOTE

The UDP service port is not the port that will be used for Web administration of the Web Listener. While the Web Administration Listener is configured for port 8888 by default, the Web Listener for user requests is usually configured for port 80.

Finally, you will see the dialog boxes shown below that confirm the completion of the installation. You can select the Back button in the dialog box shown in the first illustration to change any configuration choices. If you select the OK button, the configuration files will be created.

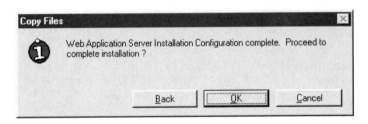

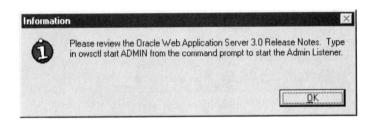

You are now ready to configure the WAS Admin Listener. Use a browser to go to the main WAS Admin page by using a URL of the format: *http://<server>:<admin port>*. On our test machine, we used the following URL:

```
http://aadkoli-lap.us.oracle.com:8888
```

You will see a dialog box similar to the one shown here, where you can provide the admin username and password for WAS configuration:

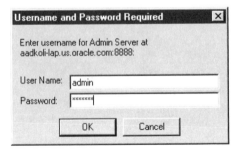

You will see the main WAS Admin page as shown in Figure 3-12.

We will take the link for *Default Configuration* for now. This will create database user accounts named *www_dba* and *www_user*, Database Access Descriptors (DADs), and install the required database objects, including PL/SQL packages, on the database. Figure 3-13 shows a sample screen for the default configuration.

We will provide the SQL*Net connect string along with a valid login for a DBA on the database, as shown in Figure 3-14, and submit this information. This information will be used to create a DAD.

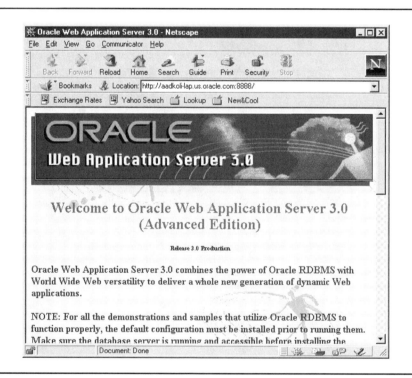

FIGURE 3-12. *Main Admin screen for WAS*

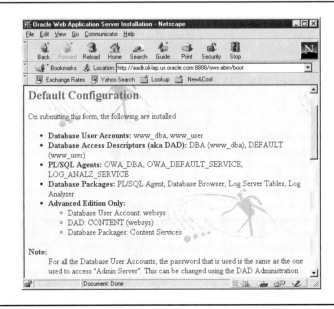

FIGURE 3-13. *Default configuration of WAS*

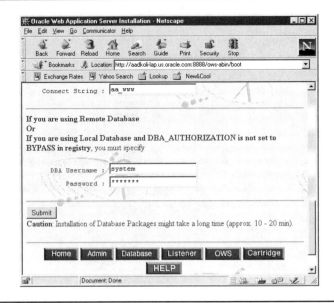

FIGURE 3-14. *Configuration of a DAD*

NOTE
WAS 3.0 uses SQL*Net 2.x to connect to a database server. WAS 4.0 is expected to be released by September 1998 and will support Net8.

You will see a screen similar to the one shown in Figure 3-15, which will provide a log of the activity.

This procedure should take about five minutes. At the end of it, you will see a screen that confirms the successful completion of the procedure as well as a reminder to restart the Web listeners. Figures 3-16 and 3-17 show portions of this screen.

You should spend a few minutes trying out the sample applications provided with WAS 3.0 to confirm that the configuration is normal. Go to the main Administration page and take the link for Sample Apps, as shown in Figure 3-18.

You will see a screen similar to Figure 3-19, from which you can install the demo packages and run demos.

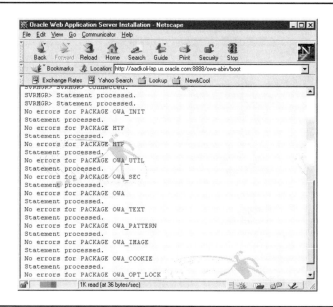

FIGURE 3-15. *Log of WAS installation*

FIGURE 3-16. *Successful completion of installation*

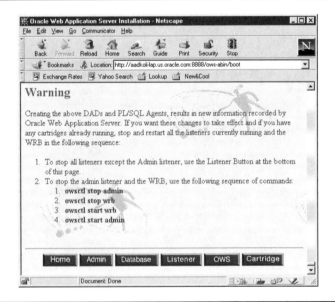

FIGURE 3-17. *Warning to restart the listener*

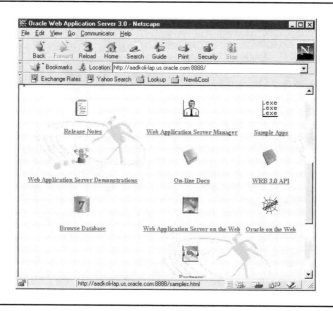

FIGURE 3-18. *Link to Sample Apps from WAS Admin screen*

FIGURE 3-19. *Screen for WAS demos*

Install the demo package for the user *www_dba*, which was created previously from the default installation of the WAS. Figures 3-20 and 3-21 show screen shots for creating demo packages.

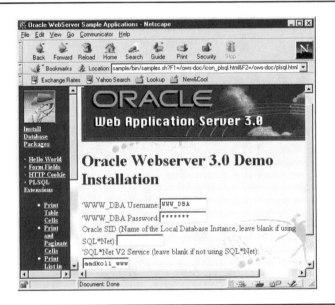

FIGURE 3-20. *Creating demo packages for WAS*

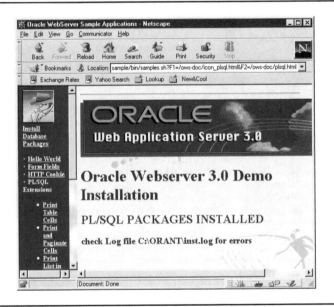

FIGURE 3-21. *Successful completion of demo installation*

Follow the links in the Demo page and ensure that the demos run properly. If you have any problems, look at a log file named **\orant\inst.log** for diagnostic information.

Once the WAS is installed, you are ready to install Developer 2000. Again, the Oracle Installer can be used to perform a default installation. Shown here are some dialog boxes that you will see during this installation:

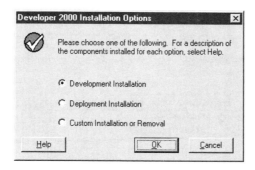

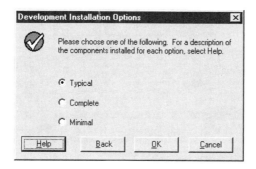

After the installation is complete, build a sample form using Forms Builder. We will use a form named **test.fmx** on the DEPT table belonging to the *SCOTT/TIGER* account and deploy this form on the Web using the Forms Listener and WAS.

Step 1 Deploy the **.fmx** on the WAS.

Copy the **test.fmx** file to either the folder **orant\bin** or into any other folder that is included in the PATH defined by the FORMS50_PATH variable. We will copy our form into the **\apps\web\html** folder.

NOTE
*You can edit the FORMS50_PATH by using
Registry Editor. Expand
HKEY_LOCAL_MACHINE->SOFTWARE->
ORACLE to locate the variable FORMS50_PATH.*

Step 2   Start the Forms Server.

You can start the Forms Server (or listener) on Windows NT 4.0 by
selecting Start | Programs | Developer 2000 R2.1 | Forms Server Listener.
This will start a process named **F50SRV32.EXE** that is visible in Task
Manager, as shown here:

```
Windows NT Task Manager                    _ □ X
File  Options  View  Help

Applications  Processes  Performance

Image Name        PID    CPU   CPU Time   Mem Usage  ▲
Deskmenu.exe       99    00    0:00:00       68 K
strtdb80.exe      106    00    0:00:00       48 K
mnaddrsrv.exe     110    00    0:00:00      708 K
TNSLSNR80.EXE     122    00    0:00:00       84 K
primservice.exe   126    00    0:00:00       44 K
RpcSs.exe         129    00    0:00:03      380 K
AtSvc.Exe         134    00    0:00:00      136 K
tcpsvcs.exe       138    00    0:00:00      192 K
spsdock.exe       142    00    0:00:00      200 K
spspwr.exe        147    00    0:00:00     1012 K
tapisrv.exe       150    00    0:00:00      200 K
rasman.exe        164    00    0:00:00      520 K
mnrpcnmsrv.exe    178    00    0:00:00      732 K
F50SRV32.EXE      181    00    0:00:00     1316 K
mnorbsrv.exe      194    00    0:00:01      900 K
wrbcfg.exe        199    00    0:00:02      900 K
wrblog.exe        204    00    0:00:01      948 K
WINWORD.EXE       205    00    0:39:54     4640 K
wrbasrv.exe       210    00    0:00:00      812 K  ▼

                                  End Process

Processes: 41    CPU Usage: 4%    Mem Usage: 114016K / 193804K
```

You can use the End Process button in Task Manager to shut down the
Forms Server, if required.

Step 3   Deploy application to end users.

The end goal is to provide a URL for users to access the form application.
We will step through the bare minimum configuration to make the **test.fmx**
application available to the user.

The first task is to create virtual directories for Forms on the Web Server.
Access the Web Listener Configuration screen from the WAS Admin screen
and configure the general listener on port 80. If you chose the default
installation for WAS, this listener is named *www*. Click on the Directory
link to configure the virtual directories. Figure 3-22 shows this screen.

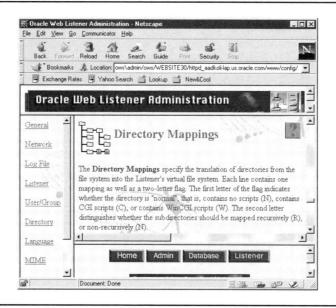

FIGURE 3-22. *Configuring virtual directories*

Create the virtual directories for Web forms as shown here:

File-System Directory	Flag	Virtual Directory
c:\orant\forms50\java	NR	/web_code/
c:\apps\web\html	NR	/web_html/
c:\orant\forms50\java	NR	/web_jars/

Figure 3-23 shows the configuration screen for our installation.

NOTE
Refer to the section "Deploying Applications on the Web" in the chapter titled "Developer 2000 Guidelines for Building Applications" in the Developer 2000 documentation for further information.

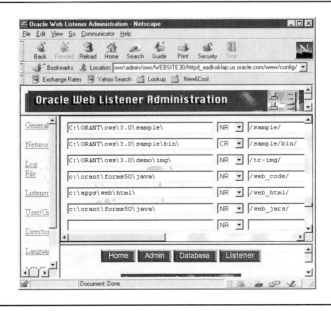

FIGURE 3-23. *Virtual directories for forms*

After this, you need to choose between a cartridge and noncartridge implementation. A cartridge implementation requires you to create a Forms cartridge handler. The Forms cartridge handler builds the initial HTML file dynamically. A cartridge implementation requires you to install the Oracle Web Request Broker on your application server. In contrast, a noncartridge implementation does not require the Web Request Broker. You need to create a static HTML file that includes hardcoded information specific to an application. We will choose a noncartridge implementation at this time.

Start by copying a static HTML template provided by Oracle. Open the file in a text editor and modify the text and applet tags as per your application needs. Place the file in the virtual directory **web_html** that you defined for HTML files. For our example, we will make a copy of the static template **static.htm** and name the file **test.htm**:

```
C:\apps\web\html> copy c:\orant\tools\devdem20\web\static.htm test.htm
```

We will edit the **test.htm** file and provide information for the **test.fmx** application created previously. The applet definition is shown below:

```
<!-- applet definition (start) -->
<APPLET CODEBASE="/web_code/"
CODE="oracle.forms.uiClient.v1_4.engine.Main"
ARCHIVE="/web_jars/f50web.jar" HEIGHT=20 WIDTH=20>
<PARAM NAME="serverArgs" VALUE="module=test
userid=scott/tiger@aa_web">
</APPLET>
<!-- applet definition (end) -->
```

CAUTION
Some of the above information is case-sensitive. The 'C' and the 'M' in the CODE argument above need to be uppercase.

Note that the **.fmx** extension is not required for the module name. Also, the complete physical path to the **test.fmx** file is not required since it is in the path defined by the FORMS50_PATH variable. The *userid* parameter includes the Oracle user, the password, and the connect string for SQL*Net.

We are now ready to test the application. We will use the JDK Applet Viewer provided by Sun Microsystems. Start **appletviewer** from the command prompt and pass the URL to the **test.htm** file that is in the virtual directory **web_html**:

```
C:\orant\JDK1.1\jdk\bin> appletviewer
http://aadkoli-lap.us.oracle.com/web_html/test.htm
```

You should see a screen similar to the one shown in Figure 3-24 for the **test.fmx** application.

Note that you can run the application in any browser that supports Java 1.1.1 or higher. We recommend that you test the application in **appletviewer** for now as it is easier to debug the application since it ignores all HTML tags and only processes the code for the applet. To install **appletviewer**, click Start | Programs | Developer 2000 R2.1 | Install JDK

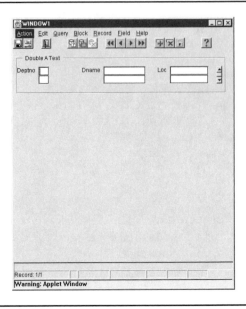

FIGURE 3-24. *Sample application in Applet Viewer*

Applet Viewer. Specify a destination folder of **c:\orant\jdk 1.1** for the installation. Ensure that the following environment variable is set using the System applet under the Control Panel:

```
CLASSPATH=C:\ORANT\JDK1.1\JDK\CLASSES.ZIP
```

Also ensure that the PATH variable includes the folder **c:\orant\jdk1.1\jdk\bin**.

Third-Party Products

If you wish to use third-party development tools and applications against an Oracle8 Server, you will need to use Open Database Connectivity (ODBC). The installation of the Oracle8 Server is identical to the stand-alone installation. If you are using third-party products in a client/server configuration, you will need to install Net8 software on the server and the client as described in the client/server installation section earlier in this chapter. Test a loopback connection on the server using **tnsping80.exe**.

Next, install the Oracle ODBC driver on the client and configure the ODBC data sources that you need. You can access the ODBC Administrator utility by clicking on Start | Settings | Control Panel | ODBC. You will see a screen similar to this one:

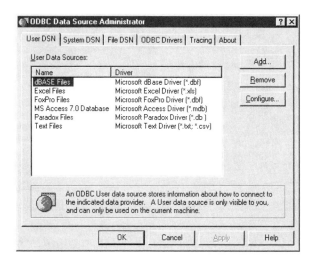

You can add a *System* data source or a *User* data source based on your needs. To add a *System* data source, select the System DSN tab and click on the Add button to see a screen similar to the one shown below. This is a listing of all the ODBC drivers installed on your machine.

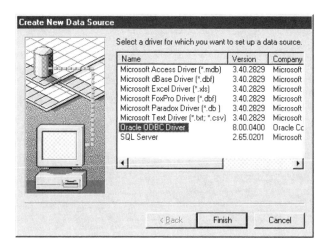

Select the Oracle ODBC driver and click on the Finish button to see a screen similar to the one shown here:

Enter appropriate information to create the data source. You need to provide a name for the data source. If you are connecting to Oracle using Net8, provide the Net8 alias for the Service Name entry. If you have a stand-alone installation and you are connecting to a local Oracle8 Server, provide '2:' as the Service Name entry. This illustration shows our test configuration for ODBC:

Click on the OK button to see a screen similar to the one shown here:

To test the ODBC connection, use the Oracle ODBC test program. Click on Start | Programs | Oracle for Windows NT | Oracle ODBC Test to see a screen similar to the one shown below. Click on the Connect button and select the Machine Data Source tab.

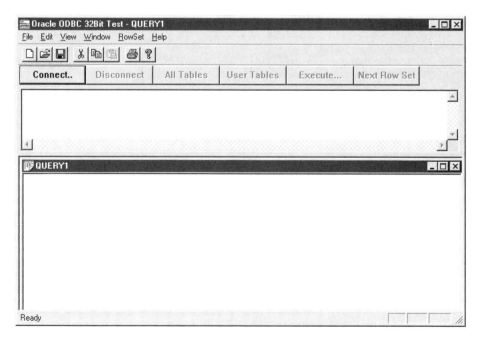

Select the data source named *Test* created previously, as shown here:

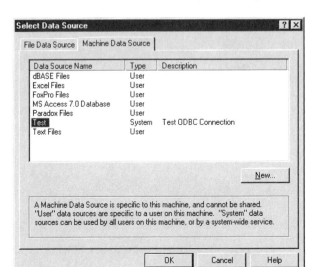

Click on the OK button to see a Login dialog box similar to the one shown below. Log in to the database and execute a sample query.

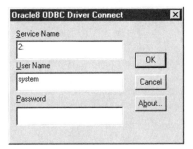

Non-Oracle RDBMS

If your site demands that you connect an Oracle client application to a non-Oracle RDBMS, you can do so using ODBC technology. While this is not in the scope of this book, we will cover this situation here for completeness. You will first need to create an ODBC data source as described in the previous section. After this, you must install a piece of software called Oracle Open Client Adapter for ODBC that is available on the Developer 2000 media. Use the custom installation process in Oracle Installer and select the component as shown in Figure 3-25.

You can connect to the ODBC data source by using a service name (instead of a Net8 connect string) of the format: *odbc:<datasource>*. Note that the string 'odbc:' is required. You can also provide the string *odbc:** to get a listing of all available ODBC resources and then pick the ODBC resource of your choice for the connection. Refer to product documentation for Oracle Developer 2000 for details of this configuration.

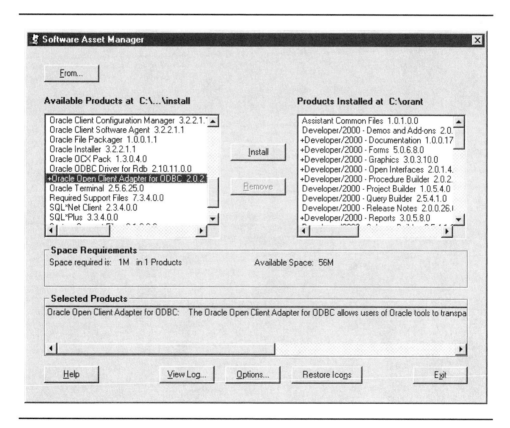

FIGURE 3-25. *Installing the Oracle Client Adapter*

CHAPTER
4

Advanced Installation of Oracle8

e looked at basic installation in client/server and three-tier
environments in Chapter 3. The topics that we discussed
included installation of the Oracle8 Server, Web Application
Server, development tools, and Net8. Many additional
features are available in the Oracle8 Server as cartridges or
add-on options. In this chapter, we will look at the cartridges and options
bundled with the Oracle8 Server. We have also included sections on
distributed databases, replication, and parallel servers, with focus on
Windows NT implementation. The Parallel Query option (PQO) is also
discussed.

NOTE
You might need to obtain special licenses for
these options and cartridges.

Partitioning Option

The Oracle8 Server allows for partitioning of tables and indexes into smaller
pieces called *partitions*. Partitions provide for improved manageability and
availability. A mechanism called *range partitioning* is used to create the
partitions, which allows users to define ranges of data in a partition. The
data is partitioned based on a *range partition key*. Partitions for the same
table or index segment can be created in separate tablespaces. If a
tablespace goes offline, the remaining partitions are available to
applications. This allows for partial availability.

Installation of the Partitioning Option

You must choose to install the Oracle8 Partitioning Option for the Oracle8
Server to use this enhanced feature. There are no special configuration
requirements to use partitions. During installation of the Oracle8 Server, you
must simply choose to install this option. If you have an existing installation,
you must choose the Custom Installation option and expand the product
component Oracle8 Enterprise Edition Cartridges and Options for

installation. Pick the Oracle8 Partitioning Option from the list. When installed, this option will be displayed in the banner information when you connect to the database, as shown below:

```
Oracle8 Enterprise Edition Release 8.0.4.0.0 - Production
With the Partitioning and Objects options
PL/SQL Release 8.0.4.0.0 - Production
```

Using Partitions

If you choose to install the partitioning option, SQL and PL/SQL extensions will be installed automatically. An additional set of views are created in the data dictionary. Extensions are made available in the CREATE TABLE, ALTER TABLE, CREATE INDEX, and ALTER INDEX commands to support partitioning.

You can use Schema Manager or issue SQL commands using any SQL tool to create and modify partitions. If you use Schema Manager, you must create the table manually, as shown below. The wizard does not support partitions.

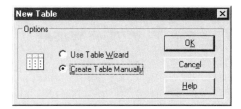

In Schema Manager, you must select the Partitions tab to define partitions as per your requirements, as shown in Figure 4-1.

Indexes can also be partitioned. Refer to *Oracle8 SQL Reference* for more information on SQL extensions for support of partitions. Partitions can be reorganized using Schema Manager or SQL. Data Manager also supports partitions for export and import.

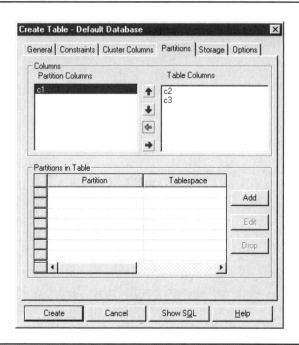

FIGURE 4-1. *Defining partitions in Schema Manager*

Objects Option

The Objects option of Oracle8 Server provides support for user-defined types (termed object types), object extensions in SQL and PL/SQL, extensions in precompilers, and Oracle Call Interface (OCI). The object type translator (OTT) is required to support object types in precompilers and OCI. Object views allow you to map relational data onto object types. Support for updatable views is also available along with an INSTEAD OF trigger.

Installing Objects Option

The Objects option must be installed during the installation of Oracle8 Server. Choose to install the component Oracle8 Objects Option. No additional configuration is required. OTT is also installed as a part of this option. As with partitioning, the banner information will show the Objects option after it is installed. If you have a database already installed, you can add the Object options by performing a custom installation and installing the component Oracle8 Enterprise Edition Cartridges and Options. Pick the Oracle8 Objects Option from the list.

Using Objects

Use the SQL extensions CREATE TYPE, ALTER TYPE, and DROP TYPE to define object types. Once defined, object types can be used with few restrictions in tables. One such restriction is that you cannot use object types in partitioned tables. Schema Manager supports object types and object views.

ConText Cartridge (CC)

Oracle8 ConText Cartridge (CC) allows for querying with text- or theme-based searches. The *text processing* and *linguistic processing* features allow for text, theme, and linguistic searches. Linguistic processing is only available for English at this time. Refer to the Oracle documentation for CC for a complete description and usage information on the cartridge. On Windows NT, start with the **c:\orant\doc\cartridg.804\a58161\toc.htm** file for online documentation on CC. The *Oracle8 ConText Cartridge QuickStart* manual provides an overview of the product.

Installing ConText Cartridge

Use the Oracle Installer to install CC. The executables and files associated with CC are installed by this procedure.

Verify that the SHARED_POOL_SIZE parameter on your database is set to at least 12Mb (CC requires a shared pool of over 11.5Mb). Edit the INIT.ORA and change this setting if necessary. Shut down and restart the database if you have changed the SHARED_POOL_SIZE setting.

Also ensure that the *contains* function is enabled via ConText by setting the following parameter in the INIT.ORA file:

```
text_enable = TRUE
```

Once the INIT.ORA is configured, use the Services applet to ensure that the service *OracleConTextService80* is started.

Start a ConText server with the *DDL* (D), *query* (Q), and *linguistics* (L) personality. On Windows NT, use **ctxsrv80.exe** from the command line as shown below:

```
ctxsrv80 -user ctxsys/ctxsys -personality dlq
```

Finally, use Database Assistant to add the database objects, including packages and roles for CC. Use the Modify a Database option in Database Assistant and choose to install the ConText Cartridge. You can also choose to install the demo at this time.

> **NOTE**
> *The setup for the demo will most likely take over an hour (it took over 90 minutes on our test installation). During this, progress will appear like it has halted or hung at 79 percent for almost an hour. At this stage, an import is being performed and indexes required for the demo are being created. An import session will be active for the user CTXSYS on your database. You can query the V$SESSION view as shown below to get information on this session:*

```
SVRMGR> select status, program, username from v$session where
username='CTXSYS';
STATUS    PROGRAM                                    USERNAME
--------  -----------------------------------------  -------------------------
ACTIVE    C:\orant\bin\imp80.exe                     CTXSYS
1 row selected.
```

The above procedure creates users on the database named *ctxsys* and *ctxdemo* with passwords of *ctxsys* and *ctxdemo*, respectively. A tablespace named *DRSYS* is also created, along with the database roles *ctxadmin*, *ctxapp*, and *ctxuser*. Refer to the Oracle documentation for information on these roles. A log file named **c:\orant\database\spoolctx.lst** is created for the procedure. You can review this file for errors. For Windows NT–specific information on the CC, refer to the document *Oracle8 Enterprise Edition*

Getting Started 8.0.4 for Windows NT. Point your browser to the **c:\orant\doc\database.804\a55928\ch8.htm** file for online documentation.

The window running **ctxsrv80** will show an output similar to the one shown below:

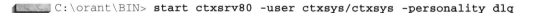

```
C:\> ctxsrv80 -user ctxsys/ctxsys -personality dlq
Oracle ConText Option: Release 2.3.6.0.0
 - Production on Mon Sep 7 12:38:23 1998
(c) Copyright 1997 Oracle Corporation.  All rights reserved.
13-38-23 09/07/98 === OCO server startup ===
13-38-23 09/07/98 Initialized CORE
13-38-24 09/07/98 Connected to database.
13-38-25 09/07/98 === Initializing dispatcher ===
13-38-25 09/07/98 === Server startup completed. ===
13-38-25 09/07/98 ..initializing ConText child heap
13-38-25 09/07/98 ..initializing ConText settings
13-38-25 09/07/98 ..reading ConText settings from database
13-38-25 09/07/98 ..opening ConText session
13-38-25 09/07/98 === Initialized Linguistics ===
13-44-15 09/07/98 Cmd 1000: begin_index, user=CTXDEMO,
polid=1061, svrcnt=1, runseq=1, opqual=C
13-44-19 09/07/98 End cmd 1000
13-44-20 09/07/98 Cmd 1001: populate_index, user=CTXDEMO,
polid=1061, svrcnt=1, svr=1, runseq=1, opqual=C
13-44-21 09/07/98 Begin document indexing
13-44-23 09/07/98 Errors reading documents: 0
13-44-23 09/07/98 Index data for 36 documents to be written
to database
13-44-23 09/07/98    memory use: 564493
13-44-29 09/07/98    index data written to database.
13-44-29 09/07/98 End of document indexing. 36 documents indexed.
13-44-30 09/07/98 End cmd 1001
13-44-31 09/07/98 Cmd 1002: end_index, user=CTXDEMO,
polid=1061, runseq=1, opqual=C
13-44-36 09/07/98 End cmd 1002
```

Running ConText Servers

You can use the **ctxsrv80** executable to run a ConText server on Windows NT. To start the ConText server in a new command window, use the **start** command as shown below:

```
C:\orant\BIN> start ctxsrv80 -user ctxsys/ctxsys -personality dlq
```

If you do not want to see a command window on your Windows NT console for the ConText server, you can use the ConText Cartridge Control utility. The executable on Windows NT is named **ctxctl80.exe**. The sample session below provides usage information for this utility:

```
C:\orant\BIN> ctxctl80
*** ConText Option Servers Control ***
Servers on AADKOLI-LAP.
Type help for a list of commands.
command> help
The following commands are available:
  help [command]                              - commands information
  status                                      - show running servers
  start n [ling | query | ddl | dml | load]... - start n servers
  stop pid... | all                           - stop server processes
  quit                                        - terminate ctxctl
  exit                                        - terminate ctxctl
  errmsg errcode                              - get message text
command> start 1 ling query ddl
Enter ConText Option database SID. Default is <ORCL>:
Enter ConText Option administrator password for SID <ORCL>: ctxsys
+--------------------------------------------------------+
| Results of start ConText Servers on this server        |
+---------+-------+-------+-------+-------+-------+-------+
| STATUS  |PID/ERR| LING. | LOAD  | QUERY |  DDL  |  DML  |
+---------+-------+-------+-------+-------+-------+-------+
| SUCCESS |  129  |   X   |       |   X   |   X   |       |
+---------+-------+-------+-------+-------+-------+-------+
| Needed  |       |   1   |   0   |   1   |   1   |   0   |
+---------+-------+-------+-------+-------+-------+-------+
| Created |       |   1   |   0   |   1   |   1   |   0   |
+---------+-------+-------+-------+-------+-------+-------+
command> exit
C:\orant\BIN> ctxctl80
*** ConText Option Servers Control ***
Servers on AADKOLI-LAP.
Type help for a list of commands.
command> status
+------------------------------------------------+
| List of ConText Servers running on this server |
+-------+-------+-------+-------+-------+-------+
|  PID  | LING. | LOAD  | QUERY |  DDL  |  DML  |
+-------+-------+-------+-------+-------+-------+
|  129  |   X   |       |   X   |   X   |       |
```

```
+=======+=======+=======+=======+=======+=======+
| Total |    1 |    0 |    1 |    1 |    0 |
+-------+-------+-------+-------+-------+-------+
command> stop 129
+---------------------------------+
| ConText servers STOP status     |
+------------+---------+---------+
| Process Id | SUCCESS | FAILURE |
+------------+---------+---------+
|       129 |    X    |         |
+============+=========+=========+
| Total      |    1    |    0    |
+------------+---------+---------+
```

ConText Demos

On Windows NT, the demos are created in the folder
c:\orant\ctx80\demo. The demo for text-based queries is created in the
subfolder **ctxplus** and the demo for linguistic processing is created in the
subfolder **ctxling**.

The instructions for the demo are available in their respective folders in
files named **readme.txt**. You should read these file before attempting to run
the demo. Run the demos as the Oracle user *ctxdemo* with the password
ctxdemo. A sample run of the demo in the **gist.sql** file is shown below for
your reference:

```
SQL> connect ctxdemo/ctxdemo
Connected.
SQL> @C:\orant\ctx80\demo\ctxling\genling
Clearing theme table...
Clearing article table...
Initializing ling_tracking table
Creating linguistic callback function LING_COMP_CALLBACK...
No errors.
Submitting all articles for linguistic extraction...
All articles submitted.  Use @status to see the status of
pending linguistic requests.
```

Once you have submitted the articles for linguistic extraction, you
should check for the status of the process by using the **status.sql** script.
When the number of requests is down to zero, you can issue queries. This

process can take up to 15 minutes. We ran the sample **gist.sql** as shown below:

```
SQL> @c:\orant\ctx80\demo\ctxling\status
Linguistic Requests left: 35
Request Errors....
SQL> @c:\orant\ctx80\demo\ctxling\status
Linguistic Requests left: 8
Request Errors....
SQL> @c:\orant\ctx80\demo\ctxling\status
Linguistic Requests left: 0
Request Errors....
SQL> @gist
Points of View
Enter value for 1: 20
1 GENERIC
2 Chiron Corporation
...
...
11 shares outstanding
...
...
16 specialization
17 rights
Which point of view gist to print: 11
Enter value for 1: 20
Technology: Ciba-Geigy Invests in Biotechnology, Buying 7.9% of
Chiron for $20 Million by Brenton R. Schlender
```

ConText Cartridge Workbench (CCW)

The ConText Cartridge Workbench (CCW) consists of GUI administration tools, document viewers, and an I/O utility. All CCW tools can be launched from the ConText Cartridge Workbench program group. Click Start | Programs | ConText Cartridge Workbench to access these tools. The GUI administration tools include Configuration Manager and a System Administration Tool. Point your browser to the file **c:\orant\doc\cartridg.804\a57700\ch01.htm** for details on CCW. System Administration Tool can be used to manage the ConText Cartridge using GUI (it is specific to Windows NT and Windows 95). Figure 4-2 shows a screen to manage the ConText server from this tool.

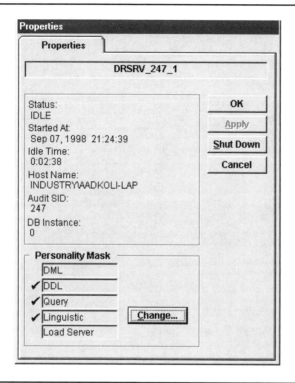

FIGURE 4-2. *Managing ConText server*

To install CCW, you must install Web Application Server (WAS). Programs are available to set up the viewer and the Configuration Manager. The setup will invoke the Oracle Installer and configure the Web listener on port 80. You must provide the password for the user *ctxsys* and the *admin* user for WAS. Figure 4-3 shows a sample screen from the setup of the viewer.

Image Cartridge (IC)

The Image Cartridge (IC) provides extensions to Oracle8 Server for imaging applications. Image storage, retrieval, and conversion are supported through object datatypes. IC uses binary large objects (BLOBs) and external files (BFILEs), the new storage attributes available with Oracle8 Server.

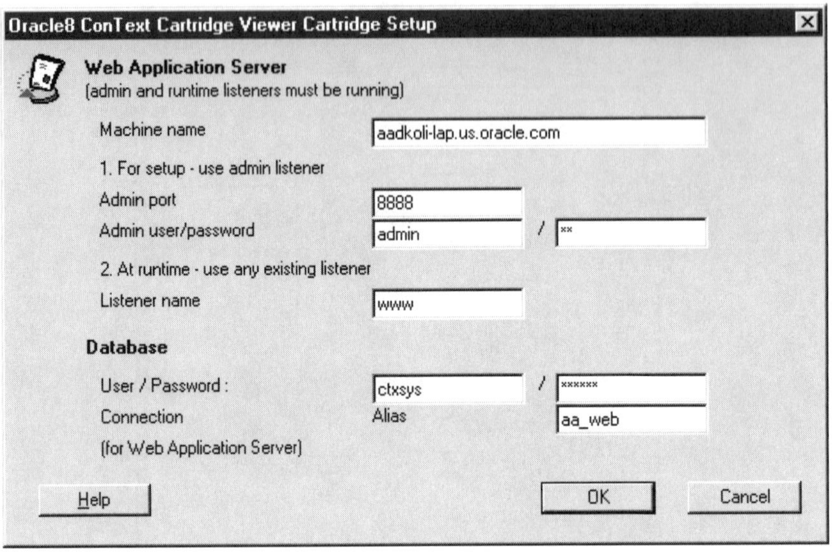

FIGURE 4-3. *Viewer Cartridge Setup*

Installing Image Cartridge

Image Cartridge needs the Objects option. If you chose to install IC while installing Oracle8 Server, no additional configuration is required. If you did not select this cartridge for installation, use the Oracle Installer to install IC. If you are adding IC to an existing installation, choose to perform a custom installation and select Oracle8 Image Cartridge from the list of cartridges. The executables and files associated with IC are installed by this procedure.

Edit the **c:\orant\ord80\img\admin\ordiinst.sql** file and make the following changes:

I. Change connection information.

Provide the password for the user *internal* in the script.

2. Remove the line to create user *ordsys*.

Delete the line that creates the user named *ordsys*, as this user was created when you installed IC. If you have changed the password for the user *ordsys*, provide the new password in the script.

3. Provide complete path information for SQL scripts.

Modify the following two lines and provide complete path information to these scripts as shown below:

```
@@ordispec.sql
@@ordibody.plb                                    ORIGINAL LINES
@c:\orant\ord80\img\admin\ordispec.sql           MODIFIED LINES
@c:\orant\ord80\img\admin\ordibody.plb
```

Run the script from Server Manager and not SQL*Plus, as you will get some errors in SQL*Plus while creating the types. SQL*Plus 8.0 also does not recognize the user *internal*. You might also see the following error message when you run this script:

```
ORA-02304: invalid object identifier literal
```

This error is caused by the fact that the object types *ORDImgB* and *ORDImgF* already exist with the object id that you are attempting to use. Delete the object types by executing the following commands before executing **ordiinst.sql** again to avoid the ORA-2304 error.

```
SVRMGR> connect ordsys/ordsys
Connected.
SVRMGR> drop type ordimgb;
Statement processed.
SVRMGR> drop type ordimgf;
Statement processed.
```

Point your browser to the file **c:\orant\doc\database.804\a55928\ch8.htm** for Windows NT–specific information on Image Cartridge.

As an alternative, you could use Database Assistant to install IC and the demo. Use the Modify a database option in Database Assistant to install IC.

Image Cartridge Demos

A demo of IC is available in the folder **c:\orant\ord80\img\demo**. Edit the script **imgdemo.sql** and provide the password for the user *internal*. Modify or delete the lines creating the user *scott* and granting roles to *scott* as required.

CAUTION
*The online documentation has an error in the location of the **imgdemo.sql** script. It is located in the folder **c:\orant\ord80\img\demo** and not the **c:\orant\ord80\img\admin** folder.*

You will need either the Microsoft C Compiler or the Borland C Compiler to create an executable for the demo. Use the command file **make.bat** for Microsoft C and **bmake.bat** for Borland C.

Visual Information Retrieval (VIR) Cartridge

Visual Information Cartridge (VIR) can be used in applications that require retrieval and manipulation of images. Its primary purpose is to store and retrieve image data from Oracle8 Server using the Image Cartridge.

Installing Visual Information Retrieval Cartridge

If you chose to install VIR when you installed the Oracle8 Server, no additional configuration is required. If you did not, then you must install the Image Cartridge before installing VIR (refer to the earlier section in this chapter on Image Cartridge). Use the custom installation process in Oracle Installer to install VIR. The post-installation tasks can be completed using Database Assistant or by executing the SQL script **c:\orant\ord80\vir\admin\ordrinst.sql** manually. The VIR objects are owned by the Oracle user *ordsys*. You might see the following error message while this script is being executed:

```
ORA-02304: invalid object identifier literal
```

Refer to the earlier section titled "Installing Image Cartridge" for a discussion of this error message, which can be ignored. Execute the three commands shown below if you do not want to see the error messages:

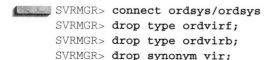

```
SVRMGR> connect ordsys/ordsys
SVRMGR> drop type ordvirf;
SVRMGR> drop type ordvirb;
SVRMGR> drop synonym vir;
```

NOTE
*Comment out or delete the line CREATE USER ORDSYS and the GRANT statement immediately below that in the **ordrinst.sql** file as this user was already created when Image Cartridge was installed.*

If you get any compilation errors while executing **ordrinst.sql**, execute **c:\orant\ord80\img\admin\ordiinst.sql** first.

Visual Information Retrieval Demos

The files related to the demo are available in the **c:\orant\ord80\vir\demo** folder (and not **c:\orant\ord80\vir\admin** as per the documentation). Execute the script **virdemo.sql** from this folder. Delete or comment out the lines in this script that attempt to create the user *scott* and grant roles to this user in order to avoid error messages from this part of the script.

You will need either the Microsoft C Compiler or the Borland C Compiler to create an executable for the demo. Use the command file **make.bat** for Microsoft C and **bmake.bat** for Borland C.

TIP
The VIR cartridge has been licensed by Oracle Corporation from third-party vendors. Visit http://www.virage.com and http:// www.viisage.com for more information on this cartridge.

Time Series Cartridge (TS)

It is often necessary for database applications to analyze data using timestamps. Time Series (TS) Cartridge uses Oracle8 objects and therefore requires that you install the Objects option before you install TS. Historical information can be derived from time-related data using TS.

Installing Time Series Cartridge

Time Series Cartridge also needs the Objects option. If you chose to install TS while installing Oracle8 Server, no additional configuration is required. If you did not select this cartridge for installation, use the Oracle Installer to install TS. If you are adding TS to an existing installation, choose to perform a custom installation and select Oracle8 Time Series Cartridge from the list of cartridges. The executables and files associated with TS are installed by this procedure.

NOTE

TS and Image Cartridge use the same Oracle user named ORDSYS. If you have installed Image Cartridge before TS, you will see some errors because this user already exists. Ignore these errors.

Use Database Assistant to install TS by using the Modify a database option or follow the manual configuration process described below.

Edit the **c:\orant\ord80\ts\admin\ordtinst.sql** file and make the following changes:

1. Add statements to create the user *ordsys* if it does not exist already. Ensure that the user has been assigned the *CONNECT* and *RESOURCE* roles. Also ensure that the user has the *CREATE LIBRARY* and *GRANT ANY PRIVILEGE* privileges.

2. Provide complete path information for SQL scripts, if necessary.

Again, run the script from Server Manager and not SQL*Plus as you will get some errors in SQL*Plus while creating the types, as shown below:

```
SVRMGR> connect ordsys/ordsys
Connected.
SVRMGR> @c:\orant\ord80\ts\admin\ordtinst.sql
```

You might see some errors with the text "ORA-955 name is already used by an existing object". Point your browser to the file **c:\orant\doc\database.804\a55928\ch8.htm** for Windows NT–specific information on Time Series Cartridge.

Time Series Cartridge Demos

There are five demos available with TS. These are installed in the **c:\orant\ord80\ts\demo** folder under five separate subfolders. A **readme.txt** file is available in each of these subfolders with instructions on running the demo. The demo in the **usage** subfolder is the easiest to run for the purposes of testing. Modify the file **demo.sql** and provide the passwords for the user *internal* in two locations before running the script. Again, run the script from Server Manager, from the folder **c:\orant\ord80\ts\demo\usage**.

TIP
*Spool the output of the **demo.sql** script to a file before you execute it.*

Spatial Cartridge (SC)

Spatial Cartridge (SC) can be used to work on spatial data such as two-dimensional maps. Maps typically contain roads and boundaries along with points representing cities. SC allows you to write applications for such spatial data.

Installing Spatial Cartridge

If you chose to install SC while installing Oracle8 Server, no additional configuration is required. If you did not select this cartridge for installation, use the Oracle Installer to install the cartridge. A user named *mdsys* with the password *mdsys* is created as part of this procedure (the Oracle documentation erroneously uses *manager* as the password for this user).

Run the script **c:\orant\md80\admin\catmd.sql** from SQL*Plus. This script runs for over 20 minutes.

CAUTION
*The **catmd.sql** script must be executed from SQL*Plus. It will not run under Server Manager.*

Point your browser to the file **c:\orant\doc\database.804\a55928\ch8.htm** for Windows NT–specific information on SC.

Spatial Cartridge Demos

Even though the Windows NT–specific documentation does not mention any demos, the generic demos for SC are available on Windows NT. View the file **c:\orant\doc\cartridg.804\a53264\sdo_scri.htm** in a browser for information on the demo SQL scripts available. These are also installed in the **c:\orant\md80\admin** folder.

Replication

Oracle8 Server on Windows NT supports *replication*. Replication allows sites to create a distributed database system by copying and maintaining objects across multiple sites. In certain situations, replication can improve performance, and in some other situations it can provide for redundancy. An example of better performance is where an application can query a local snapshot to get the required data and not access the network. Redundancy is provided automatically since more than one database can provide the required data.

Types of Replication

Two types of replication are available with Oracle8: 1) basic replication, and 2) symmetric replication. Basic replication provides a read-only view of data. Replicas of data are created on the Local node by creating *snapshots* of data from a Master node. Since these are read-only copies, applications must access the Master node if they need to modify data. Oracle8 Server supports basic replication using *snapshots* and *database links.* A variety of data dictionary objects are used to support replication.

Symmetric (also called *advanced*) replication allows for data replicas that are automatically updated throughout the system. Applications can modify data on any participating node and these changes are reflected automatically in all nodes. The Oracle Servers will ensure that there is global transaction consistency. Data integrity is maintained.

NOTE

Refer to Oracle8 Server Replication *for detailed information on replication.*

Replication Terminology

There is extensive terminology behind replication. We will provide an overview of some terms before we look at the implementation on Windows NT.

Replication Catalog

The Replication Catalog consists of a set of data dictionary tables and views that are required to maintain and administer replication. Every master and snapshot site has a Replication Catalog. Information in the catalog is also used to coordinate replication between sites.

Replication Sites

A variety of replication sites are defined in a system. A *master* site contains a copy of all objects to be replicated. Complete copies of the master objects are maintained on the master site. A *snapshot* site supports read-only or updatable snapshots of data from the master site.

Replication Group

A set of database objects to be replicated can be placed in a *replication group.* Typically, a replication group consists of objects that are a logical entity and belong to one application.

Oracle Replication Manager (REPMGR)

Oracle Replication Manager (REPMGR) is a GUI tool that allows sites to manage replication. It is available as a part of Oracle Enterprise Manager (OEM). REPMGR can be used to set up and manage master sites, snapshot sites, and schemas, and to define replication groups and parameters across the enterprise. A wizard interface is built in to REPMGR. Oracle Corporation recommends that one replication administrator manage replication across the enterprise. Table 4-1 provides information on launching REPMGR.

One additional bit of configuration is required for REPMGR. Modify the role *EXECUTE_CATALOG_ROLE* as shown below:

```
SVRMGR> grant execute on sys.dbms_repcat_admin to
execute_catalog_role;
Statement processed.
```

The above change is required since REPMGR uses the Oracle user *system* to connect to the database. The user *system* will need *EXECUTE* privileges on the DBMS_REPCAT_ADMIN package. Since the

Method	Procedure
OEM Console	1. Use shortcut for Oracle Replication Manager 2. Select Tools	Applications	Oracle Replication Manager
Program group	Click on Start	Programs	Oracle Replication Manager	Oracle Replication Manager
Oracle Administrator Toolbar	Create a shortcut to **c:\orant\bin\repmgr.exe**
Command line	Execute **c:\orant\bin\repmgr.exe**

TABLE 4-1. *Launching Oracle Replication Manager*

EXECUTE__CATALOG_ROLE role has been assigned to the user *system*, it is easier to modify the role.

We will illustrate REPMGR when we create a mock setup of advanced replication later in this chapter.

Installation of Replication

Replication is an available option on Oracle8 Server for Windows NT. If you chose to install the starter database (*typical* installation), your database is already ready for replication. If you created a database using Database Assistant, you need to select the option to set up the database for replication, as shown in Figure 4-4.

To ensure that replication is set up on your database, you can query the data dictionary using the following query:

```
SVRMGR> select object_name,object_type from all_objects
where object_name like 'REPCAT%';
```

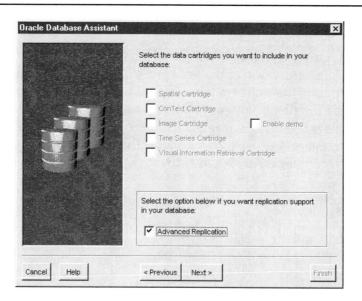

FIGURE 4-4.   *Setting up a database for replication*

Before you use replication on your site, also ensure that the INIT.ORA has the following parameters set:

```
shared_pool_size =  10000000
global_names = true
job_queue_processes = 2
job_queue_interval = 60
job_queue_keep_connections = false
distributed_lock_timeout = 60
distributed_transactions = 16
open_links = 4
snapshot_refresh_interval = 60
snapshot_refresh_keep_connections=false
snapshot_refresh_processes = 2
```

Minimum values for these parameters are also shown above. If you created your database with the replication option, these parameters would have been set for you.

We will illustrate basic and advanced replication to provide you with a feel for the configuration of replication. We will manually configure basic replication, but use REPMGR for advanced replication.

Our Test Configuration for Replication

We will provide a description of the test configuration that we will use for replication. We used the starter database named *ORCL* that was created using the Oracle Installer on our test machine *aadkoli-lap*. We created a second database named *ORC0* using Database Assistant with the replication option. Net8 Assistant was used to modify the **listener.ora** file to enroll both databases with the listener, as shown below:

```
SID_LIST_LISTENER =
   (SID_LIST =
      (SID_DESC =
      (GLOBAL_DBNAME = aadkoli-lap)
      (SID_NAME = ORCL)
   )
   (SID_DESC =
      (GLOBAL_DBNAME = Oracle8)
      (SID_NAME = ORC0)
   )
   )
```

We created a Net8 alias in the **tnsnames.ora** file for each database. The alias for the database *ORCL* was named *MAST* and the alias for the database *ORC0* was named *CHILD*.

A user named *scott* was created on each database, and we used the **c:\orant\dbs\demobld.sql** script to create test tables for the user *scott* on the database *ORCL*.

NOTE
The starter database has the user scott *and the demo tables. However, you must create the user* scott *if you used Database Assistant to create the database.*

Basic Replication

We will illustrate basic replication by setting up the tables EMP and DEPT for replication.

Step 1   Create a database link on *ORC0* that can be used to connect as the user *scott* to the database *ORCL*:

```
SVRMGR> connect system/manager@child
Connected.
SVRMGR> create public database link oracle connect to scott
identified by tiger using 'mast';
Statement processed.
```

The name of the database link must be the same as the name of the database if the following parameter is set in the INIT.ORA:

```
global_names = TRUE
```

Step 2   Create a snapshot log on the master node.

Oracle8 Server supports two kinds of refreshes: 1) complete refresh, and 2) fast refresh. A complete refresh replaces all the data on the Snapshot node with data from the Master node by executing a fresh query. A fast refresh modifies the Snapshot node by applying the changes on the Master node since the last refresh (incremental changes). A snapshot log is necessary to keep a log of changes, and is required for fast refreshes:

```
SVRMGR> connect system/manager@mast
Connected.
SVRMGR> create snapshot log on scott.emp;
Statement processed.
```

```
SVRMGR> create snapshot log on scott.dept;
Statement processed.
```

Step 3 Create the snapshots on the Snapshot node.

A snapshot provides a read-only view of the table on the Snapshot node. You can create a snapshot by using the CREATE SNAPSHOT command:

```
SVRMGR> connect system/manager@child
Connected.
SVRMGR> create snapshot scott.emp as select * from
scott.emp@oracle;
Statement processed.
SVRMGR> create snapshot scott.dept as select * from
scott.dept@oracle;
Statement processed.
```

Step 4 Create a refresh group.

A refresh group allows you to create a bundle of objects for replication. Typically, a refresh group contains the objects required for one application:

```
SVRMGR> connect system/manager@child
Connected.
SVRMGR> execute dbms_refresh.make ( \
    2> name=> 'scott.refgrp', \
    3> list=> 'scott.dept,scott.emp', \
    4> next_date=> sysdate, \
    5> interval=> 'sysdate + 1/96');
Statement processed.
SVRMGR> commit;
Statement processed.
```

Note that we have set a refresh interval of 15 minutes (1/96 of a day).

Step 5 Test replication.

First, execute a query on the Snapshot node to query the EMP table:

```
SVRMGR> connect scott/tiger@mast
Connected.
SVRMGR> select count(*) from emp;
COUNT(*)
----------
        14
1 row selected.
SVRMGR> connect scott/tiger@child
Connected.
```

```
SVRMGR> select count(*) from emp;
COUNT(*)
----------
        14
1 row selected.
SVRMGR> connect scott/tiger@mast
Connected.
SVRMGR> delete from emp where empno in(7902,7934);
2 rows processed.
SVRMGR> commit;
Statement processed.
SVRMGR> select count(*) from emp;
COUNT(*)
----------
        12
1 row selected.
SVRMGR> connect scott/tiger@child  ———— Allow 15 minutes for this replication
Connected.                                as per our refresh interval.
SVRMGR> select count(*) from emp;
COUNT(*)
----------
        12
1 row selected.
```

The change from the DELETE operation should reflect in the Snapshot node. Of course, you can query the data dictionary to see pending replication jobs.

Advanced Replication

Now that we have seen the manual configuration of basic replication, we will illustrate multimaster advanced replication using REPMGR. We will use the same configuration as we did for basic replication and use the SCOTT.EMP and SCOTT.DEPT tables in this example.

Step 1 Create Net8 aliases.

Create Net8 aliases for the master sites. We recommend that you create Net8 aliases using the same names as the database SID. We created aliases named *Oracle* and *ORC0* for our databases. If you do not use the SIDs for the aliases, Step 2 below will give an error message as the database links created by REPMGR will not be valid.

Step 2 Set up master sites.

Invoke the Setup Wizard in REPMGR and select the option to set up master sites. Click on New and add the two master sites *ORACLE* and *ORC0* as shown in Figure 4-5.

The Oracle user *system* is used to create the replication administrator, propagator, and receiver accounts. We will use the default *repadmin* user. Specify the refresh interval as shown in Figure 4-6.

Similarly, set the parameters for scheduling purges. The wizard will provide an opportunity for you to confirm your settings and then complete the required configuration. Database accounts will be created for the replication administrator, propagator, and receiver (*repadmin* in our example), and appropriate database links will be created on all the master sites. Public database links will also be created by using the database name since global naming is enabled (GLOBAL_NAMES=TRUE in the INIT.ORA). REPMGR will also test the links created for the master sites at this time. A log file named **repsetup.log** will be created in the **c:\orant\bin** folder for this procedure. Ensure that there are no errors in this log file before proceeding to the next step.

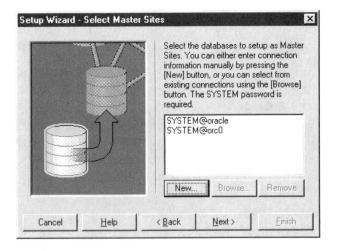

FIGURE 4-5. *Adding Master nodes*

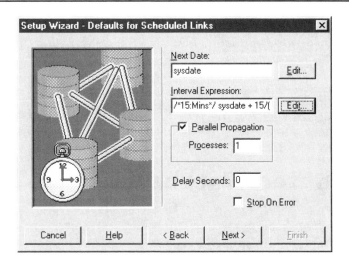

FIGURE 4-6. *Setting the refresh interval*

Step 3 Create the master groups.

A replication group at a master site is called a master group. You can create a master group by using REPMGR. Select the database connection for a master site and select File | New | New Master Group from the menu. Provide a name for the master group and add objects for replication. Also, provide destination information as shown here:

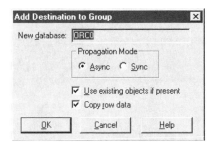

Select properties for replication in the ensuing dialog box.

Step 4 Configure conflict resolution parameters.

Conflict resolution ensures that data converges on all master sites and also avoids cascading errors. Refer to Chapter 5 of *Oracle8 Server Replication* in the Oracle documentation set for information on conflict resolution.

Step 5   Grant access to replicated objects.

Use Security Manager or the GRANT command in SQL to grant appropriate access to the replicated objects on the various sites.

Distributed Databases

In the previous section, we saw how Oracle8 Server supports a distributed system through replication. In replication, multiple copies of data are created and accessed by applications. Oracle8 Server also supports a *pure* distributed system. In a pure distributed system, applications access multiple nodes on the network for data. However, only one copy of data is available on the network. For example, an application may access the EMP table from one node and the DEPT table from another node using database links. Only one copy of these tables is available in the system.

Oracle8 Server supports distributed databases using database links. Support for heterogeneous databases (containing at least one non-Oracle database in the system) is also available on Windows NT.

Refer to *Oracle8 Distributed Database Systems* for information on distributed systems. Start with the file **c:\orant\doc\database.804\a58247\ds_ch1.htm** in the online documentation. Support for distributed systems is automatically available when you install Oracle8 Server on Windows NT.

Net8 is required on clients and servers to support distributed databases. We recommend that you install the Advanced Networking Option of Net8 and enable encryption for secure data transmission. We have also discussed encryption in Chapter 7 of this book.

Oracle Parallel Server

Oracle8 on Windows NT supports the Oracle Parallel Server (OPS) architecture. OPS allows multiple instances across nodes on a network to access a single database. This provides for better scalability and better availability. Each Windows NT node can run one instance. The database files must be available on shared drives (logical disks) on the network.

We will not go into the details of OPS. However, we will cover the requirements for OPS on Windows NT in this section. You must install the Oracle8 Enterprise Edition for OPS. A second layer named the Oracle Parallel Server Option Server must also be licensed separately and installed on top of Oracle8 Server. A tool called Oracle Parallel Server Manager is also bundled with the OPS option. This allows DBAs to manage different instances from OEM Console.

Hardware Requirements

In addition to the general requirements for Oracle8 Server detailed in Chapter 3, Oracle Corporation recommends 96Mb of RAM on each OPS node. A dedicated database for the OEM repository is required.

Software Requirements

The OPS option requires the Windows NT 4.0 Server. As mentioned previously, Oracle8 Enterprise Edition is required for the OPS option.

Shared Disks

OPS requires shared raw partitions for the datafiles, log files, and control files. While each instance maintains its own log files and control files, the datafiles must be shared. In addition, all instances need to access the online redo log files of other instances.

Windows NT Specific Information on OPS

The *Oracle Parallel Server Getting Started* provides information on OPS. Point your browser to **c:\orant\doc\paraserv.804\a55925\chap1.htm** for online documentation on OPS.

Parallel Query Option

Oracle8 Server provides full support for Parallel Data Manipulation Language (PDML). DML operations can be performed in parallel using parallel query servers. Query servers must be configured in the INIT.ORA file. Parameters like PARALLEL_MIN_SERVERS and PARALLEL_MAX_SERVERS allow DBAs to control the minimum and maximum number of query servers. Oracle8 Server manages the servers dynamically. The Parallel Query option in Oracle8 works almost identical to Oracle7, except for the fact that Oracle7 only supported querying while Oracle8 supports all DML.

Applications can use parallel query servers either implicitly or explicitly. You can use the PARALLEL clause to define the degree of parallelization (the number of query servers used in the operation) while creating the table or use the PARALLEL hint in the query. We provide an example here for your benefit.

Set the following parameters in the INIT.ORA:

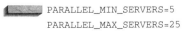

```
PARALLEL_MIN_SERVERS=5
PARALLEL_MAX_SERVERS=25
```

You can use the PARALLEL clause to create a table as shown below:

```
SQLWKS> CREATE TABLE TEST (c1 VARCHAR2(10) NULL, c2 VARCHAR2(10) NULL)
PARALLEL ( DEGREE 5 );
Statement processed.
```

A query on the table uses the parallel servers. DBAs can monitor parallel query servers using data dictionary views, as shown here:

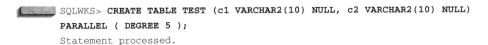

```
SQLWKS> SELECT * FROM TEST;
SVRMGR> select * from v$pq_slave;
```

SLAV	STAT	SESSIONS	IDLE_TIME_	BUSY_TIME_	CPU_SECS_C	MSGS_SENT_	MSGS_RCVD_	IDLE_TIME_	BUSY_TIME_	CPU_SECS_T	MSGS_SENT_	MSGS_R#
P000	BUSY	17	0	0	0	1	3	0	0	0	17	51
P001	BUSY	17	0	0	0	1	3	0	0	0	17	51
P002	BUSY	17	0	0	0	1	3	0	0	0	17	51
P003	BUSY	17	0	0	0	1	3	0	0	0	17	51
P004	BUSY	17	0	0	0	1	3	0	0	0	17	51

```
5 rows selected.
```

The Parallel Query option is not to be confused with the Parallel Server option. The Parallel Server option allows many instances to use a common database and requires you to install the Oracle Parallel Server. The Parallel Query option is available with every Oracle8 Server. Refer to the *Oracle8 Tuning* manual for information on this option.

Oracle Documentation Formats

All Oracle8 documentation is available online in HTML as well as Adobe Acrobat (**.pdf** files) format. The default installation provides you with documentation in HTML format. You can install the Acrobat documentation by copying files from the folder named **pdfdoc** on the media. A set of release notes and **readme.txt** files are also available with special notes for individual products in their respective folders.

CHAPTER
5

GUI-Based Approach to
Oracle Administration

he Oracle8 Server on Windows NT delivers the complete functionality of Oracle8 on a user-friendly operating system. In the first four chapters, we introduced Windows NT and Oracle8 concepts. We also looked at the installation and configuration of Oracle8 on Windows NT 4.0. In the remainder of this book, we will provide Oracle-related information that will help DBAs perform their job efficiently on Windows NT. We will begin by looking at the responsibilities and common tasks for Oracle DBAs. After this, we will provide a comprehensive look at the GUI tools and utilities provided by Oracle8 on Windows NT for DBAs. Most tasks on Windows NT can be completed using these GUI tools. In the next chapter, we will look at character-mode tools available with Oracle8. We will revisit the tasks performed in this chapter using a command line interface (CLI). Whether you prefer the GUI or the CLI, these two chapters should arm you with all the information that you need to be a DBA on Windows NT. Many DBA tasks are routine and can be scripted using batch (**.bat**) files. You can automate many tasks by scheduling batch files for execution. DBAs in real life use a combination of GUI and CLI to perform their tasks.

The information in the rest of this book supplements the information provided by Oracle8 documentation and applies to Oracle8 Servers on other platforms. However, we will keep our focus on Windows NT.

Who Are Oracle DBAs?

Oracle DBAs are a group of one or more privileged users who own and manage Oracle databases. DBAs are similar to *system administrators* for an operating system. (Windows NT 4.0 has a special group of privileged users called *administrators* while UNIX has a privileged group named *root.*) Oracle DBAs are trusted users who are expected to perform tasks ranging from installation to maintenance. Routine maintenance tasks include managing users, database space, backup and recovery, and performance tuning. While the system administrators on some sites also have DBA responsibilities, most large sites have specialized DBAs. It is critical that DBAs have a thorough understanding of all aspects of administration to keep downtimes to a minimum. Difficult situations can turn into a crisis because of errors made by DBAs, and can prove to be very expensive.

The Oracle database has a special role named *DBA* that can be granted to a user. This role includes system and object privileges that are required by typical DBAs. If this role does not satisfy the requirements of your site, you can create your own role or customize the existing *DBA* role by adding or removing privileges. This can be done using Security Manager or the GRANT and REVOKE commands in SQL.

Tasks and Responsibilities of DBAs

Oracle DBAs are expected to perform well-defined tasks on a regular basis. However, the number of DBAs that are required to do the job is site dependent. We have seen sites that maintain primary and secondary DBAs with specific responsibilities. We have also seen other sites that have a dedicated DBA for every database on-site. For other mission critical sites, 24 x 7 coverage is important and one or more DBAs are always kept on call. We have listed typical DBA tasks in this section. This list is by no means comprehensive. If you have a new Oracle site and are planning to create a team of DBAs, you must ensure that most of the skills listed here are covered by the team. Your site may also have some special needs in addition to those listed here. You should also build some redundancy into your team of DBAs by having overlapping skills and responsibilities.

Installation

Perhaps the most obvious task for DBAs is installation. DBAs need to perform installations of the Oracle Server, tools, and applications. Successful DBAs should be able perform installations with minimal guidance from documentation. DBAs should also be able to install in a variety of environments, including client/server and three-tier systems. If your site has a heterogeneous environment of network protocols and operating systems, you should be able to install Oracle software in multiple operating environments. Along with this, Oracle DBAs need to be familiar with the Oracle Installer technology.

DBAs at large sites, who are responsible for many users, must be comfortable performing an installation across a network. On Windows NT, you can create logical network drives and use these as staging areas for installation. These staging areas can be used for installations across a network.

Upgrades

Most software is revised on a regular basis. Oracle software is no different. Newer versions of Oracle software provide enhanced functionality and fix software issues or bugs. Oracle DBAs need to keep their site current to take advantage of the latest versions of software.

Oracle software packages have version numbers in the format A.B.C.D where the degree of change reduces from left to right. A major revision change is reflected in the first digit (A) and minor bug fixes are reflected in the last two digits (C and D). The second digit (B) usually reflects an enhancement or a change required for porting the software to a new platform. Upgrades that involve a change in the last two digits (C and D) are normally trivial, while upgrades that involve a change in the first two digits (A and B) require planning. A revision change reflected by a change in the first digit (A) requires scheduling, and may involve some downtime. You must plan such upgrades in a time slot that has the least impact on users. Many sites schedule such upgrades on weekends. A major revision change such as an upgrade from Oracle7 to Oracle8 requires a database migration. Upgrades in versions that change the last three digits (B, C, and D) usually do not require a database migration.

NOTE

Almost all Oracle software is built for open systems. Products are first developed on a "base" operating system (platform) and then ported to other operating systems. The same product could have a slightly different version number on two operating systems. The base platform is typically one or two minor releases ahead of other ports. At this time, either Windows NT 4.0 or Sun SPARC Solaris 2.5.x are used as the base port for the majority of Oracle products.

We will look at migration on Windows NT in detail in Chapter 8. In any case, an upgrade should always be performed with care, and if it fails, you must be in a position to revert to the previous version. For example, during an upgrade from Oracle7 to Oracle8, you should create a full backup of the database before you attempt the upgrade. It is imperative that you have a usable backup because you cannot revert an Oracle8 database to Oracle7! If possible, you should keep a backup of the entire Oracle directory structure before you attempt a major upgrade.

Capacity Planning

DBAs need to be actively involved with capacity planning on-site. They must be aware of the growth patterns of the business and the impact of this growth on database applications, including the size of the database(s). It is important to plan for proper hardware based on future projections. It is likely that buying extra hardware along with the computer will be less expensive than upgrading components at a later point in time. When you buy hardware for your database needs, plan your hard disk and memory requirements keeping growth in mind. It is not uncommon for Oracle databases to grow on the order of megabytes per day!

If you have a site that has very high database activity and a lot of input/output (I/O) to the database, you should consider disk striping. The number of disk controllers can also impact performance. We will discuss I/O further in Chapter 7 under performance tuning.

If you are deploying database applications on the Web, capacity planning can be a daunting task. It is hard to predict growth and transaction rates in large networks such as the Internet. Distributed solutions can help balance loads in these situations. We have introduced distributed databases and replication in Chapter 4.

Space Management

Oracle DBAs need to manage the logical structure of the database based on the needs of the application(s). Many applications require specific structures for data storage. Tablespaces need to be sized appropriately. Storage parameters like *INITIAL EXTENT, NEXT EXTENT*, and *MAXEXTENTS* need to be selected with care. You must consider all types of segments for proper space management. Space management for index segments, rollback segments, and temporary segments can be relatively simple with proper planning.

User Management

DBAs must be able to create and manage users on the databases. Every user must be granted roles and privileges as per application demands. In addition to the roles and privileges granted on the database, DBAs must ensure that users do not compromise security at the file system level. We recommend that you use the NTFS if you want to ensure security at the file system level. Otherwise, users who are part of the Administrators group in Windows NT can use their operating system privileges to acquire unauthorized privileges on an Oracle database, which is not a desirable situation.

Manage Database Objects

Oracle DBAs are required to create and manage database objects. These objects include tables, indexes, synonyms, and so forth that are required by applications, as well as system objects required by Oracle such as the data dictionary. Database schemas also need to be managed. It might be necessary to move database objects to a different tablespace. If you are using the *partitions* feature of Oracle8, additional management might be necessary.

Auditing

If your site requires additional monitoring of database access, you will be required to set up appropriate auditing features to track users. Additional objects need to be created in the database for auditing.

Performance Tuning

Performance is always a big concern at many sites. Performance tuning is an iterative process and requires close monitoring on a daily basis. DBAs on Windows NT can use Performance Monitor to measure the performance of the operating system, CPU usage, virtual memory, and database performance. Chapter 1 provides information on Performance Monitor. We will also discuss tuning in more detail in Chapter 7.

Backup and Recovery

The Oracle8 Server provides a variety of backup mechanisms that allow DBAs to create robust backups. It is important to design a backup procedure that meets the demands of your site. DBAs also need to tune the frequency of backups based on the site needs. The goal is to minimize downtime if recovery is ever required. The backup strategy you choose to use will directly impact downtime. Archived redo log files need to be managed properly in order to perform full recovery in case of a database crash. We will cover backup and recovery for Windows NT later in this chapter. You can also refer to *Oracle8 Backup & Recovery Handbook* (Osborne/McGraw-Hill, 1998) in the Oracle Press series for comprehensive coverage of this subject.

Training

DBAs should also be involved in user training. Many issues can be avoided if appropriate training is provided to application developers and users. We have seen a site that had 1,000 plus users who had the habit of turning off their PCs at the end of the day without a graceful exit! DBAs on the site had to get involved with training the users to get out of this habit.

Some application developers do not understand the impact on the database when they are designing an application. With training, some issues can be avoided at the application design stage itself.

Troubleshooting

Oracle DBAs need to troubleshoot issues from time to time. They need to tackle issues ranging from connection issues to tuning. Some large sites maintain a 24 x 7 help desk that helps users with issues. Experienced DBAs can ensure that minimal checks have been performed before reporting a problem to Oracle technical support staff. DBAs need to be comfortable with diagnostic tools like SQL traces and alert logs.

TIP
Oracle Enterprise Manager provides facilities for "lights-out-management." You can set up alerts including automatic paging and e-mail based on certain events on your database. Refer to the section on Oracle Enterprise Manager later in this chapter for details.

Becoming a DBA

Before we discuss the tools and utilities available with Oracle8, we will see how you can connect to Oracle as an authorized DBA. This is because you need to connect as a DBA to use most of these utilities effectively. In order to be an authorized DBA, you need to connect to Oracle as a user with *DBA* privileges. You can use the built-in *DBA* role to get these privileges or define a separate role for privileges that makes sense for your site. The authentication of such a login can be performed by Oracle itself or through external means such as the operating system. We will look at the different means of authentication in the following sections.

The *DBA* Role

As mentioned previously, there is a special role named *DBA* in Oracle. Any Oracle user that is granted this role can become a DBA and is automatically assigned certain system privileges. Oracle maintains user and role information within the database. Any user with the *DBA* role can grant *DBA* privileges to other users. We will cover the system privileges associated with the *DBA* role later in this section.

NOTE
Oracle provides two built-in users with DBA *privilege. One user is called* SYS *and has the password* CHANGE_ON_INSTALL *and the second user is called* SYSTEM *and has the password* MANAGER. *Be sure to change the passwords for these accounts on your production system.*

You can grant the *DBA* role to an existing Oracle user or create a new user and grant the *DBA* role to that user. You can use the GRANT command in SQL or use Security Manager to grant the *DBA* role to a user. Security Manager is available as part of Oracle Enterprise Manager (OEM). Tools like SQL Plus 8.0, SQL Worksheet, or Server Manager can be used to issue ad hoc SQL commands on Oracle8 for Windows NT. Table 5-1 provides information on how you can access these tools.

We will look at an example of how Security Manager can be used to grant the *DBA* role to a user.

Tool or Utility	From Program Group or Shortcut	From Command Line
Security Manager	1. Start | Programs | Oracle Enterprise Manager | Security Manager 2. Use the shortcut to Security Manager on Administration toolbar 3. Use the shortcut to Security Manager on OEM console	Execute **c:\orant\bin\vac.exe**.
SQL Plus 8.0	Start | Programs | Oracle for Windows NT | SQL Plus 8.0	Execute **c:\orant\bin\plus80w.exe**
SQL Worksheet	1. Start | Programs | Oracle Enterprise Manager | SQL Worksheet 2. Use the shortcut to SQL Worksheet on Administration toolbar 3. Use the shortcut to SQL Worksheet on OEM console	Execute **c:\orant\bin\vaw.exe**.
Server Manager	None	Execute **c:\orant\bin\svrmgr30.exe**.

TABLE 5-1. *Accessing Tools to Manage Roles*

Example: We will create a user called *SYSAD* and grant the *DBA* role to this user using Security Manager.

The solution is to use Security Manager or appropriate SQL commands to create the user *SYSAD* and grant the *DBA* role to the user. The steps are described below.

1. Start Security Manager and connect to the Oracle database as a user with *DBA* privilege. We will use the user *SYSTEM*.

2. Select the Users node and select the Create shortcut or User | Create from the menu. You will see a dialog box similar to the one shown here:

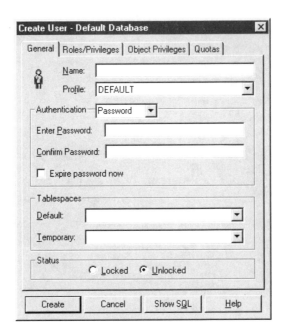

3. Enter the name for the new user and the password. For now, choose to authenticate using a password. Designate the default and temporary tablespaces from the list of available tablespaces. Ensure that the account is active by selecting the Unlocked radio button. We will enter information for a new user named *SYSAD* as shown below:

```
User: SYSAD
Profile: DEFAULT
Authentication: Password
Enter Password: aa
Confirm Password: aa
Default Tablespace: USER_DATA
Temporary Tablespace: TEMPORARY_DATA
```

4. Click on the Roles/Privileges tab and select the roles that you want to give to the user. Click on the down arrow to grant the roles to the user. We will grant the *RESOURCE* and *DBA* roles to this user. Here's the screen for our example:

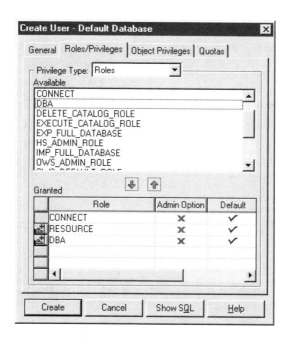

TIP

You can select contiguous multiple options by using the SHIFT key while making the selections. Similarly, use the CTRL key to select non-contiguous options.

You can also assign object privileges and resource quotas if you wish. We will take default object privileges and quotas.

5. Click on the Create button to create the user.

TIP

You can use the Show SQL button to see the SQL command issued for this task. Cut and paste this command into a SQL script that creates a user and grants roles for your future use.

6. Exit from Security Manager.

If the built-in *DBA* role is not suitable for your needs, you can grant individual system and object privileges for your DBA-level users. A better solution, though, is to create a custom role for your site.

External Authentication

Oftentimes it is convenient to use the same names for Oracle users as the operating system users. Oracle provides for external authentication using the NT operating system. You must configure Oracle to allow external authentication by setting the following parameters to the INIT.ORA file:

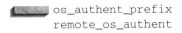

```
os_authent_prefix
remote_os_authent
```

The first parameter allows you to specify a character string that prefixes the Oracle username and the second parameter must be set to TRUE in order to allow for external authentication. It is convenient to set the OS_AUTHENT_PREFIX parameter to a null string so that the NT username and the Oracle username match.

NOTE
On prior releases of Oracle, the default value for OS_AUTHENT_PREFIX was OPS$. If the NT username was SYSAD, then you would need to create a user named OPS$SYSAD in Oracle. In Oracle8, you can set the OS_AUTHENT_ PREFIX to any string that is convenient. If you set the parameter to a null string, the NT and Oracle user would be identical. So, you could create an Oracle user named SYSAD for an NT user named SYSAD.

If you are using external authentication, you should also disable remote authentication by setting the following parameter in the INIT.ORA:

```
remote_login_passwordfile = none
```

On our test installation, we will edit the **c:\orant\database\initorcl.ora** file and add the following parameters to it:

```
os_authent_prefix = ""
remote_os_authent = true
remote_login_passwordfile = none
```

Continuing with our previous example, we would need to create a user named *SYSAD* on Windows NT as well as on Oracle. While creating the user, you must notify Oracle that the authentication will be done externally. The Security Manager screen for external authentication of the user *SYSAD* is shown here:

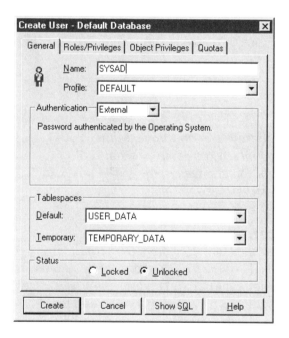

If the user *SYSAD* logs in to the Windows NT machine, then he or she could connect to the Oracle database by substituting the username and password with a forward slash ('/'). The Login dialog box in this case is shown here:

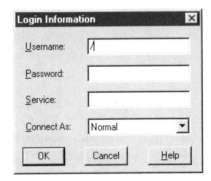

Similarly, from the command line the user *SYSAD* could use SQL Plus 8.0 to connect to Oracle by using the command

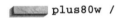 `plus80w /`

REMEMBER
The changes in the INIT.ORA file take effect when the database is started the next time. You will need to bounce (shut down and start up) the database for the changes in the INIT.ORA file to take effect.

The User *internal*

Oracle recognizes a special user named *internal*. This special user is authenticated outside of the Oracle database. You must set the password for this user while installing Oracle. The user *internal* is required in situations where you are creating a database manually and there are no users defined as yet—sort of the chicken and the egg problem! So, if you want to issue the CREATE DATABASE command to create a new database, you must connect as the user *internal* and then issue the CREATE DATABASE command.

CAUTION
There is another method of validation using a password file. Refer to the next section for more details. The password for the user internal is impacted when you create a password file.

You can also use the user *internal* to connect to an existing database. If you choose to do this, you will be connected to Oracle under the schema named *SYS*. (There is another role named *SYSDBA* that also has the same effect. The next section provides details on this role.) This makes the user *internal* a privileged user. You must take extra precaution to ensure that the password for the user *internal* does not fall into the hands of malicious users.

The user *internal* is expected to be de-supported in Oracle8 version 8.1. We therefore recommend that you create your own users with the *SYSDBA* role instead of relying on the user *internal*.

CHANGING THE PASSWORD FOR INTERNAL You must use the **oradim80** utility to change the password for the user *internal*. The procedure requires you to delete the SID and re-create it with a new password as shown below:

```
C:\> oradim80 -delete -sid orcl
C:\> oradim80 -new -sid orcl -intpwd <new password>
```

The Password File

Some sites require remote administration of Oracle databases from clients that do not have any Oracle software. In such situations, you can use the Oracle password file facility. A password file is created by using the Oracle password file utility ORAPWD. On Windows NT, the executable is named **orapwd80.exe**. For usage, execute it from the command line:

```
C:\> orapwd80
Usage: orapwd file=<fname> password=<password> entries=<users>
  where
    file - name of password file (mand),
    password - password for SYS and INTERNAL (mand),
    entries - maximum number of distinct DBA and OPERs (opt),
  There are no spaces around the equal-to (=) character.
```

The utility creates a password file as specified by the FILE argument. You must provide a full path to the file. The file must be named using the format: *pwd<database name>.ora*. The password that you specify at the command line applies to the users *SYS* and *internal*.

If you are using the starter database that was created by the Oracle Installer, a password file named **c:\orant\database\pwdorcl.ora** is created for you automatically and you do not need to create your own password file. This password file contains entries for the users *SYS* and *internal*. When you grant other Oracle users the *SYSDBA* or the *SYSOPER* role, these users are added to the password file automatically.

TIP
*The password file **pwdorcl.ora** is hidden and will not show up on your directory listing under normal conditions. You can use the **attrib** command to change the attributes of the file, but we recommend that you leave this hidden. An alternate solution is to use Windows NT Explorer to set appropriate options for hidden files using the View | Options menu item.*

You must also set the REMOTE_LOGIN_PASSWORDFILE parameter in the INIT.ORA file to an appropriate value before Oracle uses the password file for authentication. If this parameter is set to *NONE*, Oracle ignores the password file; if it is set to EXCLUSIVE, only one database can use the password file; and if it is set to SHARED, multiple databases can share a password file (this parameter is set to SHARED for the starter database on Oracle8 Server Version 8.0.4).

A user must be granted the *SYSDBA* or *SYSOPER* role before he or she can connect remotely using a password file for authentication. A copy of the INIT.ORA parameter file is also required on the client. Also note that Net8 software is required on the client for the remote connection.

NOTE
SYSDBA *is a built-in role that allows remote users to perform all* DBA *tasks.* SYSOPER *is a built-in role that allows users to start up and shut down the database.*

Finally, since external authentication is not supported if you are using a password file, you must disable it by setting the parameter REMOTE_OS_ AUTHENT to FALSE.

We will look at an example of how the *SYSDBA* and *SYSOPER* roles can be used in a real-life situation.

Example: You have a Windows NT machine with an Oracle8 database named *ORCL* running on it. You have a system operator named *JDOE* who should have the privileges to start up and shut down the database remotely. You also need to ensure that another user named *JDBA* can administer the database remotely.

The solution is to add an entry for *JDOE* and *JDBA* in the password file and set the REMOTE_LOGIN_PASSWORDFILE to either EXCLUSIVE or SHARED. Make a copy of the INIT.ORA file on the client from which remote access is required. The steps are described below.

1. Connect to the database as *SYS* or *INTERNAL* and grant the *SYSOPER* role to the user *JDOE* and the *SYSDBA* role to the user *JDBA* using Security Manager. This operation will add entries for *JDOE* and *JDBA* into the password file **c:\orant\database\pwdorcl.ora**.

2. Edit the file **c:\orant\database\initorcl.ora** on the server and set the REMOTE_LOGIN_PASSWORDFILE parameter to EXCLUSIVE. Also ensure that external authentication is disabled as shown below:

3. ```
   remote_login_passwordfile = exclusive
   remote_os_authent = false
   ```

   Copy the **initorcl.ora** file to the client that will be used by *JDOE* and *JDBA* for remote administration:

   ```
   C:\> copy c:\orant\database\initorcl.ora f:\oracle\initorcl.ora
   ```

   The above assumes the logical drive 'F' is mapped to a network drive on the client.

Now *JDOE* can connect to the remote Oracle server from the client as *SYSOPER* by using the CONNECT AS clause. The login screen is shown here:

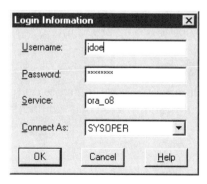
   ```

Note that *ora_o8* must be a valid Net8 connect string. Similarly, *JDBA* can connect as *SYSDBA* using the Net8 connect string.

CAUTION

When you connect to the database using the SYSDBA or SYSOPER role, you will be connected to the SYS schema, and not your own schema. In our example above, JDOE and JDBA will not be attached to their own schemas, but the SYS schema. The following example proves this behavior:

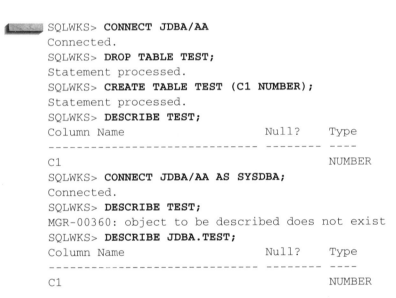

```
SQLWKS> CONNECT JDBA/AA
Connected.
SQLWKS> DROP TABLE TEST;
Statement processed.
SQLWKS> CREATE TABLE TEST (C1 NUMBER);
Statement processed.
SQLWKS> DESCRIBE TEST;
Column Name                         Null?    Type
----------------------------    --------    ----
C1                                           NUMBER
SQLWKS> CONNECT JDBA/AA AS SYSDBA;
Connected.
SQLWKS> DESCRIBE TEST;
MGR-00360: object to be described does not exist
SQLWKS> DESCRIBE JDBA.TEST;
Column Name                         Null?    Type
----------------------------    --------    ----
C1                                           NUMBER
```

Needless to say, the password file must be protected from unauthorized users. We recommend that you place this file on an NTFS file system, because Windows NT does not impose file-level security on FAT file systems.

Using Windows NT Groups

It is common for large Oracle sites to define roles on the database with certain privileges and then assign these roles to users on the database. Large groups of users can be managed easily by assigning proper privileges to the role. Roles in Oracle provide the same advantages as *groups* in operating systems.

You can configure Oracle to assign roles to a user based on the operating system group in Windows NT. For example, if the Windows NT user named *SYSAD* belongs to the *DBA* group in Windows NT, you can configure Oracle to automatically assign the *DBA* role to the user *SYSAD* when he or she connects to the database. Note that the name of the Windows NT group and the Oracle role name must be identical in order for this to work. The role needs to be granted to the user in Oracle and must be valid. The following INIT.ORA parameters must be set:

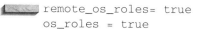

```
remote_os_roles= true
os_roles = true
```

The REMOTE_OS_ROLES parameter allows Oracle to inherit roles for remote clients while the OS_ROLES parameter provides the same effect for local users. We will demonstrate the use of OS_ROLES in the example below.

Example: The user *JDOE* needs to be assigned to the *DEVELOPER* role automatically at connect time. The user also needs to be configured for external authentication.

The solution is to create the user *JDOE* and configure the user to be identified externally using the steps detailed earlier in the "External Authentication" section of this chapter. Grant the *DEVELOPER* role to the user *JDOE* in Oracle. Use Windows NT User Manager to ensure that the Windows NT user belongs to the group named *DEVELOPER*, then add appropriate INIT.ORA parameters to enable OS roles.

1. Create the user *JDOE* using Security Manager. Ensure that the password is validated externally from the operating system. Grant the *DEVELOPER* role to the user.

2. Using User Manager, assign the Windows NT user *JDOE* to the *DEVELOPER* group. Here's a sample of the screen from User Manager:

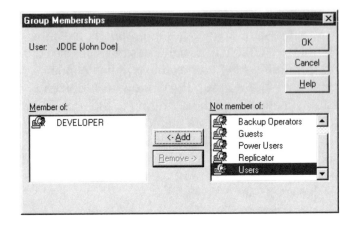

3. Add the following parameters to the **c:\orant\database\initorcl.ora** file:

```
remote_os_roles= true
os_roles = true
```

4. Shut down the database and start it up again for the changes in the INIT.ORA to take effect.

5. When the user *JDOE* connects to the database, the role *DEVELOPER* will be automatically assigned to the user.

Precreated DBA Accounts

Oracle provides two accounts with *DBA* privileges—*SYS* and *SYSTEM*. These are reserved users. All system objects owned internally by Oracle belong to the user (the schema) *SYS*. You must not alter any database objects owned by SYS at any time. The user *SYSTEM* can be used to create database objects required by Oracle tools such as Developer 2000. The default password for the user *SYS* is *CHANGE_ON_INSTALL* and the password for the user *SYSTEM* is *MANAGER*. You must remember to change the passwords for these users on your database.

Rights and Privileges of the DBA Role

As mentioned previously, the built-in *DBA* role provided by Oracle has many rights and privileges associated with it. These privileges allow users assigned this role to perform almost all the tasks that are necessary for DBAs. The *DBA* role includes other roles, system privileges, and object privileges.

Table 5-2 provides a summary of the rights and privileges included in the predefined *DBA* role.

   If this role is not suitable for DBAs on your site, you should modify it or create a new role that is tailored to your requirements.

GUI Tools and Utilities for DBAs

So far in this chapter, we have looked at the roles and responsibilities of DBAs. We have also provided information on how one can connect to the Oracle database as a DBA. Most DBA tasks must be performed as a DBA-level user. In the remainder of this chapter we will take a look at GUI tools and utilities that Oracle provides on Windows NT. We will look at equivalent CLI tools in the next chapter.

Oracle Database Assistant (ODA)

Oracle Database Assistant is a graphical tool with a wizard interface that allows you to create a new database. You can also modify or delete an existing database. Windows NT allows you to have multiple Oracle databases running simultaneously on your machine. Each database must have a unique database name, also called the *system identifier* (SID) or *instance name*. The Oracle Database Assistant (ODA) will create a unique Windows NT service for each database. You can manage each service using the Services applet under the Control Panel.

Roles/Privileges	Rights and Privileges Included
Roles	DELETE_CATALOG_ROLE, EXECUTE_CATALOG_ ROLE, EXP_FULL_DATABASE, IMP_FULL_ DATABASE, SELECT_CATALOG_ROLE
System privileges	Almost all privileges except for database startup and shutdown, creating a database
Object privileges	Execute on SYS.DBMS_DEFER_QUERY and SYS.DBMS_DEFER_SYS

TABLE 5-2. *Roles and Privileges for the DBA Role*

Creating a Default Database

We will create a starter database using a default structure. To launch the ODA, click on Start | Programs | Oracle for Windows NT | Oracle Database Assistant.

Select the option to create a database and click on the Next button to navigate to the next screen in the wizard. You can choose to create a database with the default structure or create a custom database. We will choose to create a *typical* database at this time, as shown in Figure 5-1.

The next screen in the wizard allows you to include database cartridges of your choice. We have covered installation of cartridges in Chapter 4 and we will not repeat that information here.

Next, you can choose to copy database files from your media or create new database files. If you choose to copy the database files from your media, the creation process will be quicker because the data dictionary and PL/SQL packages are precreated. We will choose to create new database files as shown in Figure 5-2.

You will see a dialog box confirming the name of the database. Database Assistant will automatically pick a name for the database using the convention *ORCx*, where *x* takes the value 0 to 9.

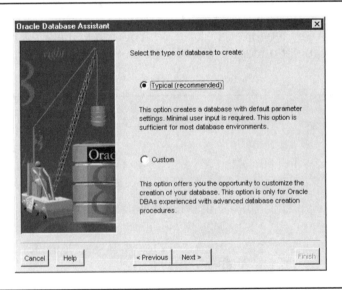

FIGURE 5-1. *Choosing the database type*

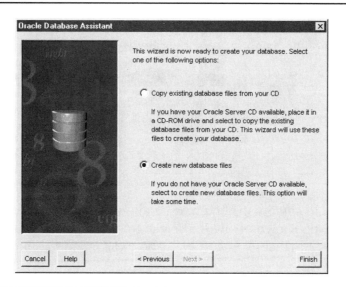

FIGURE 5-2. *Creating database files*

TIP
If you do not like the default name assigned to the new database, you will need to choose the option to create a custom database in the screen shown in Figure 5-1.

If you want this new database to be available to remote clients, the database will need to be made known to the Net8 listener. Add an entry to the **listener.ora** file as shown here:

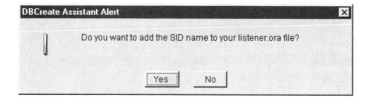

You will see a screen that displays the status of the database creation process. At the end of the procedure, you will see a dialog box confirming the creation of the database, as shown here:

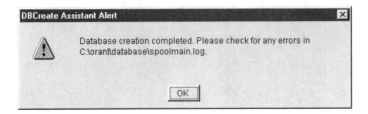

You should confirm that the new database service is running by using the Systems applet. Shown below is a screen from our test installation. Note that there are two instances named *ORCL* and *ORC0* running simultaneously on the machine.

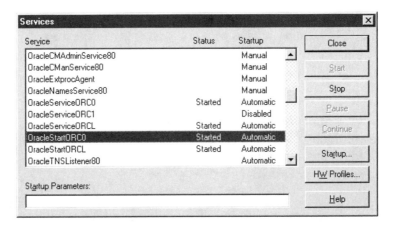

TIP
The default password for the user INTERNAL on Windows NT is ORACLE. Oracle passwords are case-insensitive.

You can create Net8 service names to access this new database using the Net8 Easy Config utility.

Creating a Custom Database

The ODA can also be used to create a custom database. You can create databases with the physical structure of your choice. You will need to provide specific information for the data files, control files, and log files that you want to create. You can also specify values for certain INIT.ORA parameters that you want, along with identifier information for the database (SID).

We will step through the process of creating a custom database for your benefit. Again launch the ODA by selecting Start | Programs | Oracle for Windows NT | Oracle Database Assistant. Choose the option to create a custom database. Again, we will not install any cartridges. The next screen should look similar to the one shown in Figure 5-3. You can pick a set of INIT.ORA parameters including the character set in this screen based on the anticipated size of your database.

You can then set the name of the database, the password for the user *INTERNAL*, and the name for the parameter file. Figure 5-4 shows a sample screen.

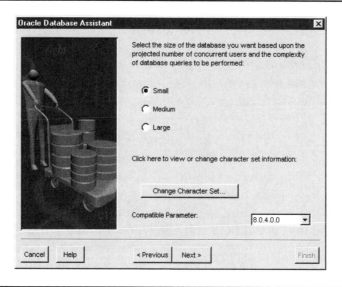

FIGURE 5-3. *Choosing INIT.ORA parameters*

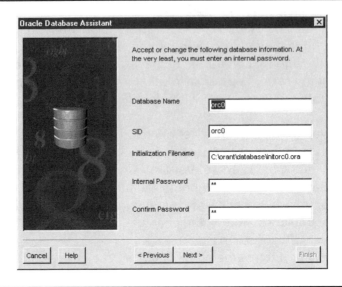

FIGURE 5-4. *Setting Database Name, Password, and Initialization File*

TIP
The convention is to name the parameter file
init<sid>.ora. *It is convenient to name the file*
using this convention and place it in the
c:\orant\database *folder, as this is the default*
location for the file. If you do not choose the
default name and location for the parameter
file, you will need to provide the location
explicitly every time you start up the database.

The next screen, shown in Figure 5-5, allows you to provide parameters pertaining to the control files.

You should plan on mirroring your control files on separate disks. In this manner, if you lose one disk, a copy of the control file is available on another disk. Oracle manages the mirroring automatically. The next screen in the wizard allows you to provide specifications for tablespaces and associate datafiles with tablespaces.

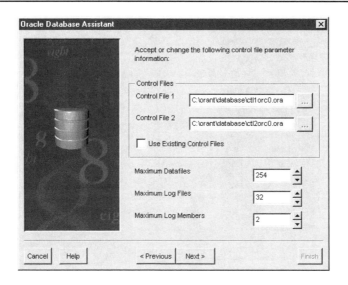

FIGURE 5-5. *Setting Control File specifications*

Enter appropriate values for tablespaces by using the tab control. The next two screens allow you to provide information on redo log files, archiving, and checkpoints. Figures 5-6 shows a sample screen where you can set the archiving parameters. We strongly recommend that you plan on mirroring your online redo logs for redundancy.

We will choose to enable archiving. The next screen enables you to size your SGA appropriately. Figure 5-7 shows a sample screen.

Tuning the SGA is a very critical task for DBAs. We will cover this subject in greater detail when we discuss performance tuning in Chapter 7. The last screen in the wizard allows you to designate the folders for system and user trace files.

Finally, you will see a dialog box similar to the one shown in Figure 5-8 where you can confirm the start of the database creation process.

Again, you will see a dialog box that shows the progress bar, and on completion of the procedure you will see a message confirming the creation of the database.

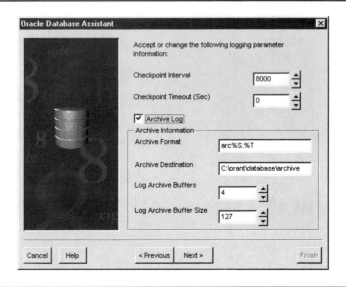

FIGURE 5-6. *Setting archiving and checkpoints*

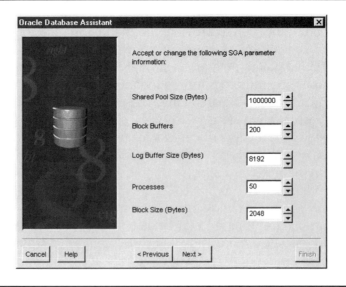

FIGURE 5-7. *Sizing the SGA*

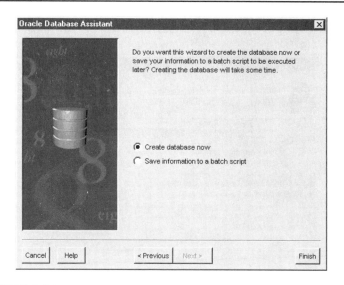

FIGURE 5-8.   *Starting database creation*

TIP
*If your site requires a specific database structure
for an application, you should use the ODA to
create a script for the creation of the database.
You can do so by selecting the option, Save
information to a batch script, in Figure 5-8. You
can make the script portable by using variables
for filenames.*

Modifying a Database

DBAs may need to add cartridges to enhance the functionality of the
Oracle8 Server. The ODA can be used to add cartridges and also to
configure the Multi Threaded Server (MTS). The software for the cartridge to
be added needs to be installed prior to modifying the database. We will
demonstrate the addition of the cartridge for the ConText option.

First, use the Custom Install procedure to install the ConText option. In
the Installer, choose to install the option labeled *Oracle8 Enterprise Edition
Cartridges and Options 8.0.4*. You will see a list of available options and

cartridges from which you can select the cartridge that you want to install. We will choose to add the ConText cartridge, as shown here:

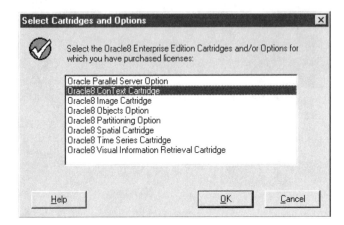

Exit the Installer and start ODA to add this cartridge to the database. Choose the Modify a Database option and follow instructions in the wizard until you see a screen similar to Figure 5-9.

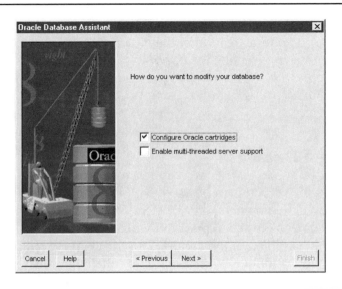

FIGURE 5-9. *Adding a cartridge*

The next screen allows you to pick the cartridge that you want. In our sample installation, only the ConText cartridge is highlighted because it is the only one we have installed. Figure 5-10 shows the screen for our installation.

NOTE

The ConText cartridge requires that the SHARED_POOL_SIZE parameter in the INIT.ORA be set to at least 12Mb. You will see an error message if your shared pool is not large enough. If you get an error, you need to increase the SHARED_POOL_SIZE in the INIT.ORA and bounce the database.

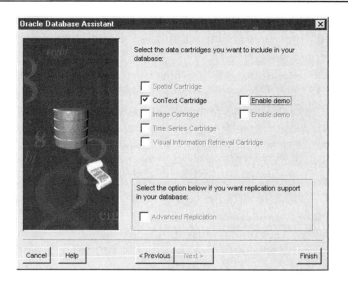

FIGURE 5-10. *Adding the ConText cartridge*

When you click on the Finish button, you will see a progress bar for the installation followed by a dialog box, shown here, confirming the successful completion of the procedure:

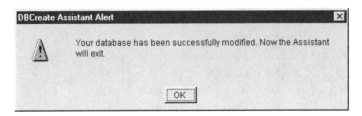

We will have discussed cartridges in more detail in Chapter 4.

Deleting a Database

You can also use ODA to delete a database. Deleting a database includes deletion of associated database files, log files, and control files. The corresponding Windows NT services need to be removed and some entries need to be deleted from the registry. Choose the Delete a Database option in ODA to delete a database. You will see a screen in the wizard similar to the one shown in Figure 5-11, where you can select the database that you want to delete. Click on the Finish button to delete all files and services related to the database.

On our test installation, all files related to the database were deleted except the INIT.ORA file. You can delete this file manually.

Under normal conditions, you should avoid deleting a database manually using Windows NT Explorer because you will see error messages when the associated services fail to start. However, if you ever get into a situation where an Oracle service associated with a database has been "orphaned," you should try to restore a configuration that works during Windows NT startup. (A process can be orphaned if you have deleted the files belonging to the database manually.) When Windows NT is being loaded, you will get an opportunity to restore the "last configuration" in the blue screen. Choose this option during startup to restore a working configuration. If this does not solve the problem, you can use Registry Editor to delete the entries related to the service.

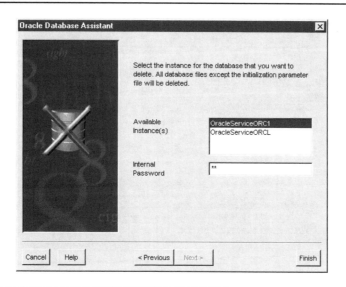

FIGURE 5-11.   *Deleting a database*

TIP
Use the Find function in Registry Editor to find the entry for the service and delete it.

Oracle Enterprise Manager (OEM)

Oracle Enterprise Manager (OEM) includes a set of tools and utilities that allow DBAs to perform a majority of tasks across the enterprise from a console. An Administrator Toolbar provides quick access to these tools and utilities. You can administer multiple databases across the network, schedule jobs across nodes, monitor events, and even distribute software across a network using OEM. The OEM Console can be used to launch all the tools using a GUI. Figure 5-12 shows the OEM Console.

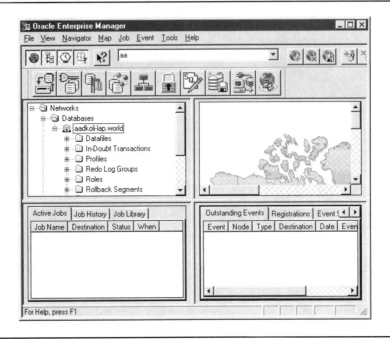

FIGURE 5-12. *OEM Console*

You can click on Start | Programs | Oracle Enterprise Manager | Administrator Toolbar or execute **c:\orant\bin\vom.exe** to start Administrator Toolbar. You should add it to the NT Start menu for easy access and customize it for your needs. To customize the toolbar, move the mouse onto the toolbar and right-click to get access to the Customize menu item. Select the Applications tab and add or remove shortcuts to applications to your taste.

You can navigate to a variety of machines and services available across the enterprise from the Navigator. These services include databases, nodes (machines), and Net8 and Web listeners. These services can be discovered automatically if the Oracle Intelligent Agent is available on the node. If the Intelligent Agent is not available, the services can be manually discovered. The communication between OEM Console and intelligent agents is done through a *communication daemon*. Daemon Manager can be used to control the communication daemon. A listing of discovered services is stored in a cache known as the *discovery cache*. Jobs can be scheduled on a node or database and their progress monitored from OEM Console. For example, a database backup can be scheduled from the OEM Console. You can also configure a variety of events that you want to track across the enterprise and track these events from the OEM Console. For example, you can track the **alert.log** file for errors and trigger an event when an error occurs. It is also possible to trigger e-mail and pager alerts when an event occurs. An integrated map system allows you to monitor network objects with a graphical display. OEM stores information about services, jobs, and events internally in a set of tables called the *OEM repository*. A separate repository needs to be built for each user using Repository Manager. If a repository does not exist for the user, it is created when the user uses OEM for the first time. In the following sections, we have provided a detailed look at the components in OEM and also included examples wherever appropriate.

Repository Manager (RM)

OEM maintains information on tasks performed by each administrator in Oracle tables as part of a repository. The repository is unique to a user across the enterprise and can be created on any accessible database on the network. You can create, validate, or delete a repository using Repository Manager (RM). As mentioned previously, the repository is created in the user's schema. There is also a provision to store discovered nodes to a file. If you are creating repositories for multiple users, it is quicker to create a list of discovered nodes in a file and use it to create a list of available nodes on multiple repositories. Automatic discovery of nodes for each user can be time-consuming. We will cover the common repository tasks in the next few sections.

CREATING A REPOSITORY   The repository can be created using Repository Manager (RM). Click on Start | Programs | Oracle Enterprise Manager | Repository Manager to launch RM. You will see the first screen of the wizard, similar to that shown in Figure 5-13.

Choose the option to create a repository and follow instructions in the wizard. You must select the option to create or validate components for OEM. You will be asked for login information for the repository. You can create the repository on any database on the network. We will create the repository for the user *SYSTEM*.

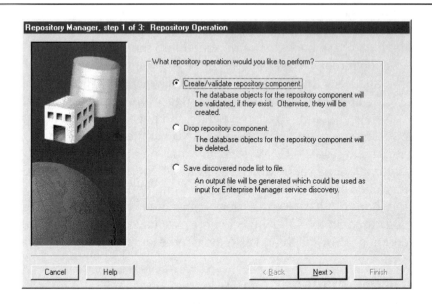

FIGURE 5-13. *Repository operation using Repository Manager*

CAUTION
Do not connect as SYSDBA *or* SYSOPER *while creating the repository. If you do so, you will be attached to the SYS schema and not your own. The repository needs to be available under your own schema.*

Click on the Finish button to create the repository. You will see a dialog box listing the repository components that will be created.

NOTE
A repository for Software Manager is also recommended by RM because we have installed Software Manager on our machine.

Click on the OK button after noting the repository components being created to start the process of repository creation. At the end of successful completion, you will see a dialog box similar to the one shown here:

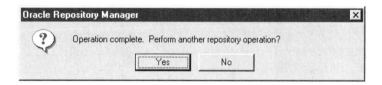

If a user attempts to connect to the OEM Console and does not have a repository, a warning message is displayed and the user will not be allowed to proceed without creating the requisite repository.

VALIDATING A REPOSITORY   If you want to validate the status of the repository for a particular user, you can use this feature of RM. It is also possible that the structure of the repository might change when you upgrade the Oracle Server software. You can perform a repository upgrade without losing historical data for a user by validating the repository.

The procedure for validating a repository is identical to that of creating a repository. If you choose the option to create or validate a repository, RM will automatically validate an existing repository for the user.

STORING DISCOVERED NODES TO A FILE   OEM maintains a list of discovered nodes in the repository. You can create a list of these discovered nodes on a file by using RM. Once this list is created on a file, you can replicate this information to other repositories. This is quicker than discovering nodes while creating a repository for each user. You will be given a chance to specify the name of the file and the name of the repository owner (user) while creating the repository.

DELETING A REPOSITORY   Occasionally you will be required to drop a repository for a user. You can also perform this task via RM. You will see a dialog box similar to the one shown below that will provide a warning of the repository components that are being dropped.

```
Oracle Repository Manager                                          [x]

      WARNING! Dropping repository sub-components is irreversible.  Continue with the indicated operations?

        Sub-component                     Operation                 ▲

        Enterprise Manager                Drop
  (i)   Software Manager                  Drop
        Oracle Expert                     Drop
        Oracle Trace                      Drop
                                                                    ▼

                      [    OK    ]     [  Cancel  ]
```

Once a repository is dropped, you will have to rebuild the repository and rediscover services if you ever need to use the repository under the same schema again.

Discovering Services

Once a repository is built for a user, OEM can keep track of services available on all available nodes. For this to work, you must create a list of nodes for OEM to track. After you create this list, you must update the OEM repository with the services available on each node. The recommended solution is to allow OEM to automatically discover services on a node. This can be accomplished if Oracle Intelligent Agent (OIA) is running on the node. OEM is capable of extracting a list of available services from OIA version 7.3.3 or higher. However, if you do not have OIA running on the machine, you can manually configure the available services on a node. We will illustrate service discovery on our Windows NT machine.

The first step is to start the OIA on the machine. On Windows NT, you can accomplish this by using the Services applet under the Control Panel. Ensure that a service named *OracleAgent80* is running on your machine.

Start OEM and connect to the database as a DBA user. We will connect as the user *SYSTEM*. Select Navigator | Service Discovery | Discover New Services to access the wizard for service discovery.

Add the nodes on which you want to discover services in order. We will discover services on our test machine named *aadkoli-lap*, as shown here:

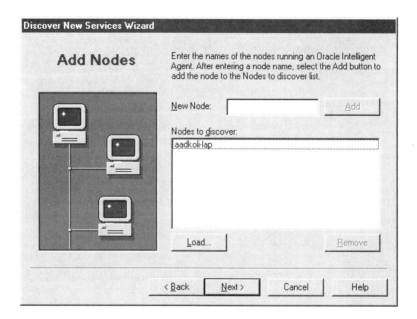

TIP

If you have created a list of nodes on a file, you can load the nodes to be discovered by clicking on the LOAD button. Refer to the section titled "Storing Discovered Nodes to a File" earlier in this chapter.

Click on the Next button to see a screen similar to the one shown in Figure 5-14.

You can specify an interval at which service discovery will be initiated automatically by the daemon. You can also set the option to update your Net8 configuration file (the **tnsnames.ora** file) automatically when a new service is discovered. This can be helpful on large networks where there are several nodes.

TIP

You should schedule an immediate discovery of services the very first time you use a repository.

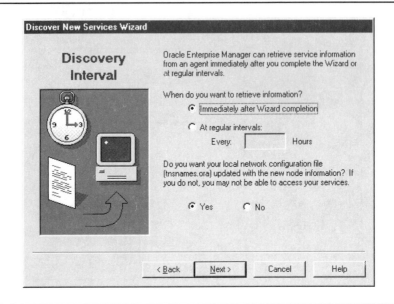

FIGURE 5-14. *Setting discovery interval*

Next, you will see a summary screen which will confirm the options you have selected for service discovery. Click on the Finish button to start service discovery.

You will see a progress report for the discovery process and, finally, a dialog box confirming that the service discovery has completed successfully.

Once you have discovered services on a node, you can get details from the OEM Navigator. Figure 5-15 shows a sample screen that provides a listing of datafiles on our sample database.

You can also get a listing of other services, such as listeners, from OEM Navigator.

Refreshing Services

If new nodes or new services on nodes are added to your enterprise, you need to refresh the OEM repository with this information. You can do so by selecting Navigator | Service Discovery | Refresh Services. A wizard will

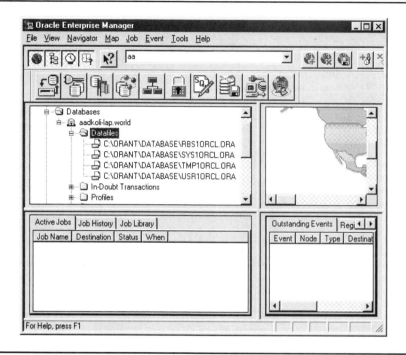

FIGURE 5-15. *Listing of available services on a discovered node*

guide you through the discovery process. We will illustrate the discovery of a new service on our node.

We will start the Oracle Web Admin Listener using the Services applet. After this, we will use OEM to refresh the services on the node *aadkoli-lap*. Shown here is a dialog box with an alert about the new Web service:

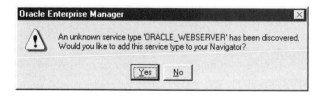

After the new services are added to the repository, we will confirm the availability of the new services in OEM Navigator. Shown here is the new service for the Web Server on our installation:

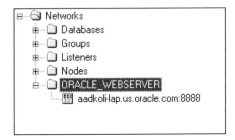

You can use OEM to visually check if a service is available. If a particular service is not available, you will see an alert (a red icon) next to the service, as shown here:

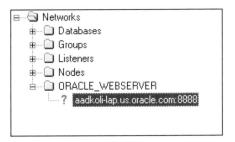

TIP

OEM allows you to filter the services shown in the Navigator and also to obtain a split view of services. You should customize the Navigator for your needs. Select a node in the Navigator and right-click the mouse or use the Navigator menu, as shown next.

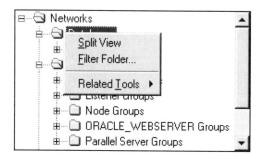

Setting Preferred Credentials

As we have seen so far, OEM keeps track of a variety of services like nodes, databases, and Net8 and Web listeners in the repository. You can set preferred credentials for each service in OEM. These credentials will be used when OEM attempts to connect and use a service. To set the credentials, select File | Preferences on OEM Console. You will see a screen similar to the one shown here:

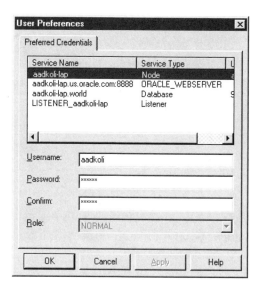

You must set credentials based on the requirements of your site. We will provide some tips on some common Oracle services.

CREDENTIALS FOR A NODE OEM uses credentials for a node to connect to a node. These credentials are used when OEM needs to connect to a node and execute a job. For example, if you have scheduled a job on the machine *aadkoli-lap*, a process will need to log in to the machine at the scheduled time and execute the job. In order to do this, it will need to log in as a Windows NT user with appropriate rights and privileges. For Windows NT systems, you need to ensure that the NT user has the privilege Log on as a batch job. Start User Manager by clicking on Start | Programs | Administrative Tools (Common) | User Manager. Select the user and invoke Policies | User Rights. Select the check box labeled Show Advanced User Rights. Select Log on as a batch job from the list of rights. Ensure that the users or groups that will be executing jobs from OEM are given this right. You can use the Add button to add users and groups to the list. Shown here is a sample screen from our installation:

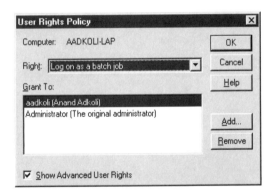

If you attempt to execute a job on Windows NT as a user without this Windows NT privilege, you will get an error with the text "Failed to Authenticate User."

If you have other nodes on your network, such as UNIX nodes, you must ensure that the credentials used for these nodes have the permissions to write to the **$ORACLE_HOME/network** directory.

CREDENTIALS FOR A DATABASE OEM can be used to perform all the routine administrative tasks on a database, from starting up and shutting down a database to backup and recovery. You should provide a user with the *DBA* role at the very minimum. However, it is more practical to provide database credentials for a user who has the *SYSDBA* role because privileged operations like STARTUP and SHUTDOWN require this role. Backup Manager also requires the *SYSDBA* role for backup and recovery. Shown here is a screen with a user named *SYSAD* on our installation with the *SYSDBA* role:

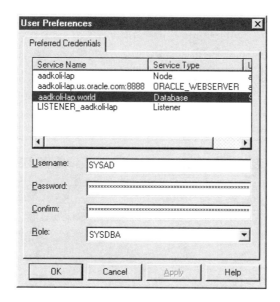

CREDENTIALS FOR LISTENERS   The credentials you provide for listeners depend on the listener. For example, for an Admin Web Listener, you can provide the credentials for the *ADMIN* user.

OEM Maps
OEM allows you to create visuals of your site configurations. You can associate a bitmap with a map. You can then drag services to an appropriate place on the map to indicate a physical location. You can also create many maps, each providing the layout of a different part of your network or even a different geographic area.

We will illustrate this functionality with a small example. From the OEM Console, add a map of the United States by selecting Map | Create Map from the menu. Associate a bitmap with this map. We will select the built-in

usa.bmp file. Let us assume the database *aadkoli-lap.world* is in California. You can drag the service associated with the database on to the portion of the map representing California and create a new map named AA. Similarly, you can create other maps for other portions of your network. You can choose to view resources at a site by selecting the appropriate map, as shown in Figure 5-16.

OEM Groups

OEM allows you to create collections of services called *groups*. Groups for databases, listeners, nodes, and parallel servers are precreated. You can also create new custom groups. For example, if all the databases for the west

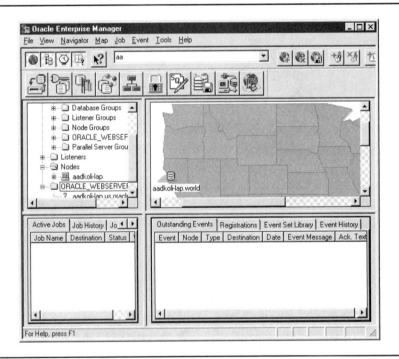

FIGURE 5-16. *Creating maps in OEM*

coast operations of your business are in California, you can create a group named *West Coast* and drag all the database nodes into this group using the mouse. Once the group is created, you can drag the entire group onto an appropriate map, as shown here:

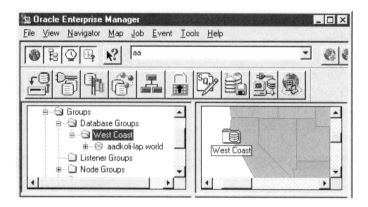

TIP

If your site has several DBAs, create one group for each DBA. This will help you visually keep track of responsibilities for each DBA.

Scheduling Jobs

One of the advanced features of OEM allows you to schedule jobs (or tasks) for routine administration. Jobs can be one-time or repetitive. The tasks are executed by Tool Command Language (TCL) scripts. OEM has predefined TCL scripts for the common tasks. You can write your own SQL scripts, batch files, or TCL scripts to enhance functionality to suit your needs.

You can track the jobs in OEM Console (left, lower pane). A listing of active jobs, a history of completed jobs, and details of jobs along with their names and descriptions are available. A library of all the available jobs can also be viewed. We will illustrate this feature with a simple example.

Example: You need to schedule an emergency shutdown of your databases on the West Coast. You want to send a broadcast message on the network and shut down the database.

We will step through the process of scheduling a job named *AA Broadcast* that performs the above task.

Step 1   Create a new job.

Select Job | Create Job in OEM console to create a new job. Select the General tab and complete the fields for the Job Name and Description. Select a destination for the job from the available destinations. We will use the group named *West Coast* that contains all the databases on the West Coast. We will not create this job as a fixit job. (A fixit job is usually another script that "fixes" a specific issue. If you designate the job as a fixit job, it is available for use when you define an event set. Event sets are discussed later.) Shown here is part of the sample screen from our installation:

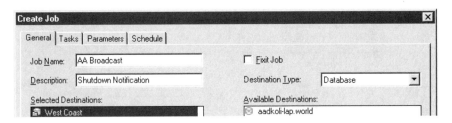

Step 2   Add the tasks to be included in the job.

Select the Tasks tab and add two tasks to the job. The first task is for the broadcast message and the second task is for the database shutdown operation. Figure 5-17 shows the screen for our sample installation.

Step 3   Provide task parameters.

In this step, we will provide the required parameters for the task. Select the Parameters tab and specify the message text for the broadcast task, as shown here:

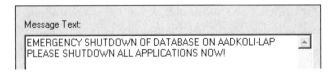

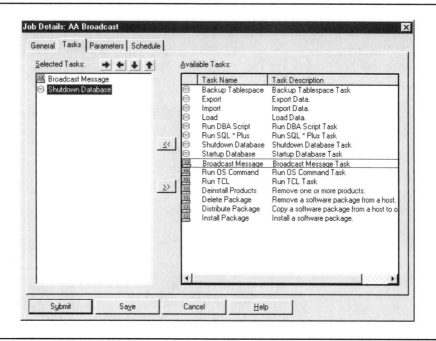

FIGURE 5-17.   *Adding tasks to an OEM job*

Similarly, specify the parameters for the Database Shutdown task as shown below. Note that we are performing an *IMMEDIATE* shutdown. We will use our preferred credentials for the task (the *SYSAD* user with *SYSDBA* role).

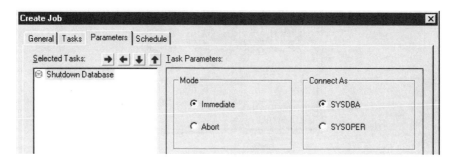

Step 4 Scheduling a job.

The final step in creating a job is to schedule it. This can be done by selecting the Schedule tab, as shown here. We have chosen to execute this task immediately because we have an emergency. OEM also allows you to schedule jobs repetitively.

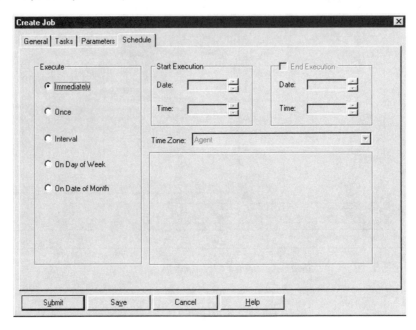

Click on the Submit button to submit the job. The job named *AA Broadcast* is added to the list of active jobs, as shown here:

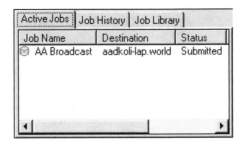

After the job is completed, it is added to the job history, as shown here:

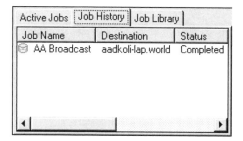

You can view details on the job (the log). Select Job | Show Details (or double-click on the job in the history using the mouse) and you will see a screen similar to the one shown here:

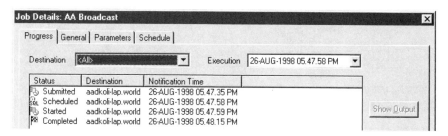

You can double-click on any of the steps or click on the Show Output button to view details of the step. If you encounter any errors, you can get detailed information here.

The above example provides an overview of the process of scheduling a job for your enterprise. You can create more complicated tasks as per the requirements of your site. We will discuss another example of a job—to create a database backup—later in this chapter when we discuss Recovery Manager.

Events and Alerts

We have seen how OEM can be used to manage services on an enterprise. In this section, we will see how OEM can be used to generate alerts (or flags) based on events. You can choose to generate alerts via e-mail or pager messages when a certain event occurs on the enterprise. You should create a list of events that are important to your site.

The first step is to define the messaging systems. Select Event | Configure Services from OEM Console and configure the e-mail and/or paging services. Figure 5-18 shows a sample screen for configuring paging services on our site.

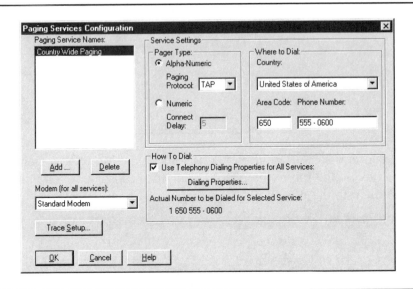

FIGURE 5-18. *Configuring paging services in OEM*

Similarly, configure e-mail services as shown here:

The next step is to define a list of administrators to whom the alerts will be sent. You can define this list by selecting Event | Administrator List from OEM Console. Click on the Add button, then add contact details for the administrator as shown here:

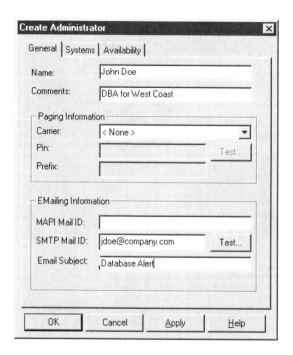

Click on the Systems tab and add a list of systems and services that are under the control of this administrator. Click on the Availability tab and specify the working hours for this administrator. You can also choose the alerting mechanism (paged messages, e-mail, or all). You can add more than one administrator to your list.

The next step is to create an event set. Select Event | Create Event Set on OEM Console to create an event set. Specify the identification details for the event, including a unique name, as shown here:

Select the Events tab and add the events you want to the set. Figure 5-19 shows a sample screen for errors in the **alert.log** file.

TIP

Add events that are of a critical nature on your site to the event set. For example, if your site is running a database in ARCHIVELOG mode, you should ensure that there is an alert generated when the archive destination is full.

Click on the Parameters tab and specify appropriate values for your event set. You can schedule a fixit job based on the event. (You must create a job and designate it as a fixit job for it to be available while creating an event

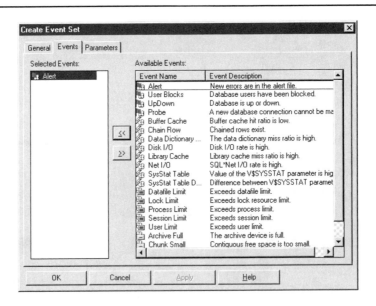

FIGURE 5-19. *Adding events to an event set*

set. Please refer to the section on creating jobs earlier in this chapter for more information on fixit jobs.) A good example of a fixit job would be to move files from the archive destination to an alternate destination when the archive destination is full.

Once an event set is created, you must register it. Select Event | Register Event Set to see a screen similar to the one shown here:

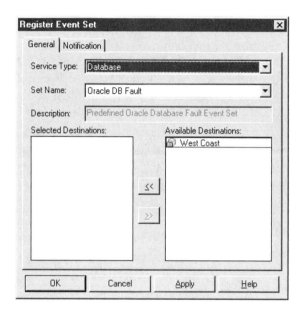

Specify the event set and the destination along with the notification type and click on the OK button. You can view information on events in OEM Console (lower-right pane). Click on the Registrations tab to confirm that your event set is registered.

Oracle Instance Manager (OIM)

Oracle Instance Manager (OIM) is a GUI utility that can be used to manage an Oracle instance. You can start up and shut down an Oracle database, edit initialization parameters, control user sessions, and manage in-doubt transactions (in-doubt transactions apply to distributed databases systems only) using OIM. In this section, we will cover the major functions of OIM.

Table 5-3 lists the methods that can be used to launch Oracle Instance Manager.

You should use an Oracle user who has the *SYSDBA* or *SYSOPER* role when you use OIM. This will allow you to use privileged operations such as STARTUP and SHUTDOWN.

MANAGING DATABASE STARTUP AND SHUTDOWN   OIM can be used to start up and shut down the database. When you select the database in the Navigator, you will see a tab control in the main screen, as shown in Figure 5-20.

The Status tab provides the current status of the database. You can start up and shut down the database by selecting the appropriate radio buttons. These options are also available in the Database menu of OIM. During startup, you can choose to create the instance, mount the database, and

Method	Procedure
OEM Console	1. Use shortcut for Oracle Instance Manager 2. Select Tools I Applications I Oracle Instance Manager
Program group	Click on Start I Programs I Oracle Enterprise Manager I Instance Manager
Oracle Administrator Toolbar	Use shortcut to Instance Manager
Command line	Execute **c:\orant\bin\vai.exe**

TABLE 5-3.   *Launching Oracle Instance Manager*

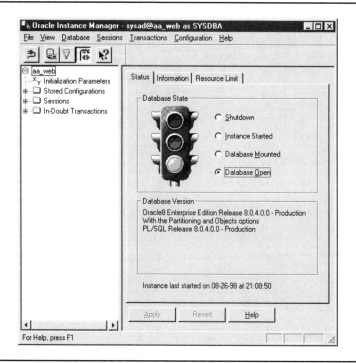

FIGURE 5-20. *Main screen of Oracle Instance Manager*

open the database. The startup options in OIM are equivalent to the
following commands:

```
startup nomount <pfile>
startup mount <pfile>
startup <pfile>
```

OBTAINING DATABASE INFORMATION   Select the Information tab
in the main screen. It includes information on the online redo log files and
archived redo log files. Information on the SGA is also available. Figure 5-21
shows a sample screen with this information.

FIGURE 5-21. *Database Information tab in Instance Manager*

You can change the database archiving mode using the Database menu in OIM. Manual archiving can also be initiated from the same menu.

OBTAINING RESOURCE USAGE INFORMATION   In the main screen, the Resource Limit tab provides information on resource usage on the database. The comparison between current utilization and availability of resources is available here. Figure 5-22 shows a sample screen from our installation.

MANAGING INITIALIZATION PARAMETERS   You can view the initialization parameters in the INIT.ORA file when you select the corresponding node in the Navigator. A tab control is available to see basic, instance-specific, advanced, and derived parameters.

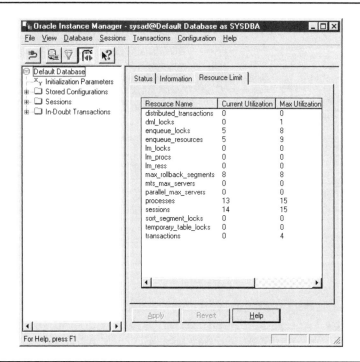

FIGURE 5-22. *Checking resource usage in Instance Manager*

TIP
The advanced and derived parameters are only visible when you select View | Advanced Mode in OIM.

To change the setting for a parameter, edit the property sheet. Be sure to save the configuration. Once a configuration has been saved, you can export it to a file. Navigate to the Configurations node, select a configuration, and choose Configuration | Export to File from the OIM menu to save the configuration to a file. On Windows NT, the **c:\orant\sysman\ifiles** folder is used by OIM as the default location for initialization files.

MANAGING SESSIONS   You can use OIM to manage sessions against Oracle. Shown here is part of a screen from our installation:

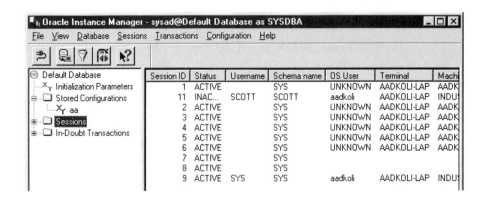

If you have the privileges, you can kill sessions from OIM. Select the session of your interest and then Sessions | Disconnect to kill the session. This is equivalent to the ALTER SYSTEM KILL SESSION command in SQL.

The Sessions menu also has an item that allows you to open the database in *restricted* mode. When you open a database in restricted mode, nonprivileged users will not be allowed to connect to the database. This mode is normally used during database recovery when you do not want users issuing transactions to the database. You can come out of restricted mode by selecting Sessions | Allow All from OIM.

MANAGING IN-DOUBT TRANSACTIONS   Transactions fail at times in distributed database systems. You can use OIM to force commits and rollbacks in distributed systems. A list of in-doubt transactions can be obtained by selecting the corresponding node in the OIM Navigator. You can force a rollback or commit by selecting the appropriate option under the Transactions menu.

Oracle Security Manager (OSM)

Oracle Security Manager (OSM) is a GUI utility that allows DBAs to manage users, roles, and profiles on Oracle databases. In this section, we will cover the major functions of OSM.

Table 5-4 lists the methods that can be used to launch Oracle Security Manager.

You should use an Oracle user who is assigned the *DBA* role when you use OSM because this role has the system privileges CREATE USER, CREATE ROLE, and CREATE PRIVILEGE. Of course, you can create a special user and assign any combination of the above privileges to this user for OSM operations.

MANAGING ROLES   Roles are used to help ease the task of managing user rights and privileges. A role in Oracle has a similar function to a *group* in operating systems. Oracle provides some predefined roles that are listed in Table 5-5.

Method	Procedure
OEM Console	1. Use shortcut for Oracle Security Manager 2. Select Tools I Applications I Oracle Security Manager
Program group	Click on Start I Programs I Oracle Enterprise Manager I Security Manager
Oracle Administrator Toolbar	Use shortcut to Security Manager
Command line	Execute **c:\orant\bin\vac.exe**

TABLE 5-4.   *Launching Oracle Security Manager*

Name of Role	Description
CONNECT	1. CREATE and ALTER SESSION 2. CREATE database objects like tables, clusters, database links, sequences, and synonyms 3. Does not include CREATE privileges for procedures, object types, and triggers
RESOURCE	1. CREATE tables, procedures, clusters, and sequences 2. Create procedures, object types, and triggers
DBA	Refer to Table 5-2
AQ_ADMINISTRATOR_ROLE	Administration of advanced message queues
SELECT_CATALOG_ROLE	HS_ADMIN_ROLE Select on data dictionary
EXECUTE_CATALOG_ROLE	HS_ADMIN_ROLE EXECUTE on system packages
DELETE_CATALOG_ROLE	Deleting catalogs
IMP_FULL_DATABASE	Full database imports
EXP_FULL_DATABASE	Full database exports
RECOVERY_CATALOG_OWNER	Owner of recovery manager catalog
HS_ADMIN_ROLE	For non-Oracle data sources
AQ_USER_ROLE	Users of advanced queues (advanced messaging)
SNMPAGENT	1. Select on select views in catalog 2. ANALYZE objects

TABLE 5-5.   *Predefined Oracle Roles*

TIP
*Query the DBA_ROLES view to get the
above listing.*

To create, modify, or remove a role, launch OSM and expand the Roles
node. You will see a screen similar to the one shown in Figure 5-23.

You can expand each of the roles listed to view other roles included
within the role. The system and object privileges associated with the role are
also listed. Use the Role menu or the shortcuts available in the toolbar to
create a new role. You can also use Role | Create Like to copy an existing
role, which can be then modified to meet your requirements. When you

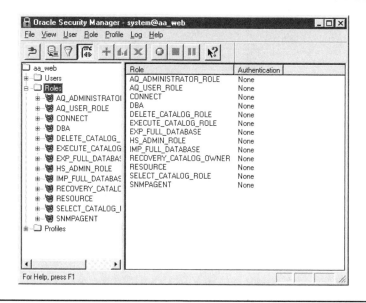

FIGURE 5-23. *Managing roles in OSM*

create a role, you can use the available tab control to add other roles, system privileges, and object privileges to the role. Other properties like passwords can also be set for the role. Shown here is a sample screen:

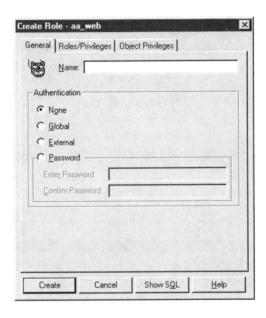

Similarly, use Role | Remove or Role | Add Privileges to Roles to remove or modify an existing role.

TIP

Use the right button of the mouse to get quick access to functions available based on the context. For example, select the Roles node and right-click the mouse to get access to the items that apply in the context (i.e. Create, Add Privileges to Roles and Filter Folder). However, if you select an existing role, the right-click will also give you access to the Remove and Show Dependencies items.

MANAGING USERS   User management is a routine chore for DBAs. OSM allows you to create or delete users and assign roles, privileges, and quotas to the user.

Again, the OSM Navigator can be used to obtain access to the Users node. New users can be created and existing users can be removed. Roles and privileges can be assigned either during the creation of the user or to an existing user.

Another important aspect of user management is to manage passwords. Passwords can be reset or expired using OSM. Occasionally, it is required to lock a user account to block access to the database. These functions are also available through OSM.

TIP

If you want to restrict access to the database for a user, you should lock the account. Do not delete the user unless you want to drop the database objects associated with that user's schema. You could also reset the password to achieve the same result.

MANAGING PROFILES   Profiles are used in Oracle to control the resources used by a user. These resources include CPU and space on the database. Oracle8 also allows for better password management. We will discuss this feature in Chapter 7. Profiles can also be managed using OSM and are used like roles. Once a profile is created, you can assign the profile to a user. Profiles can be modified at any time.

Oracle provides a built-in profile named *DEFAULT*. This is automatically assigned when a user is created. Some sites prefer to modify the *DEFAULT* profile to control resource usage. Initially, all the resource levels are set to *UNLIMITED* for this profile.

LOGGING FEATURE OF SECURITY MANAGER   OSM includes a logging feature that is useful to create SQL scripts for common user management tasks. To start logging, select Log | Record from the menu. Perform the task in OSM and then select Log | Stop. You will be prompted for a filename. This can be used as a SQL script to perform the same task at a later time. We will demonstrate this feature with the example below.

Example: Create a SQL script that will create a user and assign the *CONNECT* role to the user. Specify default and temporary tablespaces for the user.

The solution is to use the logging feature of OSM. The steps are outlined below:

1. Start recording to log by selecting Log | Record.

2. Create the user using OSM. Specify the default and temporary tablespaces, then assign a password and the *CONNECT* role to the user.

3. Stop recording by selecting Log | Stop.

4. When prompted, specify a filename for the script. You will see a script similar to that listed below:

```
REM
REM
REM
CREATE USER "TEST" IDENTIFIED BY "aa" DEFAULT TABLESPACE
"USER_DATA" TEMPORARY TABLESPACE "TEMPORARY_DATA" PROFILE
DEFAULT ACCOUNT UNLOCK
/
GRANT "CONNECT" TO "TEST"
/
ALTER USER "TEST" DEFAULT ROLE ALL
/
EXIT;
```

Replace the username, the role, the tablespace information, and the password with SQL variables and this will become a generic script.

TIP

*Place your SQL scripts in the **c:\orant\ sysman\scripts\sql** folder as this is the default location used by OEM on Windows NT.*

Storage Manager (OSTM)

Oracle Storage Manager (OSTM) is a GUI utility that allows DBAs to manage storage on a database. Oracle has logical units of storage called tablespaces. Tablespaces are associated with physical storage, namely datafiles. Rollback segments are used to store *undo* information by Oracle. OSTM can be used to manage tablespaces, datafiles, and rollback segments.

Table 5-6 lists the methods that can be used to launch Oracle Storage Manager.

Method	Procedure
OEM Console	1. Use shortcut for Oracle Storage Manager 2. Select Tools | Applications | Oracle Storage Manager
Program group	Click on Start | Programs | Oracle Enterprise Manager | Storage Manager
Oracle Administrator Toolbar	Use shortcut to Storage Manager
Command line	Execute **c:\orant\bin\vag.exe**

TABLE 5-6.   *Launching Oracle Storage Manager*

You should use an Oracle user who is assigned the *DBA* role when you use OSTM because this role has the system privileges CREATE TABLESPACE and CREATE ROLLBACK SEGMENT. You can create a special user and assign the above privileges to this user for OSTM operations.

MANAGING TABLESPACES   Tablespaces are logical units of storage defined in Oracle. Tablespaces can be created and dropped using OSTM. When a tablespace is created, you need to associate one or more datafiles with it. The datafiles provide the physical storage for the data while the tablespace provides logical storage for the data. Oracle needs to have one tablespace named SYSTEM that is available at all times for normal functioning. You can choose to create other tablespaces based on your needs. If you want, you could have a database with just the SYSTEM tablespace. This is, however, highly inadvisable. Rollback segments are also objects that are stored in a tablespace and can be considered as scratch pads that are used to make copies of data before being modified. When a database is created, a special rollback segment named SYSTEM is defined automatically. You can create other rollback segments based on your needs. (The number of transactions and the rate of transactions must be considered while sizing rollback segments.)

OSTM Navigator provides nodes for tablespaces, datafiles, and rollback segments. When a new tablespace is created, you can specify the datafiles that are associated with it. You can also specify the storage parameters like *INITIAL EXTENT* and *NEXT EXTENT*. Additional attributes like marking the tablespace for temporary segments can also be provided. The tablespace can be marked *ONLINE* or *OFFLINE*. Shown here is the screen that is used to provide tablespace specifications:

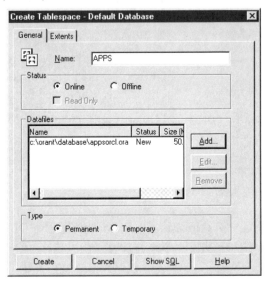

Shown next is a sample screen that can be used to provide storage parameters. Once all the specifications for the tablespace are provided, you need to click on the Create button to create the tablespace.

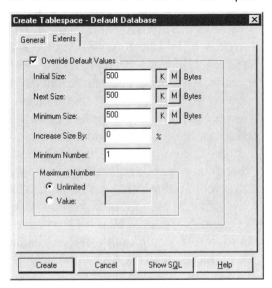

TIP
Click on the Show SQL button to see the SQL
command for your tablespace creation task,
and create a script by cutting and pasting text
from here.

OSTM can also be used to add datafiles to existing tablespaces and drop tablespaces. Menu items are available under the Tablespace menu.

Note that the status of a tablespace along with its usage is available visually when you select the Tablespaces node, as shown here:

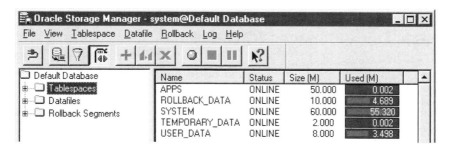

MANAGING DATAFILES   As mentioned before, datafiles are associated with tablespaces and provide physical storage for Oracle database objects. Datafiles can be managed separately using OSTM. Expand the Datafiles node in OSTM Navigator to view the available datafiles. You can take a datafile *OFFLINE* and *ONLINE*, and enable autoextension for a datafile. Autoextension is a useful feature available on Oracle7 release 7.3 and higher. When a tablespace cannot allocate extents when space is required, earlier versions of Oracle gave an error message. This can be avoided by enabling autoextension for a datafile. A datafile belonging to a tablespace will now expand automatically when additional space is required for extents.

MANAGING ROLLBACK SEGMENTS   Rollback segments are used to store *undo* information in Oracle. The optimal number and size of rollback segments on a database vary with the number of transactions and rate of transactions. Rollback segments (RBS) are created in tablespaces. Oracle allocates a transaction to a rollback segment based on an internal algorithm. A transaction can also explicitly request a particular rollback segment. In any case, OSTM allows DBAs to graphically manage RBS. You can add RBS, make them *OFFLINE* and *ONLINE,* and modify their storage parameters. The status and usage of RBS can be obtained visually using OSTM. Figure 5-24 shows a typical screen with a listing of RBS and their status.

LOGGING FEATURE OF STORAGE MANAGER   OSTM also includes a logging feature that can be used to record tasks performed. These tasks can be stored as SQL scripts for future use. Refer to the discussion on Security Manager for information on this feature. We will not repeat this information here because the logging feature of OSTM is identical to Security Manager.

Oracle Data Manager (ODM)

Oracle Data Manager (ODM) is a GUI utility that allows DBAs to perform database import and export. External (non-Oracle) data can be loaded into

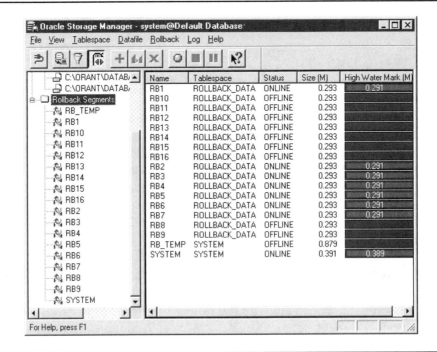

FIGURE 5-24.   *Viewing rollback segments in Storage Manager*

Oracle using Loader. The functionality of Data Manager is identical to that provided by the Import, Export, and SQL*Loader utilities.

Table 5-7 lists the methods that can be used to launch Oracle Data Manager.

You should use an Oracle user who is assigned the *DBA* role when you use ODM because this role has the system privileges *IMP_FULL_DATABASE* and *EXP_FULL_DATABASE*. You can also create a special user and assign the above privileges to this user for ODM operations. In addition, users can export their own schema.

EXPORTING DATA   Using ODM, you can export data from an Oracle database to a file. The export file can then be used to import the data into another Oracle database on any platform. There are some restrictions for the import. The rule of thumb is that you can import data into an equivalent or higher version of Oracle, but not into an earlier version.

Method	Procedure
OEM Console	1. Use shortcut for Oracle Data Manager. 2. Select Tools | Applications | Oracle Data Manager.
Program group	Click on Start | Programs | Oracle Enterprise Manager | Data Manager.
Oracle Administrator Toolbar	A shortcut to Data Manager is not available in the Administrator Toolbar. You can add a shortcut for Data Manager using the following procedure: 1. Move the mouse on to the Administrator Toolbar. 2. Right-click the mouse and select the Customize option. 3. Select the Applications tab and add **c:\orant\bin\vad.exe**.
Command line	Execute **c:\orant\bin\vad.exe**.

TABLE 5-7.   *Launching Data Manager*

TIP
If you are using a utility like **ftp** *to transfer the export file between machines, be sure to use the* **binary** *mode for data transfer.*

Data can be exported at three levels. These are referred to as *modes* in Oracle documentation. The *full database* export mode can be used to migrate the entire database from one machine to another. The *user* mode can be used to migrate the objects belonging to one user (schema) to another database, and the *table* mode can be used to export individual tables. The mode of export a user can perform obviously depends on the object privileges available to the user.

To export data, select Data | Export in ODM. You will see the Export Wizard, which consists of several screens (or pages). Table 5-8 below provides information on these screens.

TIP
*We have experienced a few failures while attempting to export data using Data Manager. If you experience an inexplicable failure, use the CLI (**exp80.exe**). We will discuss CLI export in the next chapter.*

IMPORTING DATA   The import operation is the opposite of export. An export file created with the export utility can be imported into an Oracle database (of the same or higher version). During the import, you can optionally import the data into another user's schema.

NOTE
An export/import can be used to upgrade databases. For example, an export file of an Oracle7 database can be imported into Oracle8. This is a one-way export since Oracle8 stores data in a different format.

To start the import, select Data | Import in ODM. A wizard will guide you through the import. The wizard is very similar to the one for export. You

Screen Number	Uses
1	1. Export file destination (local vs. remote). OEM console must be running for remote export. 2. Name of export file (**.dmp** extension for filename).
2	Select modes for export. If you select the database, it implies full export. Similarly, picking a user or object implies user export or table export.
3	1. Associated objects to be exported (i.e., grants, constraints, and indexes) 2. Direct path vs. conventional. Tip: Direct path is faster than conventional since it does not use the SQL layer. However, it is only available on version 7.3 and higher and is not backward compatible.
4	1. Record length. 2. Buffer size. 3. Log file for export.
5	1. Incremental export parameters. 2. Type of statistics to be used for optimization. 3. Ensure read consistency. 4. Compress extents.
6	Summary screen; last chance to change parameters for impending export operation.

TABLE 5-8. *Data Manager Export Wizard*

can select a few additional options for import. These are listed in Table 5-9.

LOADING DATA   ODM can be used to load external data in non-Oracle format. This functionality is identical to the SQL*Loader utility. Select Data | Load from the ODM menu to invoke the wizard interface for the Loader. The wizard is very similar to the one for export and import. Table 5-10 lists some of the options that are unique to the Loader.

Import Option	Description
Ignore Creation Errors	No errors will be generated for objects that preexist.
Write Index-Creation Commands to file	During import, you can choose to create a SQL script for creation of indexes.
Commit after each array insert	Choose this to break the import into smaller pieces. If this option is not selected, you will need an RBS to accommodate the entire import.

TABLE 5-9. *Import Options*

Loader Option	Description
Control File	Includes all the command-line arguments for the Load operation; can optionally include the data. Has a file extension of **.ctl** by default.
Optional Files	External datafile containing data to be loaded, a log file, a bad file to hold bad data, a discard file to hold data that was discarded during the load, and a parallel file for concurrent loads.
Records to be skipped from the beginning	First *n* records that you do not want to load.
Records to load after initial skip	Records to be loaded after skipping n records above.
Rows per commit	How often a commit should occur; this parameter impacts the RBS directly.
Minimum insert errors, Maximum discard records	Parameters to specify when the load operation should be terminated based on the errors.

TABLE 5-10. *Load Options in Data Manager*

Several sample control files are provided with Data Manager. On Windows NT, these are located in the **c:\orant\rdbms80\loader** folder. We will use Data Manager to load data using a control file in the example below:

Example: Use Data Manager to load sample data from the file **ulcase1.ctl**. The steps are shown here:

1. Select Data | Load from ODM to launch the wizard.

2. Choose the control file, as shown in Figure 5-25.

3. Click on the Finish button to begin the load. The log from our sample load is shown below:

```
Table DEPT:
  7 Rows successfully loaded.
  0 Rows not loaded due to data errors.
  0 Rows not loaded because all WHEN clauses were failed.
  0 Rows not loaded because all fields were null.
Space allocated for bind array:                49536 bytes(64 rows)
Space allocated for memory besides bind array:      0 bytes
Total logical records skipped:          0
Total logical records read:             7
Total logical records rejected:         0
Total logical records discarded:        0
Run began on Fri Aug 28 06:42:06 1998
Run ended on Fri Aug 28 06:42:07 1998
Elapsed time was:     00:00:01.41
CPU time was:         00:00:00.28
```

Schema Manager (OSCM)

Oracle Schema Manager (OSCM) allows Oracle users to create and manage database objects. OSCM can be used by DBAs as well as application developers to manage database objects. The functionality available to all levels of users is the same except that the list of objects available to users depends on the object privileges granted to them.

Table 5-11 lists the methods that can be used to launch Oracle Schema Manager.

OSCM has an interface that is identical to the other tools like Security Manager and Storage Manager. We will not delve into OSCM in the same level of detail. The Navigator allows you to select the database objects that you want to work with. You can set an option to view the objects by schema

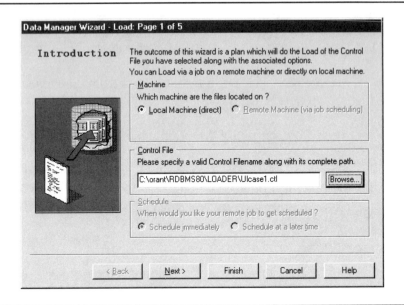

FIGURE 5-25. *Choosing the control file for the load operation*

Method	Procedure
OEM Console	1. Use shortcut for Oracle Schema Manager 2. Select Tools I Applications I Oracle Schema Manager
Program group	Click on Start I Programs I Oracle Enterprise Manager I Schema Manager
Oracle Administrator Toolbar	Use shortcut to Schema Manager
Command line	Execute **c:\orant\bin\vas.exe**

TABLE 5-11. *Launching Schema Manager*

or by object type (in the View menu). The Object menu provides access to a variety of tasks that include creation of objects, granting object privileges, and truncating tables. Oracle8 allows for partitioning of tables and indexes. Some of the operations like SPLIT PARTITION and EXCHANGE PARTITION are available under the Object menu. Again, the facility to record tasks performed in the GUI into a SQL script is available under the Log menu.

SQL Worksheet (SQLWKS)

SQL Worksheet (SQLWKS) is a GUI tool that can be used to issue ad hoc SQL and PL/SQL. SQLWKS is more advanced than SQL Plus since it is capable of executing privileged commands including database STARTUP and SHUTDOWN. SQLWKS also allows you to type multiple commands that can be submitted in a consolidated manner. (When used interactively, SQL Plus and Server Manager only allow one SQL command or one PL/SQL block to be executed at a time.) You can also edit the commands in the command window, like any text editor. The interface consists of two panes—the lower pane is used to issue SQL and PL/SQL, and the upper pane is used to view the results. You can also save the worksheet to a file. Shown here is the command and results windows of SQL Worksheet:

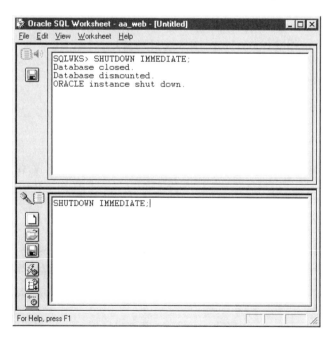

TIP
You should make it a habit to use the shortcuts (icons) on the SQLWKS for quick access to worksheet commands. The shortcut for execution of SQL and PL/SQL is especially handy.

Table 5-12 lists the methods that can be used to launch SQL Worksheet. In the next chapter, we will use CLI to perform normal DBA tasks. SQL Worksheet will feature in many of those examples.

Oracle Recovery Manager (RMAN)

Oracle Recovery Manager (RMAN) is a utility that can be used for database backup and recovery tasks across the enterprise. RMAN is available in GUI as well as CLI. If you are managing multiple databases, RMAN is the preferred method for database backups. Many database recoveries are performed under high stress, and many a time DBAs make critical mistakes in their attempt to bring up the database quickly. RMAN can minimize such mistakes because it keeps track of available backups in a *recovery catalog* and this information is used during recovery. While a recovery catalog is not mandatory, it is highly recommended. RMAN features include the ability to take incremental backups and get detailed reports of backups. Before going into the use of RMAN, we will discuss the recovery catalog.

Method	Procedure
OEM Console	1. Use shortcut for SQL Worksheet 2. Select Tools | Applications | Oracle SQL Worksheet.
Program group	Click on Start | Programs | Oracle Enterprise Manager | SQL Worksheet
Oracle Administrator Toolbar	Use shortcut to SQL Worksheet
Command line	Execute **c:\orant\bin\vaw.exe**

TABLE 5-12. *Launching SQL Worksheet*

THE RECOVERY CATALOG   The recovery catalog contains information about backups and is stored inside an Oracle8 database. This information is used to determine the backup to be used when recovery is required. Obviously, the recovery catalog itself must be available for a recovery, and therefore must be stored in a separate database. If you only have one Oracle database on your site, you should create another small database to hold the recovery catalog. Most sites have multiple databases, and catalogs can be spread across those databases. For example, a site that has two databases, A and B, can store the recovery catalog of A in B and vice versa.

The recovery catalog must be created in the schema of a user that has the role *RECOVERY_CATALOG_OWNER*. While you can use any available user on your database, it is better to create a separate user for this purpose. We will illustrate the creation of a catalog.

CAUTION
Do not use the user SYS *or* INTERNAL *to create the recovery catalog.*

Example: Create a recovery catalog for a database named PROD in a database named RCV. Register the database into the catalog (we will use the databases PROD and RCV in all our discussions on RMAN).

Step 1   Create the Owner for the Recovery Catalog.
Use Security Manager to create a user named *RMAN* in the *RCV* database. Grant the roles *CONNECT, RESOURCE,* and *RECOVERY_CATALOG_ OWNER* to this user.

Step 2   Create the Recovery Catalog.
Using a tool such as SQL Worksheet, connect to the *RCV* database as the user *RMAN* created in step 1 and run the script **c:\orant\rdbms80\admin\ catrman.sql** to create the recovery catalog:

```
SVRMGR> connect rman/rman@rcv
Connected.
SVRMGR> @c:\orant\rdbms80\admin\catrman.sql
ORA-00942: table or view does not exist
DROP TABLE    brl cascade constraints
              *
```

```
ORA-00942: table or view does not exist
DROP TABLE    al cascade constraints
                *
ORA-00942: table or view does not exist
DROP TABLE    bcb cascade constraints
     .     .     .
     .     .     .
     .     .     .
Statement processed.
Statement processed.
Statement processed.
No errors for PACKAGE DBMS_RCVCAT
Statement processed.
No errors for PACKAGE BODY DBMS_RCVCAT
Statement processed.
No errors for PACKAGE DBMS_RCVMAN
Statement processed.
No errors for PACKAGE BODY DBMS_RCVMAN
SVRMGR>
```

TIP

*If you get errors running this script from SQL Worksheet or SQL Plus, use Server Manager to execute the script. Start Server Manager by executing **svrgmr30.exe.***

Step 3 Register the Database in the Recovery Catalog.

You can use the CLI or GUI of *RMAN* to perform all tasks. In this chapter, we will demonstrate *RMAN*'s GUI. We will use CLI in the next chapter. First, ensure that the service *OracleAgent80* is running on your machine. Start OEM and connect to the production database as a user with the *SYSDBA* role. Ensure that the preferred credentials for databases are set to a user with the *SYSDBA* role (see the "Setting Preferred Credentials" section earlier in this chapter). Expand the Databases node and select the *PROD* database. Launch Backup Manager from OEM Console.

NOTE

The Backup Manager on OEM can be used to launch GUI RMAN as well as take Operating System backups. We will use the terms RMAN and Backup Manager interchangeably in this section.

You will see a dialog box similar to the one shown next. Select the radio button for Recovery Manager.

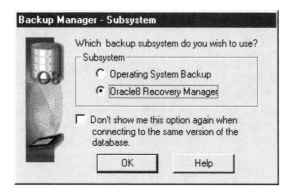

Follow instructions on the screen until you see a dialog box that warns you that the database is not registered in the recovery catalog, as shown here:

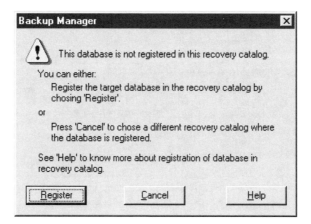

Click on the Register button to register the database into the recovery catalog. You will see a dialog box confirming that a job has been submitted for this task. You can track this job from OEM Console. Verify that the job completes successfully before using RMAN for backups.

Creating Backups

RMAN can also be used to create backups. Launch Backup Manager and choose the database that you want to back up from the Navigator. The first step is to create a *channel* for the backup. (A channel is a connection to a backup device such as a disk or a tape. Every channel is identified by a unique name.) Select Channel | Create to create a channel to your backup device. Once a channel is created, you can use Backup Wizard to create a backup. If you are familiar with RMAN, you can create a backup set directly. We will now create a backup using RMAN.

Example: Create a backup of the USER_DATA tablespace belonging to a database named *PROD* using RMAN. Assume that the database has already been registered in the recovery catalog, which resides in a database named *RCV*.

Step 1   Create a Channel for the Backup.
   Select Channel | Create from Backup Manager and create a channel that will be used for the backup. We will create a channel named *c1* to disk, as shown here:

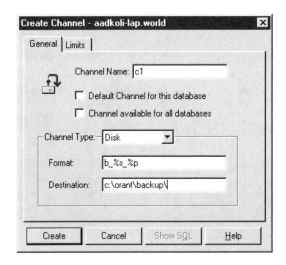

You can set the format for the filenames used for the backup as well as the destination for the backup. Optionally, you can set limits for the file sizes of the backup. This is to avoid a situation where the backup will fail because the backup media is full.

Step 2 Create the Backup.

You can create the backup by creating a backup set (a backup set consists of a set of datafiles, control files, and archived log files) or by using the wizard. We recommend that you use the Backup Wizard to create the backup.

The wizard will prompt you to select the portions of the database that you want to back up in a dialog box similar to the one shown here:

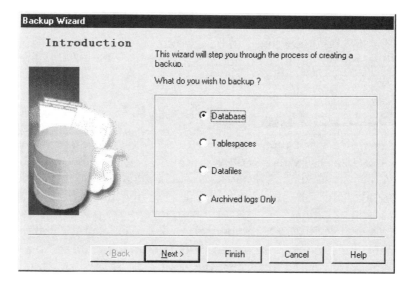

We will choose to back up tablespaces and select the tablespace USER_DATA from the list of tablespaces for backup. You will get a chance to view details for the backup job before you confirm submission of the job.

Again, the submitted job can be viewed in OEM Console. Ensure that the job was successful from OEM Console.

Database Recovery

Database recovery with RMAN is a relatively simple task. RMAN will use information in the recovery catalog to ensure that the right backup set is used for the restoration of the required files. You can use the Restore Wizard to restore the required files. The Recover menu in Backup Manager provides access to the restoration and recovery commands.

Daemon Manager (DM)

OEM uses a daemon (process) for communication between the console and intelligent agents on the network. This is called the *communication daemon*. Daemon Manager (DM) can be used to monitor the communication daemon. Table 5-13 provides a listing of methods to launch DM.

DM provides the status of jobs and events pending on a node on the network. Third-party applications that have pending jobs are also listed here. The OEM console provides a list of pending jobs and events. If any of these wait indefinitely or fail, the DM can be used to diagnose the issue.

DM has a Ping utility that can be used to check for the availability of an intelligent agent on a given node. Select Node | Ping Agent from the DM menu.

NT Backup Manager (BM)

We have seen how Backup Manager (and RMAN) can be used for Oracle backup and recovery. Oracle8 on Windows NT has another GUI tool that allows you to create database backups. This tool is unique to Windows NT and is not available on other platforms. This utility can be used to take *online* as well as *offline* backups. Online backups are possible if the database is in *ARCHIVELOG* mode. NT Backup Manager (BM) allows for partial backups. A backup is created by default in the **c:\orant\backup** folder. You must move it to another destination to avoid losing the backup.

Method	Procedure
OEM Console	Select Tools	Daemon Manager.
Program group	Click on Start	Programs	Oracle Enterprise Manager	Daemon Manager.
Oracle Administrator Toolbar	No shortcut available. Customize the toolbar and create a shortcut to **c:\orant\bin\voda.exe**.
Command line	Execute **c:\orant\bin\voda.exe**.

TABLE 5-13. *Launching Daemon Manager*

BM records information about available backups in a file named
c:\orant\backup\vsbackup.ini. When you use NT Recovery Manager for
recovery, the information in this file is used during the restoration.

To launch NT Backup Manager, click on Start | Programs | Oracle for
Windows NT | NT Backup Manager or execute **c:\orant\bin\vsbck80.exe**.
You will be prompted to provide the password for the *INTERNAL* user. After
validation, you will see a screen similar to the one shown in Figure 5-26.

You will see options for offline and online backup. An online backup is
only available when the database is in *ARCHIVELOG* mode. You can select
specific tablespaces for backup or choose to back up the entire database. It
is possible to back up the control file during an online backup. You can also
specify the destination for the backup.

TIP

*Use the CTRL or SHIFT key to make multiple
selections in the list of tablespaces. Use the
SHIFT key when the selections are adjacent to
each other and the CTRL key when the
selections are not adjacent to each other.*

FIGURE 5-26. *NT Backup Manager screen*

Example: Create an online backup of a tablespace named APPS. We will use this backup to perform a mock recovery using NT Recovery Manager in the next section. The steps are outlined here:

1. Launch NT Backup Manager after ensuring that the database is in *ARCHIVELOG* mode.

2. Choose to perform an online backup and select the tablespace APPS from the list of available tablespaces.

3. Choose the destination for the backup. We will take the default location of **c:\orant\backup**.

4. Click on the Backup button to create the backup.

NT Recovery Manager (RMGR)

NT Recovery Manager (RMGR) can be used to perform recovery using backups created by NT Backup Manager. RMGR uses information in **c:\orant\backup\ vsbackup.ini** during recovery. Again, the user *INTERNAL* needs to perform recovery. RMGR can perform automatic recovery, restore a full database backup, restore a specific datafile, and restore a control file. After restoring the specified files, recovery is performed. The NT Recovery Manager is not to be confused with the Oracle Recovery Manager (RMAN), which is a much superior and robust backup & recovery utility. RMAN is also available on all platforms whereas the NT Recovery Manager is specific to Windows NT. We have included a separate section on this utility under OEM utilities. The following example demonstrates the process to restore and recover a lost data file with NT Backup Manager.

Example: Restore and recover a lost datafile belonging to the APPS tablespace. This is a continuation from the example where NT Backup Manager was used to create a backup.

We will first simulate the loss of a datafile. We will then restore the lost datafile and perform recovery. Follow these steps:

1. We will simulate the loss of a datafile by deleting the file **c:\orant\ database\appsorcl.ora**.

2. Start RMGR and restore the datafile and perform recovery. You will see a screen similar to the one shown here:

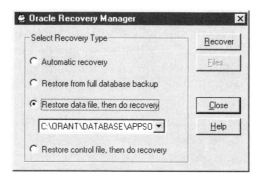

3. Choose to use the latest backup available in the folder **c:\orant\backup** and click on the OK button. You will see a dialog box confirming that the datafile **appsorcl.ora** has been restored and recovered successfully.

NOTE
While NT Backup Manager and NT Recovery Manager are easy to use and can be used to create backups and perform recovery, Recovery Manager (RMAN) is a better tool to perform backup & recovery on production sites. It is more complex to configure and use, but the benefits outweigh the additional work. One of the limitations of NT Recovery Manager is that the database is shut down while performing recovery. This is not optimal in many situations. A better solution is to take the corrupt or missing datafile offline and open the database before performing recovery on the lost datafile(s). This allows other parts of the database to be available to users and minimizes the impact of the downtime. Refer to the section on Oracle Recovery Manager (RMAN) for more information on this topic.

Oracle File Packager (OFP)

The Oracle File Packager (OFP) is a GUI tool that you use to deploy applications using the Oracle Installer. Oftentimes application developers have to write batch files or manually distribute application files to clients. With OFP, you can create an installable product that includes all the files for your applications. The directory structure for the application files can be maintained when an application is deployed on a client.

To launch OFP, click on Start | Programs | Oracle for Windows NT | Oracle File Packager or execute **c:\orant\bin\oisfp10.exe**. You will see the OFP Wizard. You can choose to create a stand-alone product or a sharable product. A stand-alone product is one that is installed on only one machine, whereas a shareable product gets installed on a server and is shared by many clients (the shared product requires the Oracle Client Software Manager for installation).

We will explain the product usage with an example.

Example: We will deploy an application that has a Forms run-time executable for managing department data using OFP. Follow these steps:

1. Start OFP and choose to install a stand-alone product.

2. Provide a name for the product and an identification string along with a brief description of the product, as shown in Figure 5-27. This information will be used to create the **nt.prd** file for the product.

3. Provide a version number (1.0.2 in our example) for the product and choose a Windows NT installation. A **.prd** file will be created based on the operating system that you choose. If you select Windows 95, a file named **win95.prd** will be created. For Windows NT, a file named **nt.prd** will be created. The **.prd** file is used by the Oracle Installer to identify a product for installation.

4. Choose a staging area for the creation of the product installation files. The default location on Window NT is the **c:\orant\oisfp** folder.

5. Include the files that need to be included in the product in a screen similar to the one shown here:

6. Assign a destination for the product installation if your application is dependent on the location.

7. Click on the Finish button to create an installable product in the specified staging area.

For our example, the **nt.prd** file is created in the **c:\orant\oisfp10\deptmgr\install** folder. To install this product, you must start the Oracle Installer and point the Installer to this folder. It will pick up information on the product automatically from the **nt.prd** file.

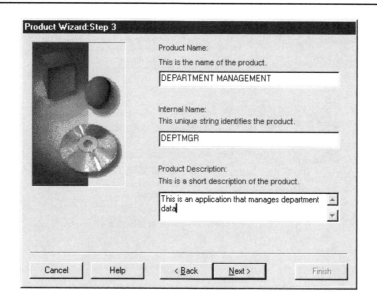

FIGURE 5-27. *Providing product identification information*

Oracle Web Publishing Assistant (WPA)

The Oracle Web Publishing Assistant (WPA) can be used to create static HTML pages based on SQL queries. The content of the HTML file can be kept current through scheduled updates. The HTML file can be viewed through any standard Web browser.

    The HTML file is created by the *OracleWebAssistant* service. Ensure that this service is running on the Windows NT machine. We will provide a small example that will demonstrate the use of this product.

Example: The management has noticed that many employees are using the Internet to get updated stock quotes. It decides to create a local table of common stock quotes on a database. A link is provided from the corporate home page to a page containing updated stock quotes. The page is refreshed every 15 minutes. The steps are outlined here:

  1. Use the WPA Wizard to create an HTML file that is based on a query of the QUOTES table, as shown in Figure 5-28.

  2. Schedule the creation of the HTML file every 15 minutes, as shown here:

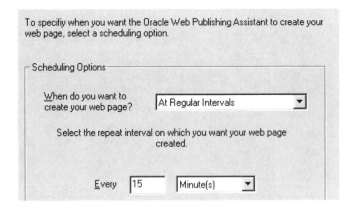

  3. Create a link to the HTML file from the corporate home page. A console on the server will show all jobs scheduled through WPA. Shown here is a sample screen on our installation:

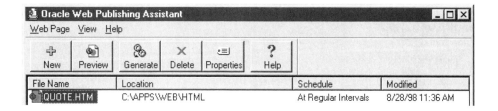

Net8 Assistant

Net8 Assistant is a GUI tool that can be used to configure the Net8 environment for Oracle clients and servers. Net8 uses configuration files on the server as well as the client. Server configuration files include the **listener.ora** file that is used for the Net8 listener configuration. Client-side configuration files include the **tnsnames.ora** and **sqlnet.ora**, which are used for name resolution. Net8 configuration has two main elements:

- Net8 Server (Listener)
- Net8 Client

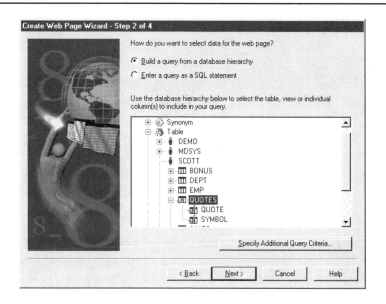

FIGURE 5-28. *Building a query for Web Publishing Assistant*

We will walk through an example of server and client configuration using Net8 Assistant.

NOTE
All Net8 configuration files reside in the
c:\orant\net80\admin *folder on*
Windows NT by default.

Configuring Net8 Listener

The Net8 Listener is a process that *listens* for incoming connection requests and makes them available to a client after suitable validation. Net8 services include database services and external services. (Oracle8 includes a new feature that can be used to execute external programs via a process called *extproc.*) The listener configuration file, **listener.ora**, contains information about the listener and the services known to the listener. Information about the listener includes the server identification and the port on which the listener process is *listening* for new connections. We will step through a Net8 Listener configuration using Net8 Assistant. For the purposes of illustration, we will configure Net8 for TCP/IP networks since these are widely used today. The procedure for configuring other network protocols is identical.

Step 1 Install Net8 Server.

If you have not already done so, install the Net8 Server software along with the necessary *protocol adapters.* You can install multiple protocol adapters based on the network protocols that you wish to use for Net8 connections. If you chose to install the Oracle8 Enterprise Edition, this software has already been installed on your machine. If you chose to perform a custom installation, ensure that you have installed the Net8 Server and appropriate protocol adapters.

Step 2 Create listener configuration files.

Start Net8 Assistant and select the Listeners node. Click on the Create shortcut or Edit | Create from the menu. You will be prompted to choose a name for the listener (a machine can run more than one Net8 Listener as long as they have unique names and configuration. For example, configure listeners on separate ports for TCP/IP-based networks). Select the general parameters from the General tab, as shown in Figure 5-29.

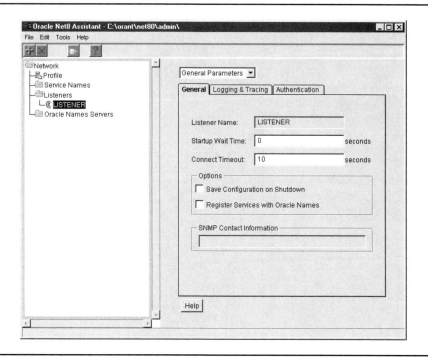

FIGURE 5-29.   *Configuring general parameters for Net8 Listener*

We will set a startup delay of zero seconds and a connection timeout of 10 seconds for the listener named *LISTENER.*

Select the Listening Locations tab and configure the protocol, host, and port information (you will see different fields here based on the network protocol that you choose). We will provide a host name of **aadkoli-lap.us.oracle.com** and choose to use port 1521, the default port, for this listener, as shown in Figure 5-30.

Next, select the Database Services tab to add database services to the **listener.ora**. We will add our starter database named *ORCL* to the list of database services. At this time, we will not prespawn any servers.

If you want to configure other services such as *extproc*, select the Other Services tab to configure these services. We will leave the default *extproc* service from our installation of Oracle8 Enterprise Edition.

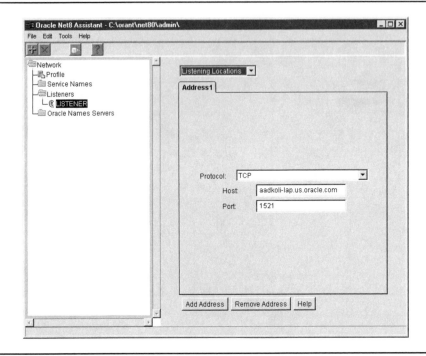

FIGURE 5-30. *Configuring listening locations for Net8 Listener*

The minimum listener configuration is now complete. Choose to save the configuration by selecting File | Save Network Configuration. The **listener.ora** file created on our test installation is shown below:

```
# C:\ORANT\NET80\ADMIN\LISTENER.ORA
Configuration File:C:\orant\net80\admin\listener.ora
# Generated by Oracle Net8 Assistant
PASSWORDS_LISTENER= (oracle)
LISTENER =
  (ADDRESS = (PROTOCOL = TCP)(HOST = aadkoli-lap.us.oracle.com)(PORT = 1521))
SID_LIST_LISTENER =
  (SID_LIST =
    (SID_DESC =
      (SID_NAME = extproc)
      (PROGRAM = extproc)
    )
    (SID_DESC =
      (GLOBAL_DBNAME = aadkoli-lap)
      (ORACLE_HOME = c:\orant)
```

```
      (SID_NAME = ORCL)
  )
)
```

Step 3   Start the Listener.

Start the listener services *OracleTNSListener80* using the Services applet under the Control Panel. We recommend that you enable the *OracleTNSListener80* service for Automatic startup.

Configuring Net8 Clients

Net8 clients need to have Net8 Client software along with the appropriate *Net8 protocol adapters* to be able to connect to Net8 listeners. Net8 clients have configuration files on the client that enable them to locate remote Oracle Servers. These files can be created using the Net8 Assistant.

NOTE
There is another utility on Windows NT named Net8 Easy Configuration Utility that can also be used to create client configuration files. We have included a separate section on this utility later in this chapter.

Net8 clients need to resolve *service names* or *aliases* to locate a remote Oracle database. This process is called *name resolution* (very similar to the concept of Domain Name Servers). There are two methods to configure clients: 1) TNSNAMES and 2) ONAMES (a third method named HOSTNAME is described in Chapter 7). We will illustrate both methods with an example.

TNSNAMES METHOD FOR NET8 NAMES RESOLUTION   This method involves the creation of two client configuration files named **tnsnames.ora** and **sqlnet.ora**. These two files together contain information that allows Net8 clients to resolve Oracle services on the network. This method is very simple to configure since the configuration files can be created on one client and then copied over to all the clients on the network. However, it can be burdensome to manage copies of **tnsnames.ora** and **sqlnet.ora** on all clients at large sites. This means that every time a database service is added or modified on the network, the client files need to be updated (the ONAMES method overcomes this issue).

We will illustrate the creation of Net8 client configuration files using Net8 Assistant.

Start Net8 Assistant and select the Service Names tab. Select the Create shortcut or Edit | Create from the menu to create a new service. Provide the protocol and associated information. Figure 5-31 shows the configuration for our client that uses the TCP/IP protocol.

The above procedure creates client configuration files named **sqlnet.ora** and **tnsnames.ora**. The **tnsnames.ora** file from our example is provided below for your reference:

```
# C:\ORANT\NET80\ADMIN\TNSNAMES.ORA
Configuration File:C:\orant\net80\admin\tnsnames.ora
# Generated by Oracle Net8 Assistant
AA.WORLD =
  (DESCRIPTION =
    (ADDRESS = (PROTOCOL = TCP)(HOST =
aadkoli-lap.us.oracle.com)(PORT = 1521))
    (CONNECT_DATA = (SID = ORCL))
  )
```

ORACLE NAMES METHOD FOR NET8 NAMES RESOLUTION

We have seen how client configuration files can be created using Net8 Assistant. It can be cumbersome to maintain updated client configuration files at large sites. Database services frequently get added and modified on the network, and administrators have to deploy fresh copies of this file to all the clients. This issue can be overcome by using Oracle Names (this is very similar in concept to the creation Domain Name Servers for TCP/IP host name resolution). With Oracle Names, a list of services is maintained on servers, either in Oracle databases or files. Net8 clients can use these services to resolve Net8 service names. When database services are added or modified on the network, administrators need to simply ensure that the Names database is updated and these changes will automatically reflect on all clients. We will illustrate Names configuration with an example. We will use an Oracle database (called the *region database*) to maintain NAMES configuration.

Step 1   Create the Names database objects.

Special database objects need to be created on the database that will act as the Names Server. Oracle recommends that you create these objects in a separate schema. We have created a user named *NAMES* who will own these objects.

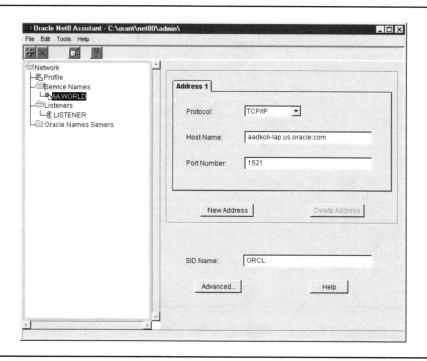

FIGURE 5-31.   *Address parameters for Net8 alias*

Execute the script **c:\orant\net80\names\namesini.sql** to create the objects in the schema for the user *NAMES*.

Step 2   Start the Oracle names service.

Use the Services applet to start a service named *OracleNamesService80*. You must install the product *Oracle Names Server* for this service to be available.

Step 3   Discover Names Server.

Start Net8 Assistant and choose to discover available Oracle Names Servers by selecting Tools | Discover Oracle Names Servers. You should see a dialog box confirming the discovery of the Names Server that was started in step 2, as shown next.

Step 4 Configure Names Server.

Exit from the Assistant and restart. Select the Names Server in the Navigator as shown in Figure 5-32.

The Monitor tab can be selected to manage the Names Server. You can shut down and start up the server from here if you wish.

Choose the Configure Server from the list box and select the Database tab to configure the Names database. Provide the connect information to the database, as shown in Figure 5-33.

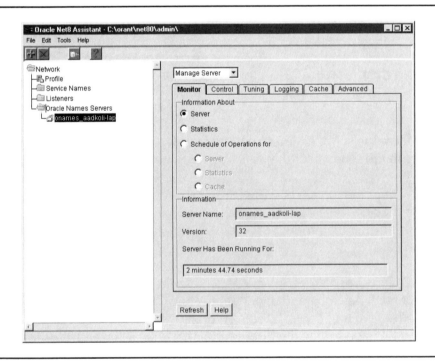

FIGURE 5-32. *Configuring Names Server*

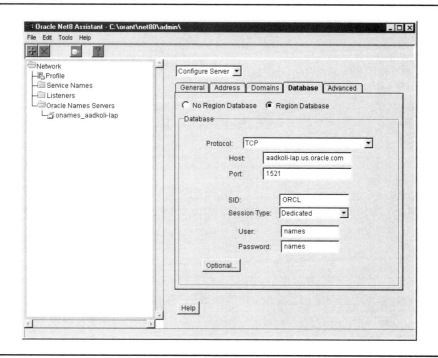

FIGURE 5-33. *Configuring Names database*

Now you can add the service names that you want to store in the Names Server. Select the option to Manage Data and add the services that you wish to store in the database. If you have an updated **tnsnames.ora** file, you can choose to load this file into the Names Server as shown in Figure 5-34.

Be sure to save the configuration changes. The **names.ora** file created on our test installation is shown below for your reference:

```
# C:\ORANT\NET80\ADMIN\NAMES.ORA Configuration
File:C:\orant\net80\admin\names.ora
# Generated by Oracle Net8 Assistant
NAMES.ADDRESSES =
  (Address = (protocol = tcp)(port = 1575)(host = aadkoli-lap))
NAMES.ADMIN_REGION =
  (REGION =
    (DESCRIPTION =
      (ADDRESS = (PROTOCOL = TCP)(HOST = aadkoli-lap.us.oracle.com)
      (PORT = 1521))
```

```
    (CONNECT_DATA = (SID = ORCL)(Server = Dedicated))
  )
(USERID = names)
(PASSWORD = names)
(NAME = LOCAL_REGION)
(REFRESH = 86400)
(RETRY = 60)
(EXPIRE = 600)
(VERSION = 134230016)
)
```

Step 5 Update the profile.

We have discussed two naming methods used by Net8 (TNSNAMES and ONAMES). You can update your profile to set your preferences for name

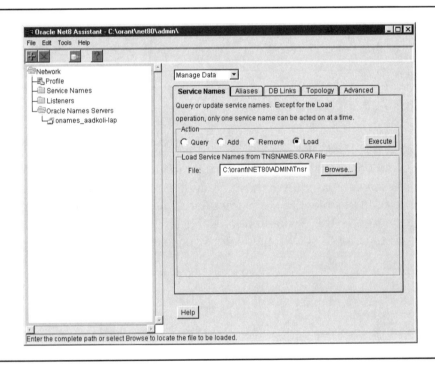

FIGURE 5-34. *Adding service names to Oracle Names*

resolution. Select the Profile node in the Navigator and provide the order of naming methods as shown in Figure 5-35.

The **sqlnet.ora** file from our installation is provided here for your reference:

```
# C:\ORANT\NET80\ADMIN\SQLNET.ORA
Configuration File:C:\orant\net80\admin\sqlnet.ora
# Generated by Oracle Net8 Assistant
NAME.DEFAULT_ZONE = world
NAMES.DEFAULT_DOMAIN = world
#sqlnet.authentication_services = (NONE)
SQLNET.EXPIRE_TIME = 0
SQLNET.ENCRYPTION_SERVER = requested
SQLNET.ENCRYPTION_CLIENT = requested
```

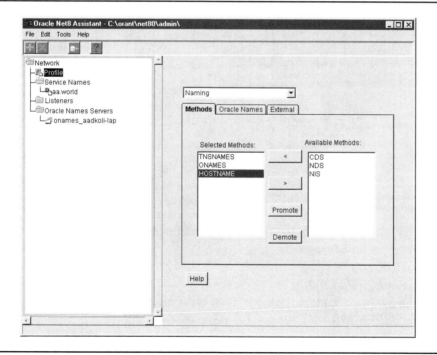

FIGURE 5-35. *Updating Net8 Profile*

The **sqlnet.ora** can also contain some additional configuration. As in Domain Name Services (DNS), you can configure multiple Oracle Names Servers on the network for redundancy. The order of preference is specified in the **sqlnet.ora** file. If you want to encrypt your data on the network, you must install the Advanced Network Option (ANO). We discuss ANO in Chapter 7. The crypto seeds and encryption type are also available in the **sqlnet.ora** file. Refer to Net8 documentation for details on these topics.

NET8 EASY CONFIGURATION UTILITY   This utility can also be used to update **tnsnames.ora** files. It is easier to use and it has a smaller footprint. However, it cannot be used to update other Net8 configuration files. Click on Start | Programs | Oracle for Window NT | Oracle Net8 Easy Config and you will see a wizard similar to the one shown here:

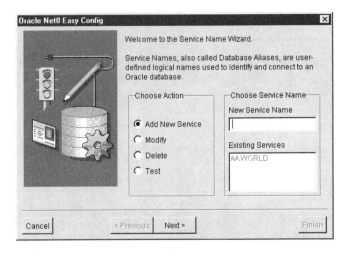

Follow instructions in the wizard to update your TNSNAMES information.

WARNING
You must avoid manually editing Net8 configuration files at all times. This can cause unpredictable errors. However, since these are ASCII text files, you can copy these files from one machine to another, regardless of operating system.

NET8 EASY CONFIG VS. SQL NET EASY CONFIGURATION
Prior releases of Net8 software were called SQL*Net. Some applications still depend on SQL*Net version 2.x for connectivity. The SQL Net Easy Configuration utility can be used to create **tnsnames.ora** files for SQL*Net 2.x. This program is also available in the Oracle for Windows NT Program group. SQL*Net 2.x configuration files reside in the **c:\orant\network\ admin** folder on Windows NT, while Net8 configuration files reside in the **c:\orant\net80\admin** folder.

NOTE
*SQL*Net 2.x was used with Oracle7 applications. SQL*Net 1.x was used with Oracle6 applications and is now obsolete.*

In the above few sections, we have provided basic information on Net8 configuration on Windows NT. There are some advanced topics such as *Connection Manager* that we have not included. We have included the configuration of Multi Threaded Server (MTS) in Chapter 7.

Miscellaneous Tools and Utilities

The Oracle8 installation on Windows NT provides additional tools and utilities that are not available on other Oracle platforms. In this section we will provide a quick overview of these tools for the sake of completion.

Oracle Migration Assistant for MS Access

Oracle8 for Windows NT delivers the full functionality of the industry's leading RDBMS on a user-friendly platform. Many sites are migrating their MS Access databases to Oracle8. The Oracle Migration Assistant for MS Access (OMA) is a GUI tool that can be used to ease this migration. It has a wizard interface that allows you to step through the process in simple steps. You can customize the migration to your requirements. We will illustrate the functionality of this tool by migrating a small MS Access database.

Example: Migrate an MS Access database to Oracle8. Transfer the objects and data in the **.mdb** file into a new Oracle schema.

Step 1   Create a list of MS Access databases to be migrated.

Start OMA and add all the **.mdb** files to a list of databases to be migrated from MS Access into Oracle. In the wizard, click the Add Database button and provide the names of all the **.mdb** files. We will add a file named **test.mdb**, as shown in Figure 5-36.

Step 2   Customize migration to requirement.

Step through the wizard and customize the migration as per your requirement. A Customize button is available on each screen that will allow you to change the options for that screen.

The first option is the customization of datatypes. MS Access and Oracle8 have different datatypes, and you can choose to specify how

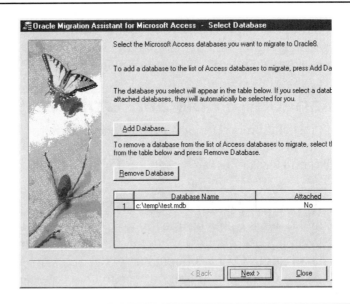

FIGURE 5-36.   *Creating a list of databases for migration from MS Access*

datatype differences are handled. For example, a CHARACTER field in MS Access can be migrated to a CHAR or VARCHAR2 in Oracle8.

Similarly, you can choose the portions of the database that you want to migrate. You can migrate the whole databases or choose to migrate just the tables and ignore the indexes and relationships. Shown here is the dialog box for this purpose:

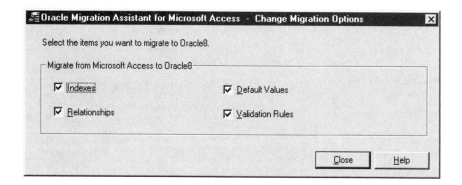

One of the screens that will follow will allow you to migrate only the structure of the database, or the structure and data.

You can choose the schema and the tablespace into which the migrated data is placed. OMA is capable of creating a tablespace that will hold the new data and place it into a new schema that will be created during the migration. You will be asked to supply a valid DBA account during the migration.

Step 3   Perform the migration.

When all the options are set to your satisfaction, you can start the migration. You will see a progress bar that displays the status of migration.

Step 4   View migration log and reports.

OMA provided a log of the migration as well as some reports. You should view these logs and reports for any error messages. Shown next is a portion of a report for our migration.

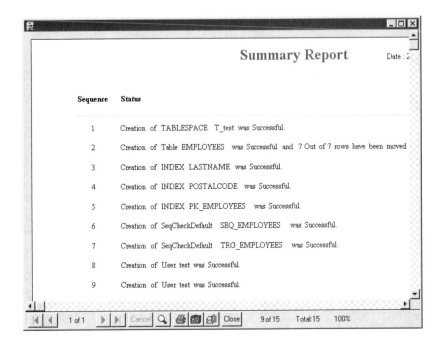

Oracle Home Selector

Some sites have multiple versions of Oracle under different directory structures. If you have multiple Oracle structures on your NT machine, you can switch between the available environments by using this utility. Click on Start | Programs | Oracle for Windows NT | Oracle Home Selector to access this utility and follow instructions on the screen.

Oracle Patch Assistant

You can obtain patches directly from Oracle's customer support site using this utility. You must have Internet connectivity in order to use this utility.

Oracle INTYPE File Assistant

Oracle8 supports object types. Users can define their own (data) types using object extensions to SQL. If you have user-defined types that you want to use in Pro*C/C++ or OCI programs, you need to use the *Object Type Translator* (OTT) for such translations. OTT uses INTYPE files for information on user types that need to be translated. You can use Oracle INTYPE File Assistant to create INTYPE files. Click on Start | Programs |Oracle for Windows NT| Oracle INTYPE File Assistant 8.0 to access this tool.

Response File Generator

Oracle Installer technology uses response files (extension of **.rsp**) to obtain information on the installation. The response files provide information for dialog boxes during installation, along with possible responses. You can customize these response files for your site using Response File Generator. The utility is available in the Oracle for Windows NT program group. The Oracle Software Manager can be used to customize your installation process.

Oracle Software Manager

Oracle provides another product named Oracle Software Manager as part of OEM tools that can also be used to distribute software across the enterprise. This product allows sites to control versions of software being deployed. You need to create bundles of software known as *packages* and deploy these packages across your enterprise. You can use Response File Generator to customize response files that can be used by Software Manager.

Data Migration Assistant

Data Migration Assistant (DMA) can be used to upgrade Oracle databases. There are many methods to upgrade to Oracle8 from previous versions of Oracle, but DMA provides a GUI solution to migration. We will discuss this further in the section on Migration in Chapter 8.

In this chapter, we have taken a look at the GUI tools available with Windows NT. In the next chapter, we will present the CLI tools available with Windows NT.

CHAPTER

6

CLI-Based Approach to Oracle Administration

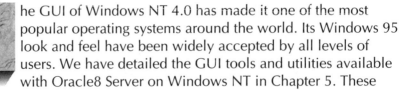he GUI of Windows NT 4.0 has made it one of the most popular operating systems around the world. Its Windows 95 look and feel have been widely accepted by all levels of users. We have detailed the GUI tools and utilities available with Oracle8 Server on Windows NT in Chapter 5. These tools allow DBAs to manage Oracle servers without learning nitty-gritty SQL or operating system commands. While it is true that Oracle Enterprise Manager (OEM) allows for a certain amount of automation, all GUI tools require some degree of user interaction. At times, this can slow down tasks and increase the probability of human errors. Experienced DBAs prefer to create batch jobs for common tasks at their site. On Windows NT, batch jobs can be files with **.bat** or **.cmd** extensions. Scripts can include SQL commands, CLI (command line interface) tool commands, and operating system commands. In this chapter, we will look at CLI solutions to common DBA tasks. We will revisit many topics in Chapter 5 with a CLI approach.

SQL Tools

Oracle Corporation provides three major tools that can be used to issue SQL and PL/SQL (procedural language /SQL) commands to the Oracle database. These tools are ANSI SQL 92 compliant and provide a combination of GUI and CLI. Certain extensions are also available for extended features of Oracle8, such as Objects. Table 6-1 lists the commands to launch these tools.

Tool	Command to Launch
SQL Plus 8.0 (GUI)	**c:\orant\bin\plus80w.exe**
SQL Plus 8.0 (CLI)	**c:\orant\bin\plus80.exe**
SQL Worksheet	**c:\orant\bin\vaw.exe**
Server Manager	**c:\orant\bin\svrmgr30.exe**

TABLE 6-1. *SQL Tools on Oracle8 for Windows NT*

Becoming a DBA

In Chapter 5 we listed the roles and responsibilities of DBAs. We have seen that many methods are available for users to authenticate themselves as DBAs. We will present the same methods in this section using CLI.

The DBA Role

A user can be created and suitable roles can be assigned using a set of SQL commands from a SQL tool. You must connect as a DBA-level user to create another user. The SQL commands are shown below:

```
SQLWKS> CONNECT SYSTEM/MANAGER@PROD
Connected.
SQLWKS> CREATE USER SYSAD IDENTIFIED BY AA DEFAULT TABLESPACE
    2>    USER_DATA TEMPORARY TABLESPACE TEMPORARY_DATA;
Statement processed.
SQLWKS> GRANT CONNECT,RESOURCE, DBA TO SYSAD;
Statement processed.
```

If your site requires you to create users frequently, you can create a SQL script that accepts the USER and PASSWORD as arguments and creates a user with the DBA role. In order to do this, you will have to create a text file that contains the following SQL script:

```
DROP USER &1;
CREATE USER &1 IDENTIFIED BY &2 DEFAULT TABLESPACE USER_DATA
    TEMPORARY TABLESPACE TEMPORARY_DATA;
GRANT CONNECT, RESOURCE, DBA TO &1;
EXIT;
```

In the SQL script above, '&1' and '&2' are parameters for the user and password. Save the file as **creatusr.sql**. Now you can execute the following from the command line to execute the script to create the user:

```
plus80w system/manager @c:\temp\sql\creatusr.sql sysad aa
```

Note that you need to use SQL Plus for this solution. SQL Worksheet cannot process a script passed as a command-line argument. We are also assuming that **c:\orant\bin** is in your path. A better solution is to create a batch file, say **creatusr.bat**, with the following text for the same script:

```
plus80w system/manager @c:\temp\sql\creatusr.sql %1 %2
```

You can execute the batch file from the command line by executing the following:

```
C:\> creatusr sysad aa
```

To modify an existing user, you must use the ALTER USER command. The following example resets the password for a user:

```
SQLWKS> ALTER USER SYSAD IDENTIFIED BY SYSAD;
Statement processed.
```

Similarly, you can assign roles using the GRANT command and revoke roles using the REVOKE command as shown below:

```
SQLWKS> REVOKE DBA FROM SYSAD;
Statement processed.
SQLWKS> GRANT DBA TO SYSAD;
Statement processed.
```

External Authentication

You can use the CREATE USER command in SQL to create the user. A special clause is required for external authentication. Continuing with our example from Chapter 5, we would need to create a user named *SYSAD* on Windows NT as well as on the Oracle database. While creating the user, you must notify the Oracle database that the authentication will be done externally, as shown below:

```
SQLWKS> CREATE USER SYSAD IDENTIFIED EXTERNALLY
    2>      DEFAULT TABLESPACE USER_DATA
    3>      TEMPORARY TABLESPACE TEMPORARY_DATA;
Statement processed.
```

In addition, you will need to set the following INIT.ORA parameters:

```
os_authent_prefix = ""
remote_os_authent = true
remote_login_passwordfile = none
```

If the user *SYSAD* logs in to the Windows NT machine, then he or she could connect to the Oracle database by substituting the username with a forward slash ('/'). The password field must be left blank. From the command line, the user *SYSAD* could use SQL Plus 8.0 to connect to the Oracle database by using the following command:

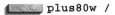

```
plus80w /
```

The User *internal*

The user *internal* can be used from any tool with no restrictions. All CLI tools support this user as shown below:

```
SQLWKS> CONNECT INTERNAL/ORACLE
Connected.
```

The Password File

CLI tools can also use the password file for authentication. The procedure to create the password file and set up the INIT.ORA is detailed in Chapter 5. We will repeat the same example here with CLI.

Example: You have a Windows NT machine with an Oracle8 database named *ORCL* running on it. You have a system operator named *JDOE* who should have the privileges to start up and shut down the database remotely. You also need to ensure that another user named *JDBA* can administer the database remotely.

The solution is to add an entry for *JDOE* and *JDBA* in the password file and set the REMOTE_LOGIN_PASSWORDFILE to either EXCLUSIVE or SHARED. Make a copy of the INIT.ORA file on the client from which remote access is required. The steps are described below.

1. Connect to the database as *SYS* or *INTERNAL* and grant the SYSOPER role to the user *JDOE* and the *SYSDBA* role to the user *JDBA* by issuing the SQL commands shown below:

   ```
   SQLWKS> GRANT SYSOPER TO JDOE;
   Statement processed.
   SQLWKS> GRANT SYSDBA TO JDBA;
   Statement processed.
   ```

   This operation will add entries for *JDOE* and *JDBA* into the password file **c:\orant\database\pwdorcl.ora**.

2. Edit the file **c:\orant\database\initorcl.ora** on the server and set the REMOTE_LOGIN_PASSWORDFILE parameter to EXCLUSIVE:

```
remote_login_passwordfile = exclusive
```

3. Copy the **initorcl.ora** file to the client that will be used by *JDOE* and *JDBA* for remote administration:

```
C:\> copy c:\orant\database\initorcl.ora
f:\oracle\initorcl.ora
```

assuming the logical drive F: is mapped to a network drive on the client.

4. Now *JDOE* can connect to the remote Oracle Server from the client as *SYSOPER* by using the CONNECT AS clause as shown below:

```
SQLWKS> CONNECT JDOE/AA AS SYSOPER;
Connected.
SQLWKS> CONNECT JDBA/AA AS SYSDBA;
Connected.
```

Using Windows NT Groups

Operating system groups can be used to define the role assigned to an Oracle user. CLI tools can use these roles just like GUI tools with no restrictions.

CLI Tools and Utilities for DBAs

Oracle Corporation provides CLI tools that cover all aspects of Oracle administration. While GUI tools are simple to use, they can be slow. Using point-and-click for simple tasks can take longer than entering the equivalent commands. Many experienced DBAs prefer CLI. In this section, we will cover the CLI tools provided by Oracle.

Oracle Server Manager

Oracle Server Manager (SVRMGR) provides a CLI to Oracle. SQL and PL/SQL commands can be passed to Oracle using SVRMGR. In the past, SVRMGR (like SQLDBA in Oracle version 6.x) was necessary for privileged operations like database startup and shutdown. With Oracle8, SQL

Worksheet can be used for all SQL and PL/SQL with no restrictions, and SVRMGR has become unnecessary. Instance Manager can also be used for database startup and shutdown.

Execute **c:\orant\bin\svrmgr30.exe** to start SVRMGR. Commands can be issued from the command prompt. We present some common tasks in Table 6-2.

Task	Description	Examples
Connect to Oracle	Use the CONNECT command to start a new session.	SVRMGR> **connect system/manager** SVRMGR> **connect sysad/aa as sysdba**
Issue a SQL command	Any valid SQL command can be issued via SVRMGR. Terminate all SQL commands with a semicolon.	SVRMGR> **select user from dual;** SVRMGR> **select * from emp;** SVRMGR> **create tablespace apps datafile** <*File*>; SVRMGR> **drop tablespace apps including contents;**
Execute a script containing SQL and PL/SQL	Use the @ sign to execute the script. The default extension for the script is **.sql**.	SVRMGR> **@c:\temp\test.sql** SVRMGR> **@c:\temp\test**
Creat a log	A log of the session can be created using the SPOOL command. The SPOOL OFF command can be used to stop spooling.	SVRMGR> **spool c:\temp\output.lis** SVRMGR> **spool off**
Start up the database	Use the STARTUP command with options like NOMOUNT and MOUNT or PFILE for parameter file.	SVRMGR> **startup** SVRMGR> **startup mount pfile=c:\myfiles\initorcl.ora**

TABLE 6-2. *Common Tasks in Server Manager*

Task	Description	Examples
Shut down the database	Use the SHUTDOWN command with options like IMMEDIATE and ABORT.	SVRMGR> **shutdown** SVRMGR> **shutdown immediate**
Execute a stored procedure	Use the EXECUTE command.	SVRMGR> **execute test;**
To re-execute a command or execute an anonymous PL/SQL block	Use the forward slash (/) operator.	See example of anonymous PL/SQL block below.
Execute anonymous PL/SQL block	Enclose the block between BEGIN and END.	SVRMGR> **DECLARE** 2> **c1 number;** 3> **BEGIN** 4> **c1 := 1;** 5> **null;** 6> **END;** 7> **/**
Get Help	Use the HELP command to get help on SVRMGR commands. Use *Oracle8 SQL Reference* for help on SQL commands.	SVRMGR> **HELP**

TABLE 6-2. *Common Tasks in Server Manager* (continued)

TIP
The command history feature of Windows NT is available in SVRMGR. Use the UP or DOWN ARROW to step through the commands issued in the session. The F7 key recalls the command history.

Executing Scripts from the Command Line

You can execute scripts from the command line directly by passing the name of the script as a command-line argument to SVRMGR. Let us look at a simple example. First create a file with the required script. We will create a file named **c:\temp\test.sql** with the following contents:

```
connect system/manager@prod
select user from dual;
exit
```

SVRMGR cannot receive Oracle user and password information from the command line directly. You must provide connect information as part of the script. You can execute the script from the command line as shown below:

```
C:\> svrmgr30 @c:\temp\test.sql
Oracle Server Manager Release 3.0.4.0.0 - Production
(c) Copyright 1997, Oracle Corporation.  All Rights Reserved.
Oracle8 Enterprise Edition Release 8.0.4.0.0 - Production
With the Partitioning and Objects options
PL/SQL Release 8.0.4.0.0 - Production
Connected.
USER
------------------------------
SYSTEM
1 row selected.
Server Manager complete.
```

You can also write batch files to execute several scripts from the command line. You can pass command-line arguments to the batch files. We will create a batch file named **test.bat** to execute the script created above. The batch file contains the following text:

```
svrmgr30 %1
```

You can execute the **test.bat** program and pass the SQL script **test.sql** as a command-line argument as shown below:

```
C:\> test @c:\temp\test.sql
```

The Export Utility

Data Manager allows you to Export Oracle data into an operating system file. We have discussed this in Chapter 5. The Export utility provides the same functionality with CLI. Execute **c:\orant\bin\exp80.exe** to run this utility. Use the command-line argument *HELP=YES* to obtain complete usage information as shown below.

```
C:\> exp80 help=yes
Export: Release 8.0.4.0.0 - Production on Mon Aug 31 12:22:19 1998
(c) Copyright 1997 Oracle Corporation.  All rights reserved.
You can let Export prompt you for parameters by entering the EXP
command followed by your username/password:
      Example: EXP SCOTT/TIGER
Or, you can control how Export runs by entering the EXP command followed
by various arguments. To specify parameters, you use keywords:
      Format:  EXP KEYWORD=value or KEYWORD=(value1,value2,...,valueN)
      Example: EXP SCOTT/TIGER GRANTS=Y TABLES=(EMP,DEPT,MGR)
               or TABLES=(T1:P1,T1:P2), if T1 is partitioned table
USERID must be the first parameter on the command line.
Keyword  Description (Default)          Keyword      Description (Default)
--------------------------------------------------------------------------
USERID     username/password            FULL         export entire file (N)
BUFFER     size of data buffer          OWNER        list of owner usernames
FILE       output file (EXPDAT.DMP)     TABLES       list of table names
COMPRESS   import into one extent (Y)   RECORDLENGTH length of IO record
GRANTS     export grants (Y)            INCTYPE      incremental export type
INDEXES    export indexes (Y)           RECORD       track incr. export (Y)
ROWS       export data rows (Y)         PARFILE      parameter filename
CONSTRAINTS export constraints (Y)      CONSISTENT   cross-table consistency
LOG        log file of screen output    STATISTICS   analyze objects (ESTIMATE)
DIRECT     direct path (N)
FEEDBACK display progress every x rows (0)
POINT_IN_TIME_RECOVER   Tablespace Point-in-time Recovery (N)
RECOVERY_TABLESPACES    List of tablespace names to recover
Export terminated successfully without warnings.
```

All three modes of export detailed in Chapter 5—database export, user export, and table export—are available. Here is an example of a DBA performing an export of all objects belonging to the user *SCOTT*:

```
C:\>exp80 userid=system/manager owner=scott file=c:\temp\scott.dmp
log=c:\temp\scott.log
Connected to: Oracle8 Enterprise Edition Release 8.0.4.0.0 - Production
With the Partitioning and Objects options
PL/SQL Release 8.0.4.0.0 - Production
Export done in WE8ISO8859P1 character set and WE8ISO8859P1 NCHAR character set
About to export specified users ...
. exporting foreign function library names for user SCOTT
. exporting object type definitions for user SCOTT
About to export SCOTT's objects ...
. exporting database links
. exporting sequence numbers
. exporting cluster definitions
```

```
. about to export SCOTT's tables via Conventional Path ...
. . exporting table                         BONUS          0 rows exported
. . exporting table                          DEPT          4 rows exported
. . exporting table                           EMP         14 rows exported
. . exporting table                      SALGRADE          5 rows exported
. exporting synonyms
. exporting views
. exporting stored procedures
. exporting referential integrity constraints
. exporting triggers
. exporting posttables actions
. exporting snapshots
. exporting snapshot logs
. exporting job queues
. exporting refresh groups and children
Export terminated successfully without warnings.
```

If you have a situation where an object has too many extents allocated, you can use export to compress the extents allocated for the object into one extent using the *COMPRESS=Y* option of Export.

The Import Utility

The Import utility can be used to import data into an Oracle database from an operating system file that was created using the export utility. Execute **c:\orant\bin\imp80.exe** to access this utility. Again the *HELP=YES* argument provides full usage information.

```
C:\>imp80 help=yes
Import: Release 8.0.4.0.0 - Production on Mon Aug 31 12:35:37 1998
(c) Copyright 1997 Oracle Corporation.  All rights reserved.
You can let Import prompt you for parameters by entering the IMP
command followed by your username/password:
     Example: IMP SCOTT/TIGER
Or, you can control how Import runs by entering the IMP command followed
by various arguments. To specify parameters, you use keywords:
     Format:  IMP KEYWORD=value or KEYWORD=(value1,value2,...,valueN)
     Example: IMP SCOTT/TIGER IGNORE=Y TABLES=(EMP,DEPT) FULL=N
              or TABLES=(T1:P1,T1:P2), if T1 is partitioned table
USERID must be the first parameter on the command line.
Keyword  Description (Default)          Keyword       Description (Default)
--------------------------------------------------------------------------
USERID   username/password             FULL          import entire file (N)
BUFFER   size of data buffer           FROMUSER      list of owner usernames
FILE     input file (EXPDAT.DMP)       TOUSER        list of usernames
SHOW     just list file contents (N)   TABLES        list of table names
IGNORE   ignore create errors (N)      RECORDLENGTH  length of IO record
GRANTS   import grants (Y)             INCTYPE       incremental import type
INDEXES  import indexes (Y)            COMMIT        commit array insert (N)
```

```
ROWS      import data rows (Y)         PARFILE      parameter filename
LOG       log file of screen output
DESTROY   overwrite tablespace data file (N)
INDEXFILE write table/index info to specified file
CHARSET   character set of export file (NLS_LANG)
POINT_IN_TIME_RECOVER  Tablespace Point-in-time Recovery (N)
SKIP_UNUSABLE_INDEXES  skip maintenance of unusable indexes (N)
ANALYZE   execute ANALYZE statements in dump file (Y)
FEEDBACK display progress every x rows(0)
Import terminated successfully without warnings.
```

We will import the data belonging to the user *SCOTT* into the schema of a user named *JOE* by using the **scott.dmp** file, created earlier in our example for export.

```
C:\>imp80 userid=system/manager file=c:\temp\scott.dmp log=imp.log
fromuser=scott touser=joe
Import: Release 8.0.4.0.0 - Production on Mon Aug 31 12:41:31 1998
(c) Copyright 1997 Oracle Corporation.  All rights reserved.
Connected to: Oracle8 Enterprise Edition Release 8.0.4.0.0 - Production
With the Partitioning and Objects options
PL/SQL Release 8.0.4.0.0 - Production
Export file created by EXPORT:V08.00.04 via conventional path
. . importing table                        "BONUS"           0 rows imported
. . importing table                        "DEPT"            4 rows imported
. . importing table                        "EMP"            14 rows imported
. . importing table                     "SALGRADE"           5 rows imported
About to enable constraints...
Import terminated successfully without warnings.
```

The above technique can be used to change ownership of objects. Perform a user export and import it into another schema using the *FROMUSER* and *TOUSER* clauses.

The Loader Utility

The Loader function available in Data Manager is also available in the CLI via SQL*Loader. Execute **c:\orant\bin\sqlldr80.exe** to launch SQL*Loader. Type **sqlldr80.exe** without any arguments to get usage information:

```
SQL*Loader: Release 8.0.4.0.0 - Production on Mon Aug 31 12:47:26 1998
(c) Copyright 1997 Oracle Corporation.  All rights reserved.
Usage: SQLLOAD keyword=value [,keyword=value,...]
Valid Keywords:
    userid -- ORACLE username/password
    control -- Control file name
```

```
      log -- Log file name
      bad -- Bad file name
     data -- Data file name
  discard -- Discard file name
discardmax -- Number of discards to allow          (Default all)
     skip -- Number of logical records to skip   (Default 0)
     load -- Number of logical records to load   (Default all)
   errors -- Number of errors to allow           (Default 50)
     rows -- Number of rows in conventional path bind array or between direct path
data saves
              (Default: Conventional path 64, Direct path all)
  bindsize -- Size of conventional path bind array in bytes  (Default 65536)
    silent -- Suppress messages during run
(header,feedback,errors,discards,partitions)
    direct -- use direct path                     (Default FALSE)
   parfile -- parameter file: name of file that contains parameter specifications
  parallel -- do parallel load                    (Default FALSE)
      file -- File to allocate extents from
skip_unusable_indexes -- disallow/allow unusable indexes or index partitions
(Default FALSE)
skip_index_maintenance -- do not maintain indexes, mark affected indexes as unusable
(Default FALSE)
commit_discontinued -- commit loaded rows when load is discontinued  (Default FALSE)
PLEASE NOTE: Command-line parameters may be specified either by
position or by keywords.  An example of the former case is 'sqlload
scott/tiger foo'; an example of the latter is 'sqlload control=foo
userid=scott/tiger'.  One may specify parameters by position before
but not after parameters specified by keywords.  For example,
'sqlload scott/tiger control=foo logfile=log' is allowed, but
'sqlload scott/tiger control=foo log' is not, even though the
position of the parameter 'log' is correct.
```

CAUTION
Using HELP=YES as an argument to
SQL*Loader crashed the product on our test
installation of Version 8.0.4.

Control files are supported by SQL*Loader. Look at the sample control
files in the **c:\orant\rdbms80\loader** folder. We will run one of the samples
here for your benefit:

```
C:\> sqlldr80 scott/tiger
control = c:\orant\rdbms80\loader\ulcase1.ctl
SQL*Loader: Release 8.0.4.0.0 - Production on Mon Aug 31 12:55:38 1998
(c) Copyright 1997 Oracle Corporation.  All rights reserved.
Commit point reached - logical record count 7
```

Terminating Unwanted Sessions

Occasionally, DBAs are required to terminate Oracle sessions by force. This can be done by issuing the SQL command ALTER SYSTEM KILL SESSION. On Windows NT, there is a utility named *ORAKILL* to kill sessions. Execute **c:\orant\bin\orakill.exe** to access this utility. We will provide a small example here to kill an unwanted SQL Plus session belonging to the user *SCOTT*:

```
C:\> orakill
Usage:  orakill sid thread
   where sid   = the Oracle instance to target
         thread = the thread id of the thread to kill (in hex)
   The thread id should be retrieved from the spid column of a query such as:
         select spid, osuser, s.program from
         v$process p, v$session s where p.addr=s.paddr
```

As seen above, the utility requires thread information and the name of the Oracle instance. We will obtain the thread information by using the query shown below to find information about a SQL Plus session:

```
SVRMGR> SELECT SPID,OSUSER,S.PROGRAM FROM
     2>    V$PROCESS P, V$SESSION S WHERE P.ADDR=S.PADDR AND
     3>    S.PROGRAM LIKE '%plus80w%';
SPID        OSUSER            PROGRAM
---------   ---------------   -----------------------------
000DC       AADKOLI           C:\orant\bin\plus80w.exe
1 row selected.
```

We will kill this session on our default instance on Windows NT with an SID of *ORCL* as shown below:

```
C:\> orakill ORCL 000DC
Kill of thread id 000DC in instance ORCL successfully signalled.
```

Datafile Verification

A utility named *DBVERIFY* is provided by Oracle to check the integrity of a database file. On Windows NT, you can access this utility by executing **c:\orant\bin\dbverf80.exe.**

```
C:\> dbverf80 help=yes
DBVERIFY: Release 8.0.4.0.0 - Production on Mon Aug 31 13:16:5 1998
```

```
(c) Copyright 1997 Oracle Corporation.  All rights reserved.
Keyword    Description         (Default)
---------------------------------------------
FILE       File to Verify      (NONE)
START      Start Block         (First Block of File)
END        End Block           (Last Block of File)
BLOCKSIZE  Logical Block Size  (2048)
LOGFILE    Output Log          (NONE)
FEEDBACK   Display Progress    (0)
```

We will verify the datafile **c:\orant\database\usr1orcl.ora** as shown below:

```
C:\> dbverf80 file='c:\orant\database\usr1orcl.ora'
DBVERIFY: Release 8.0.4.0.0 - Production on Mon Aug 31 13:29:15 1998
(c) Copyright 1997 Oracle Corporation.  All rights reserved.
DBVERIFY - Verification starting : FILE = usr1orcl.ora
DBVERIFY - Verification complete
Total Pages Examined       : 4096
Total Pages Processed (Data) : 81
Total Pages Failing   (Data) : 0
Total Pages Processed (Index): 246
Total Pages Failing   (Index): 0
Total Pages Empty          : 0
Total Pages Marked Corrupt : 0
Total Pages Influx         : 0
```

Since **dbverf80** is an external command-line utility that performs a physical data structure integrity check, you can also use it on backed up files to ensure their integrity before you use them in a restoration. Integrity checks are also much faster on an off-line database. RMAN (Recovery Manager) also has a facility to detect corrupt blocks. Refer to the *Oracle8 Backup and Recovery Guide* for details on this feature. The *Oracle8 Backup & Recovery Handbook* (Osborne/McGraw-Hill, 1998) in the Oracle Press Series also provides information about this feature along with an example.

SQL Plus Character vs. Graphical Mode

Oracle8 on Windows NT provides a character mode as well as graphical mode of SQL Plus. To execute character-mode SQL Plus, run **c:\orant\bin\plus80.exe** and to execute the graphical-mode SQL Plus, run **c:\orant\bin\plus80w.exe**. There is no difference between the functionality provided by them.

Net8 Management

Character-mode utilities are available with Oracle8 on Windows NT to manage Net8 listeners, Oracle Names, and for diagnostics. However, there are no character-mode tools to create configuration files. We will take a look at these tools in this section.

Listener Control Utility

The Listener Control utility, as the name suggests, can be used to control the Net8 listener. On Windows NT, the executable is named **lsnrctl80.exe**. The **help** command gives complete usage, as shown below:

```
C:\orant\BIN> lsnrctl80
LSNRCTL80 for 32-bit Windows: Version 8.0.4.0.0 - Production on 31-AUG-98 16:13:
46
(c) Copyright 1997 Oracle Corporation.  All rights reserved.
Welcome to LSNRCTL, type "help" for information.
LSNRCTL> help
The following operations are available
An asterisk (*) denotes a modifier or extended command:
start             stop             status
services          version          reload
save_config       trace            dbsnmp_start
dbsnmp_stop       dbsnmp_status    change_password
quit              exit             set*
show*
```

To start a listener, use the **start** command. You can start the default listener on Windows NT (named LISTENER) as shown below:

```
LSNRCTL> start
Starting tnslsnr80: please wait...
Service OracleTNSListener80 start pending.
Service OracleTNSListener80 started.
TNSLSNR80 for 32-bit Windows: Version 8.0.4.0.0 - Production
System parameter file is C:\orant\NET80\admin\listener.ora
Log messages written to C:\orant\NET80\log\listener.log
Listening on: (ADDRESS=(PROTOCOL=tcp)(DEV=164)(HOST=127.0.0.1)(PORT=1521))
Connecting to (ADDRESS=(PROTOCOL=TCP)(HOST=aadkoli-lap.us.oracle.com)(PORT=1521)
)
STATUS of the LISTENER
------------------------
Alias                    LISTENER
Version                  TNSLSNR80 for 32-bit Windows: Version 8.0.4.0.0 - Prod
uction
Start Date               29-AUG-98 15:21:38
```

```
Uptime                      0 days 0 hr. 0 min. 3 sec
Trace Level                 off
Security                    ON
SNMP                        OFF
Listener Parameter File     C:\orant\NET80\admin\listener.ora
Listener Log File           C:\orant\NET80\log\listener.log
Services Summary...
  ORCL          has 1 service handler(s)
  extproc              has 1 service handler(s)
The command completed successfully
```

On Windows NT, the default listener password is set to *ORACLE*. If you want to shut down the listener from LSNRCTL, you must supply the password as shown below:

```
LSNRCTL> set password oracle
The command completed successfully
LSNRCTL> stop
Connecting to
(ADDRESS=(PROTOCOL=TCP)(HOST=aadkoli-lap.us.oracle.com)(PORT=1521)
)
The command completed successfully
```

Most of the LSNRCTL commands can be issued from the command line. This feature is useful while writing batch files. We will provide an example of obtaining the status of a listener below:

```
C:\> lsnrctl80 status
LSNRCTL80 for 32-bit Windows: Version 8.0.4.0.0 - Production on 31-AUG-98 16:22:22
(c) Copyright 1997 Oracle Corporation.  All rights reserved.
Connecting to (ADDRESS=(PROTOCOL=TCP)(HOST=aadkoli-lap.us.oracle.com)(PORT=1521))
STATUS of the LISTENER
-----------------------
Alias                       LISTENER
Version                     TNSLSNR80 for 32-bit Windows: Version 8.0.4.0.0 -
Production
Start Date                  31-AUG-98 16:20:39
Uptime                      0 days 0 hr. 1 min. 45 sec
Trace Level                 off
Security                    ON
SNMP                        OFF
Listener Parameter File     C:\orant\NET80\admin\listener.ora
Listener Log File           C:\orant\NET80\log\listener.log
Services Summary...
  ORCL          has 1 service handler(s)
  extproc          has 1 service handler(s)
The command completed successfully
```

As shown in the following example, you could write a batch file that checks the status of the Net8 listener and start it, if it is not running:

```
:begin
lsnrctl80 status
if not errorlevel 1 goto end
echo The Listener is not running; we will attempt to start it
lsnrctl80 start listener
:end
```

The listener control utility can also be used to set Net8 trace and log file parameters. The **set** command can be used for this purpose as shown in the sample session below:

```
LSNRCTL> set trc_level
Connecting to
(ADDRESS=(PROTOCOL=TCP)(HOST=aadkoli-lap.us.oracle.com)(PORT=1521)
)
LISTENER parameter "trc_level" set to off
The command completed successfully
LSNRCTL> set trc_level admin
Connecting to
(ADDRESS=(PROTOCOL=TCP)(HOST=aadkoli-lap.us.oracle.com)(PORT=1521)
)
LISTENER parameter "trc_level" set to admin
The command completed successfully
LSNRCTL> set trc_directory
Parameter Value: c:\temp
Connecting to
(ADDRESS=(PROTOCOL=TCP)(HOST=aadkoli-lap.us.oracle.com)(PORT=1521)
)
LISTENER parameter "trc_directory" set to c:\temp
The command completed successfully
```

Names Control Utility

As we have seen in Chapter 5, Net8 clients can use Oracle Names to resolve Net8 aliases. In Chapter 5, we used Net8 Assistant to configure Oracle Names. The Names Control Utility is the CLI to Oracle Names configuration. To start the utility, execute **c:\orant\bin\namesctl80.exe**. Again, help is available within the utility.

```
C:\orant\BIN> namesct180
Oracle Names Control for 32-bit Windows: Version 8.0.4.0.0 - Production on 31-AU
G-98 16:38:09
(c) Copyright 1997 Oracle Corporation.  All rights reserved.
NNL-00018: warning: could not contact default name server
Welcome to NAMESCTL, type "help" for information.
NAMESCTL> help
The following operations are available
An asterisk (*) denotes a modifier or extended command:
delegate_domain         domain_hint             exit
flush                   flush_name              log_stats
password                ping                    query
quit                    register                reload
repeat*                 reset_stats             restart
save_config             set*                    show*
shutdown                start                   start_client_cache
startup                 status                  stop
timed_query             unregister              reorder_ns
version
```

Similarly, you can stop the Names server and start it as shown below:

```
NAMESCTL> stop
Confirm [yes or no]: yes
Server shutting down
NAMESCTL> start
Starting "names80.exe"...Service OracleNamesService80 start pending.
Service OracleNamesService80 started.
server successfully started
Currently managing name server "onames_aadkoli-lap"
Version banner is "Oracle Names for 32-bit Windows: Version 8.0.4.0.0 - Production"
Server name:                            onames_aadkoli-lap
Server has been running for:            2.82 seconds
Request processing enabled:             yes
Request forwarding enabled:             yes
Requests received:                      0
Requests forwarded:                     0
Foreign data items cached:              0
Region data next checked for reload in: 23 hours 59 minutes 58.40 seconds
Region data reload check failures:      0
Cache next checkpointed in:             not set
Cache checkpoint interval:              not set
Cache checkpoint file name:             C:\orant\NET80\names\ckpcch.ora
Statistic counters next reset in:       not set
Statistic counter reset interval:       not set
Statistic counters next logged in:      not set
Statistic counter logging interval:     not set
Trace level:                            0
```

```
Trace file name:                    C:\orant\NET80\trace\nameseb.trc
Log file name:                      C:\orant\NET80\log\names.log
System parameter file name:         C:\orant\NET80\admin\names.ora
Command-line parameter file name:   ""
Administrative region name:         root
Administrative region description:  (DESCRIPTION=(ADDRESS=(PROTOCOL=TCP)(H
OST=aadkoli-lap.us.oracle.com)(PORT=1521))(CONNECT_DATA=(SID=ORCL)(Server=Dedica
ted)))
ApplTable Index:                    0
Contact                             ""
Operational Status                  0
Save Config on Stop                 no
```

NAMESCTL supports command-line usage like LSNRCTL. This allows you to include NAMESCTL commands in batch files.

TNS Ping Utility

Oracle Net8 includes a utility named TNSPING that can be used to check connectivity through Net8. To run the utility, execute **c:\orant\bin\ tnsping80.exe** from the command line. Type **tnsping80** to get usage as shown below:

```
C:\orant\BIN> tnsping80
TNS Ping Utility for 32-bit Windows: Version 8.0.4.0.0 - Production on 31-AUG-98
 16:53:33
(c) Copyright 1997 Oracle Corporation.  All rights reserved.
TNS-03502: Insufficient arguments.  Usage:  tnsping <address> [<count>]
```

We will check the validity of a Net8 service named *PROD* from a Net8 client as shown below:

```
C:\> tnsping80 prod 2
TNS Ping Utility for 32-bit Windows: Version 8.0.4.0.0 - Production on 31-AUG-98
 16:56:58
(c) Copyright 1997 Oracle Corporation.  All rights reserved.
Attempting to contact (ADDRESS=(PROTOCOL=TCP)(HOST=aadkoli-lap.us.oracle.com)(PO
RT=1521))
OK (150 msec)
OK (60 msec)
```

Administering the Web Application Server

The Oracle Web Application Server can also be controlled using a utility named **owsctl** using a CLI. The executable is named **owsctl.exe** on

Windows NT and resides in the **c:\orant\ows\3.0\bin** folder. The following session shows a sample session that uses this utility to start and stop the *admin* listener.

```
C:\orant\OWS\3.0\BIN> owsctl
To start/stop/status the Oracle Web Listener:
  usage: owsctl [start|stop|reload|status] [listener name]
To start/stop/status the Oracle WebServer WRB or Cartridge process:
  usage: owsctl [start|stop|status] [[-e] wrb|cartridge| -p process_name] | ncx
To start/stop/status the Oracle Web Status Monitor:
  usage: owsctl [start|stop|status] -stat [listener name]
C:\orant\OWS\3.0\BIN> owsctl stop ADMIN
OWS-08809: Oracle Web Listener `ADMIN' is being terminated.
C:\orant\OWS\3.0\BIN> owsctl start ADMIN
Oracle Web Application Server 3.0.0.0
```

The **owsctl** utility can only be used by a Windows NT user who is part of the A*dministrators* group. You will get an error if you do not have sufficient privileges as shown below:

```
C:\> owsctl stop admin
Access is denied.
```

Web Application Server Configuration

The WAS version 3.x configuration files are available in the folder **c:\orant\ows\admin\ows\website30**<your host name> (the last sub-directory will change based on your host name). Each listener has a directory at this level. The **config** directory contains a file with a **.cfg** extension which is the configuration file for the listener. The following session shows the directory structure for the default WAS configuration with two listeners *admin* and *www* on our test machine:

```
C:\orant\OWS\admin\OWS\WEBSITE30\HTTPD_AADKOLI-LAP.US.ORACLE.COM> tree
Directory PATH listing for volume DRIVE_C
Volume serial number is 0012FC94 3127:16CF
C:.
+---ADMIN
|   +---CONFIG
|   +---LOG
+---WWW
    +---CONFIG
    +---LOG
```

You can edit the **.cfg** files to configure a listener.

TIP
*Protect the **.cfg** files from other users as these files contain password information. For example, the **svadmin.cfg** file exposes the password for the ADMIN user as shown below:*

```
(Users)
admin: aa
```

Recovery Manager

We looked at NT Backup Manager, NT Recovery Manager, and Backup Manager (RMAN) and their GUI functionality in Chapter 5. RMAN (Oracle Recovery Manager) is also available with a CLI. To launch RMAN, execute **c:\orant\bin\rman80.exe** from the command line. We will revisit the character version of RMAN in this section.

Recovery Catalog

RMAN uses the same recovery catalog regardless of whether you use GUI or CLI. The process of creating the recovery catalog has been covered in Chapter 5 and we will not repeat that information here.

Registering a Database in the Recovery Catalog

To register a database in the recovery catalog, you must use the **register database** command of RMAN. You must have configured Net8 to access the database that is holding the recovery catalog as well as the database that will be backed up. In our example, we will register the production database named *PROD* into the recovery catalog contained in a database named *RCV*. We have also created Net8 aliases *PROD* and *RCV* for these databases.

```
C:\>rman80 target=\"internal/oracle@prod\" rcvcat=\"rman/rman@rcv\"
Recovery Manager: Release 8.0.4.0.0 - Production
RMAN-06005: connected to target database: ORCL
RMAN-06008: connected to recovery catalog database
RMAN> register database;
RMAN-03022: compiling command: register
RMAN-03023: executing command: register
RMAN-08006: database registered in recovery catalog
RMAN-03023: executing command: full resync
```

```
RMAN-08002: starting full resync of recovery catalog
RMAN-08004: full resync complete
```

Creating Backups

To create a full backup set of your *PROD* database with five files per set and a channel *C1*, you can use the following set of commands:

```
RMAN> run {
2> allocate channel c1 type disk;
3> backup full filesperset 5
4> (database format 'aa_%p%d.%s');
5> }
```

Similarly, to create a backup set of specific datafiles, you can use the following set of commands:

```
RMAN> run {
2> copy datafile 'c:\orant\database\usr1orcl.ora' to 'd:\usr1orcl.bak';
3> copy datafile 'c:\orant\database\sys1orcl.ora' to 'd:\sys1orcl.bak';
4> copy current controlfile to 'd:\cntrlora.bak';
5> }
```

Note that the control file has been included in the backup set.

CREATING INCREMENTAL BACKUPS   Incremental backups save space and time. During an incremental backup, only copies of database blocks that have changed since the previous backup are created. Two kinds of incremental backups are available:

■ Cumulative incremental backups

■ Non-cumulative incremental backups

Cumulative backups include all blocks that were changed since the last backup at a lower level. A non-cumulative backup includes only the blocks that were changed since the previous backup at the same or lower level. A cumulative backup reduces the work during restoration, as only one backup contains all the changed blocks. Cumulative backups, however, consume more space than non-cumulative backups.

The GUI of RMAN allows you to create incremental backups. Use the following as a starting point for creating a sound backup strategy at your site. With this method, you can organize your backups such that you do not have to recover more than three days worth of data.

Create a backup methodology that creates a backup at level 0 every Sunday (note that a full backup includes all blocks ever used by the database—it is not the same as a whole database backup). You can do this by performing a non-cumulative incremental backup at level 2 on Monday, Tuesday, Thursday, Friday, and Saturday. On Wednesday, make a non-cumulative incremental backup at level 1.

Here, we illustrate this backup strategy for a specific tablespace named USER_DATA.

On Sundays, run the following script:

```
RMAN> run {
2> allocate channel c1 type disk;
3> backup incremental level 0
4> format 'sunday%t.%s'
5> filesperset 5
6> tablespace "user_data";
7> }
```

The above backup includes all used blocks in the tablespace USER_DATA. On Monday and Tuesday, run the following script:

```
RMAN> run {
2> allocate channel c1 type disk;
3> backup incremental level 2
4> format 'level2%t.%s'
5> filesperset 5
6> tablespace "user_data";
7> }
```

Schedule an incremental backup at level 1 on Wednesday as follows:

```
RMAN> run {
2> allocate channel c1 type disk;
3> backup incremental level 1
4> format 'level1%t.%s'
5> filesperset 5
6> tablespace "user_data";
7> }
```

The above backup ensures that all changes made to database blocks since Sunday are available. On Thursday, Friday, and Saturday, schedule a level 2 backup again. Finally, schedule a level 0 backup on Sunday. In this manner, if recovery is required, RMAN will not need to use a backup set older than three days.

Performing Recovery

Performing recovery using RMAN is much simpler than manual recovery. The probability of a crisis due to human errors during recovery using RMAN is also low. RMAN can be used for recovery. We will recover a database named *PROD* that is down because the USER_DATA tablespace needs to be restored. We will assume that a backup set is available and the recovery catalog is created in a database named *RCV*.

First, mount the database *PROD* using Server Manager as shown below:

```
SVRMGR> startup mount
ORACLE instance started.
Total System Global Area          5208748 bytes
Fixed Size                          47788 bytes
Variable Size                     4677632 bytes
Database Buffers                   409600 bytes
Redo Buffers                        73728 bytes
Database mounted.
```

Now RMAN can be used to restore the datafiles for the USER_DATA tablespace and to perform recovery. Note that SQL commands can be issued from RMAN. We will open the database after recovery is completed as shown below:

```
RMAN> run {
2> allocate channel c1 type disk;
3> restore tablespace "user_data";
4> recover tablespace "user_data";
5> sql 'alter database open';
6> }
```

Retrieving Information from the Catalog

Information on all backups created is recorded in the recovery catalog. To get information on the incarnation of the database and the copies of a particular tablespace available in a backup set, use commands similar to those shown below:

```
RMAN> list incarnation of database;
RMAN-03022: compiling command: list
RMAN-06240: List of Database Incarnations
RMAN-06241: DB Key   Inc Key DB Name  DB ID             CUR Reset SCN  Reset Time
RMAN-06242: -------  ------- --------  ----------------  --- ----------  -------
RMAN-06243: 1        2       ORCL      870404535         YES 22484       29-AUG-98
RMAN> list copy of tablespace 'user_data';
RMAN-03022: compiling command: list
RMAN-06210: List of Datafile Copies
RMAN-06211: Key      File S Completion time Ckp SCN    Ckp time         Name
RMAN-06212: -------  ---- - --------------- ---------- ---------------  ------
RMAN-06213: 484      5    D 29-AUG-98       264663     29-AUG-98
C:\ORANT\DATABASE\USR1ORCL.ORA
```

RMAN also provides comprehensive reports that allow DBAs to get a status of valid backups available on the database. You can check if the existing backups can restore a particular tablespace or datafile using a command similar to the one shown below:

```
RMAN> report unrecoverable tablespace "user_data";
RMAN-03022: compiling command: report
RMAN-06250: Report of files that need backup due to unrecoverable operations
RMAN-06251: File Type of Backup Required Name
RMAN-06252: ---- --------------------- ------------------------------------
```

If the tablespace USER_DATA cannot be recovered, you will see a listing of what files need to be backed up to meet the deficiency.

Creating RMAN Scripts

You can create RMAN scripts and store them in the recovery catalog or the file system. You should create scripts for regular tasks and store them in the recovery catalog so that they are always available. Human errors can be minimized by using scripts. Here is a sample script named **db_full** to create a full backup:

```
RMAN> replace script db_full {
2> allocate channel c1 type disk;
3> backup full filesperset 5
4> (database format 'dbfull%p%d.%s');
5> }
```

```
RMAN-03022: compiling command: replace script
RMAN-03023: executing command: replace script
RMAN-08086: replaced script db_full
```

To execute this script, you can use the **execute script** command as shown below:

```
RMAN> run {
2> execute script db_full;
3> }
```

NOTE
For complete details on full and incremental backups, refer to the Oracle8 Server Backup and Recovery Guide.

Creating a Database

In Chapter 5, we saw that the Oracle Installer can create a starter database during installation. This database can be customized by using OEM tools such as Storage Manager. We also presented Database Assistant, along with its wizard that can be used to create custom databases. In this section, we will take a look at how a customized database can be built using the CLI.

Oracle Corporation provides some files that can be used as templates for scripts that can be used during database creation. These files are listed in Table 6-3.

We will now illustrate the manual creation of a database named *TST*.

Step 1   Ensure that the Oracle service is running.

Use the Services applet under the Control Panel to ensure that the service *OracleServiceORCL* is running. If this service is not running, you will see the following error message when you attempt to do a **connect internal**:

```
ORA-12203: TNS:unable to connect to destination
```

If you do not have this service, choose to install a starter database from the Oracle Installer. To install the starter database, choose Custom Installation and select the component Oracle8 Enterprise Edition or Oracle8 Server 8.0.4.

File	Purpose
c:\orant\database\initseed.ora	Use this file to create a copy of an INIT.ORA parameter file for your database. Tip: For your convenience, copy this file as a file named **init\<sid\>.ora** and place it in the **c:\orant\database** directory as this is the default location and name for INIT.ORA files. If you do not do this, you will have to explicitly provide the location of the INIT.ORA every time you start up the database.
c:\orant\rdbms80\admin\build_db.sql	Use this file as a template for the CREATE DATABASE procedure. Be sure to edit the file and set the name of the database, location, and names for parameter file, control files, log files, and datafiles.

TABLE 6-3.   *Template Files for Database Creation*

Step 2   Create the parameter file.

Create a copy of the **initseed.ora** file and save it as **c:\orant\database\ inittst.ora**. Edit the parameters to read as shown below:

```
db_name=TST
control_files = c:\orant\DATABASE\ctl1TST.ora
```

Note that the database name and the control file(s) associated with it must be unique. If you have the starter database installed, it is named ORCL and has a control file named **c:\orant\database\ctl1ORCL.ora**. If you want to overwrite this database, you must use the *REUSE* clause when you specify the filenames in the above script.

Step 3   Create the script for database creation.

Create a copy of the **build_db.sql** script and save it as **c:\orant\ database\createtst.sql**. Edit the file to suit your needs. We have made changes to create a database named *TST*, as shown below:

```
---- $Header: build_db.sql 1.1 94/10/18 15:55:37 gdudey
Osd<desktop/netware> $ Copyr (c) 1994 Oracle
---- This file must be run out of the directory containing the
-- initialization file.
connect internal/oracle
startup nomount pfile=C:\orant\DATABASE\initTST.ora
spool C:\orant\DATABASE\createdb.log
--  Create database
create database TST
    logfile 'C:\orant\DATABASE\log1TST.ora' size 1M ,
            'C:\orant\DATABASE\log2TST.ora' size 1M ,
            'C:\orant\DATABASE\log3TST.ora' size 1M ,
            'C:\orant\DATABASE\log4TST.ora' size 1M
    datafile 'C:\orant\DATABASE\sys1TST.ora' size 10M  autoextend on
      next 10M maxsize 200M
    character set WE8ISO8859P1;
create rollback segment rb_temp storage (initial 100 k next 250 k);
-- Create additional tablespaces ...
-- USER_DATA: Create user sets this as the default tablespace
-- TEMPORARY_DATA: Create user sets this as the temporary tablespace
-- ROLLBACK_DATA: For rollback segments
create tablespace user_data
    datafile 'C:\orant\DATABASE\usr1TST.ora' size 3M  autoextend on
      next 5M maxsize 150M;
create tablespace rollback_data
    datafile 'C:\orant\DATABASE\rbs1TST.ora' size 5M  autoextend on
      next 5M maxsize 150M;
create tablespace temporary_data
    datafile 'C:\orant\DATABASE\tmp1TST.ora' size 2M  autoextend on
      next 5M maxsize 150M;
alter rollback segment rb_temp online;
-- Change the SYSTEM users' password, default tablespace and
-- temporary tablespace.
alter user system temporary tablespace temporary_data;
alter user system default tablespace user_data;
-- Create 16 rollback segments.  Allows 16 concurrent users with open
-- transactions updating the database. This should be enough.
create public rollback segment rb1 storage(initial 50K next 250K)
  tablespace rollback_data;
create public rollback segment rb2 storage(initial 50K next 250K)
  tablespace rollback_data;
create public rollback segment rb3 storage(initial 50K next 250K)
  tablespace rollback_data;
create public rollback segment rb4 storage(initial 50K next 250K)
```

```
     tablespace rollback_data;
create public rollback segment rb5 storage(initial 50K next 250K)
   tablespace rollback_data;
create public rollback segment rb6 storage(initial 50K next 250K)
   tablespace rollback_data;
create public rollback segment rb7 storage(initial 50K next 250K)
   tablespace rollback_data;
create public rollback segment rb8 storage(initial 50K next 250K)
   tablespace rollback_data;
-- create public rollback segment rb9 storage(initial 50K next 250K)
--   tablespace rollback_data;
-- create public rollback segment rb10 storage(initial 50K next 250K)
--   tablespace rollback_data;
-- create public rollback segment rb11 storage(initial 50K next 250K)
--   tablespace rollback_data;
-- create public rollback segment rb12 storage(initial 50K next 250K)
--   tablespace rollback_data;
-- create public rollback segment rb13 storage(initial 50K next 250K)
--   tablespace rollback_data;
-- create public rollback segment rb14 storage(initial 50K next 250K)
--   tablespace rollback_data;
-- create public rollback segment rb15 storage(initial 50K next 250K)
--   tablespace rollback_data;
-- create public rollback segment rb16 storage(initial 50K next 250K)
--   tablespace rollback_data;
-- Now bring public RBS Online as required
alter rollback segment rb1 online;
alter rollback segment rb2 online;
alter rollback segment rb3 online;
alter rollback segment rb4 online;
alter rollback segment rb5 online;
alter rollback segment rb6 online;
alter rollback segment rb7 online;
alter rollback segment rb8 online;
```

In our copy of the script, we have commented out the creation of rollback segments *rb9* to *rb16*. We have also added appropriate ALTER ROLLBACK SEGMENT statements to the bottom of the script. Be sure to change the password for the user *internal* in the above script. Choose filenames and locations to your convenience.

Here's something to watch out for: On our sample installation, the **build_db.sql** script had a syntax error in the following section:

```
create database ORCL
     controlfile reuse
     logfile 'C:\orant\DATABASE\log1ORCL.ora' size 1M reuse,
             'C:\orant\DATABASE\log2ORCL.ora' size 1M reuse,
```

```
         'C:\orant\DATABASE\log3ORCL.ora' size 1M reuse,
         'C:\orant\DATABASE\log4ORCL.ora' size 1M reuse,
 datafile 'C:\orant\DATABASE\sys1ORCL.ora' size 10M reuse autoextend on
   next 10M maxsize 200M
 character set WE8ISO8859P1;
```

There is an extraneous comma after the log file definitions. Delete the comma after the line:

```
'C:\orant\DATABASE\log4ORCL.ora' size 1M reuse,
```

Step 4   Create the database.
   Start **svrmgr30.exe** and execute the **createtst.sql** script to create the database.

Step 5   Check for errors.
   View the file **c:\orant\database\createdb.log** for any errors.

Database Startup

A database must be open in order to allow user connections. You can have four different states for a database as shown in Table 6-4.
   If you want to start a database using CLI, you can issue the commands shown in Table 6-4 from SQLWKS or SVRMGR. The ALTER DATABASE

State	Command
Database closed	See "Database Shutdown" section later in this chapter.
Instance started, database not mounted	**startup nomount**
Database mounted	**startup mount**
Database open	**startup**

TABLE 6-4.   *Four States of an Oracle Database*

command can be used to move the database from one state to the next. The following sequence of commands can be used to open the database:

```
startup nomount
alter database mount;
alter database open;
```

On Windows NT, you can use **c:\orant\bin\oradim80.exe** to manage an Oracle instance. The options for this executable are shown below for your reference:

```
-NEW                        -Create an instance by specifying the following
                             parameters:
 -SID <sid>                 -Instance name(mandatory)
 -SRVC <svcname>            -Service name
 -INTPWD <password>         -Password for the INTERNAL account(mandatory
                             unless DBA_AUTHORIZATION or
                             DBA_<sid>_AUTHORIZATION is set to BYPASS in
                             the Windows NT Registry)
 -MAXUSERS <number>         -Maximum number of users in the password file
                             (optional; default=5)
 -STARTMODE<auto,manual>    -Indicate whether to start the database
                             automatically or manually at boot time
 -PFILE <filename>          -Fully qualified pathname of file which contains
                             database initialization parameters( valid only if
                             STARTMODE is specified)
-EDIT                       -Edit an instance by specifying the following
                             parameters:
 -SID <sid>                 -Instance name(mandatory)
 -NEWSID <sid>              -New instance name(optional; use only to
                             change the instance name)
 -INTPWD <password>         -Password for the INTERNAL account(mandatory
                             unless DBA_AUTHORIZATION or
                             DBA_<sid>_AUTHORIZATION is set to BYPASS in
the Windows NT Registry)
 -STARTMODE<auto,manual>    -Indicate whether to start the database
                             automatically or manually at boot time
 -PFILE <filename>          -Fully qualified pathname of file which contains
                             database initialization parameters( valid only if
                             STARTMODE is specified)
-DELETE                     -Delete instances by specifying the following:
 -SID <sida, sidb..>        -Instance names.
 -SRVC <srvc1, srvc2..>     -Delete specific services.
-STARTUP                    -Startup services and instance by specifying the
                             following parameters:
 -SID <sid>                 -Instance name(mandatory)
```

```
 -USRPWD <password>      -Password for INTERNAL account(mandatory
                          unless DBA_AUTHORIZATION or
                          DBA_<sid>_AUTHORIZATION is set to BYPASS in
                          the Windows NT Registry)
 -STARTTYPE <srvc,inst>  -Specify whether to start only the services
                          or instance or both
 -PFILE <filename>       -Fully qualified pathname of file which contains
                          database initialization parameters
-SHUTDOWN                -Shutdown services and instance by specifying the
                          following parameters:
 -SID <sid>              -Instance name(mandatory)
 -USRPWD <password>      -Password for INTERNAL account(mandatory
unless DBA_AUTHORIZATION or
                          DBA_<sid>_AUTHORIZATION is set to BYPASS in
                          the Windows NT Registry)
 -STARTTYPE <srvc,inst>  -Specify whether to start only the services
                          or instance or both
 -PFILE <filename>       -Fully qualified pathname of file which contains
                          database initialization parameters
-SHUTDOWN                -Shutdown services and instance by specifying the
                          following parameters:
 -SID <sid>              -Instance name(mandatory)
 -USRPWD <password>      -Password for INTERNAL account(mandatory
                          unless DBA_AUTHORIZATION or
                          DBA_<sid>_AUTHORIZATION is set to BYPASS in
                          the Windows NT Registry)
 -SHUTTYPE <srvc, inst>  -Specify whether to stop only the services or
                          instance or both
 -SHUTMODE <a,i,n>       -Specify instance shutdown mode:abort, immediate or
                          normal
-? | -h | -help          -Query for help.
```

A file named **c:\orant\database\strtorcl.cmd** is created during your installation. This command file can be executed to start the default database *ORCL* and executes **oradim80.exe** with the options shown below:

```
c:\orant\bin\oradim80.exe -startup -sid ORCL -usrpwd oracle
-starttype srvc,inst
 -pfile c:\orant\database\initorcl.ora
```

Note that the password for the user *internal* is exposed in this file. You must protect this file by setting appropriate file security options.

On Windows NT, you can also start an Oracle database by starting the corresponding service. To start the default database *ORCL* on Windows NT, you need to start the service *OracleStartORCL*.

Database Shutdown

A database can be shut down when it is not required or for maintenance reasons. Table 6-5 shows the three modes of shutting down a database.

The above table also provides the commands to shut down a database using CLI. On Windows NT, **oradim80.exe** can be used to shut down a database. You can create a batch file named **shutdown.cmd** that performs an immediate shutdown of a database name *ORCL* with the following command:

```
C:\orant\DATABASE> c:\orant\bin\oradim80.exe -shutdown -sid ORCL
-usrpwd oracle - shuttype srvc,inst -shutmode I
```

If you have installed a starter database, a batch file named **c:\orant\database\orashut.bat** has been created for you. This batch file uses the **orashut.sql** script to shut down the database. To shut down a database named *ORCL*, you can execute the following command:

```
C:\> orashut internal oracle orcl c:\orant
```

The arguments for **orashut.bat** are shown in Table 6-6.

Using Windows NT for Database Startup and Shutdown

The **net** command in Windows NT can be used to start up and shut down Oracle services including the database. The following sample session starts

Shutdown Mode	Command
Normal	**shutdown**
Immediate	**shutdown immediate**
Abort	**shutdown abort**

TABLE 6-5. *Modes of Database Shutdown*

Argument Number	Description
1	Authorized user with *SYSDBA* or *SYSOPER* role
2	Password for user
3	Name of database (SID)
4	Oracle home directory

TABLE 6-6. *Command-Line Arguments for ORASHUT.BAT*

the Oracle service and the database with SID of *ORCL* and then shuts down both services using the **net** command:

```
C:\> net start OracleServiceORCL
The OracleServiceORCL service is starting.
The OracleServiceORCL service was started successfully.
C:\> net start OracleStartORCL
The OracleStartORCL service is starting..........
The OracleStartORCL service was started successfully.
C:\> net stop OracleServiceORCL
The following services are dependent on the OracleServiceORCL service.
Stopping the OracleServiceORCL service will also stop these services.
   OracleStartORCL
Do you want to continue this operation? (Y/N) [N]: y
The OracleStartORCL service was stopped successfully.
The OracleServiceORCL service is stopping.
The OracleServiceORCL service was stopped successfully.
```

CHAPTER
7

Advanced Oracle
Administration

s we have seen in Chapter 5, DBAs have to perform several routine tasks ranging from installation to tuning. In the previous two chapters we discussed the tools and utilities available to administer Oracle8 Server on the Windows NT platform. In this chapter, we will discuss some advanced tasks performed by DBAs. We begin with a discussion of Multithreaded Server and then cover the advanced options in Net8. After this, we cover administration topics involving new features of the Oracle8 Server. A section on database tuning with specific information for Windows NT is next. We have also introduced the Oracle Enterprise Manager Performance Pack. Information on server and client trace files is included. After this, we discuss the starter database on Windows NT and suggest changes that need to be made to it before using it in production. We also present information on Net8 tracing. We close out this chapter with a section on Oracle 16-bit applications under Windows NT and another on scheduling backups with NT Scheduler.

Multithreaded Server

In a client/server situation, Oracle spawns a process on the server known as the *dedicated server* for every client connection. The dedicated server acts as an interface between client processes (applications) and the Oracle Server. All client requests to the Oracle Server are routed through the dedicated server. In return, data from the Oracle Server (including error messages) is returned to the client through this process. It is common to have hundreds of client connections at sites. If each client spawns a dedicated server, it will result in hundreds of processes on the server machine. This can consume unnecessary resources. Since it is unlikely that every client connection is active at the same time, a better solution is to share server processes. This feature is called Multithreaded Server (MTS). MTS requires additional configuration in the INIT.ORA and Net8 client configuration files. In this section, we will walk through a sample MTS configuration.

NOTE
Oracle documentation also refers to the dedicated server as a "shadow" process, the "server" process, or just the "server."

Configuring MTS

MTS configuration is a two-step process: 1) configuring INIT.ORA parameters for MTS, and 2) configuring Net8 clients to use MTS. On Windows NT, Database Assistant can be used to configure MTS.

Step 1   Configuring INIT.ORA parameters for MTS.

Use the Modify a Database option in Database Assistant Wizard to add the MTS option to a database (refer to the section "Oracle Database Assistant" in Chapter 5 for more information). You will see an option to enable MTS, as shown in Figure 7-1.

You will need to configure the number of servers and dispatchers for MTS using the wizard, as shown in Figure 7-2.

Since MTS parameters are set in the INIT.ORA file, you will be prompted for the location of the INIT.ORA file associated with your database, as shown here:

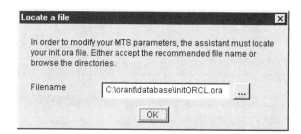

The wizard will update the INIT.ORA file with MTS parameters and remind you that the database needs to be shut down and restarted in order for the parameters to take effect. Using the above procedure, we modified the **c:\orant\database\initorcl.ora** file on our installation and added the following MTS parameters:

```
mts_listener_address = ""
mts_service = "ORCL"
mts_dispatchers = "(protocol=tcp)(dispatchers=4)(mul=no)(pool=no)"
mts_max_dispatchers = 4
mts_servers = 12
mts_max_servers = 12
```

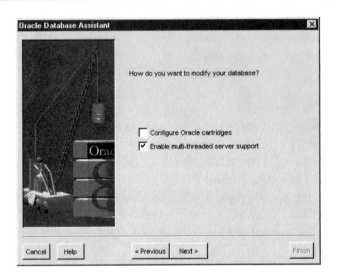

FIGURE 7-1. *Enabling MTS using Database Assistant*

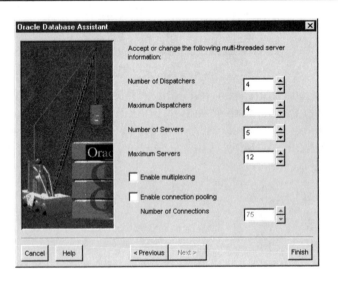

FIGURE 7-2. *Configuring MTS parameters*

Database Assistant automatically creates a backup of the original
initorcl.ora to a file named **initorcl.sav**.

Please be aware that we faced some issues when we tested the above
procedure on our sample installation of Oracle8 Enterprise Edition version
8.0.4. Firstly, the **initorcl.sav** file created by Database Assistant was invalid.
Therefore, we strongly recommend that you create your own copy of the
initorcl.ora file before you attempt this procedure. We also got the following
error message when we attempted to start up our database using the new
initorcl.ora file:

```
ORA-00101: invalid specification for system parameter MTS_DISPATCHERS
```

We modified the **initorcl.ora** file using a text editor and changed the
setting for the MTS_LISTENER_ADDRESS parameter as shown below to
resolve this issue:

```
mts_listener_address = "(address=(protocol=tcp)(host=aadkoli-lap.us.oracle.com)
(port=1521))"
```

Since the default value for MTS_LISTENER_ADDRESS is a null string, you
could also just comment out the MTS_LISTENER_ADDRESS parameter by
adding a '#' sign in front of the statement as shown below:

```
# mts_listener_address = ""
```

If you do not have access to Database Assistant, you could add the
above parameters to your INIT.ORA file manually for MTS. Remember to
shut down and restart the database.

After you have configured MTS, you should confirm that clients are using
the shared servers. You can do this by querying the data dictionary. In our
example above, we spawned four dispatchers and twelve shared servers. A
listing of the results obtained by querying the data dictionary on our
installation is shown below for your reference:

```
SQLWKS> SELECT NAME,NETWORK,STATUS FROM V$DISPATCHER;
NAME   NETWORK                                                       STATUS
-----  ------------------------------------------------------------  ----------------
D000   (ADDRESS=(PARTIAL=YES)(PROTOCOL=tcp))                         WAIT
D001   (ADDRESS=(PARTIAL=YES)(PROTOCOL=tcp))                         WAIT
D002   (ADDRESS=(PARTIAL=YES)(PROTOCOL=tcp))                         WAIT
D003   (ADDRESS=(PARTIAL=YES)(PROTOCOL=tcp))                         WAIT
4 rows selected.
```

```
SQLWKS> SELECT NAME, STATUS FROM V$SHARED_SERVER;
NAME   STATUS
-----  ----------------
S000   WAIT(COMMON)
S001   WAIT(COMMON)
S002   WAIT(COMMON)
S003   WAIT(COMMON)
S004   WAIT(COMMON)
S005   WAIT(COMMON)
S006   WAIT(COMMON)
S007   WAIT(COMMON)
S008   WAIT(COMMON)
S009   WAIT(COMMON)
S010   WAIT(COMMON)
S011   WAIT(COMMON)
12 rows selected.
```

Step 2   Configuring Net8 clients to use MTS.

There is no special configuration required on the clients to use MTS. However, you need to confirm that your clients are not explicitly requesting for a dedicated server. Ensure that the service name or Net8 alias being used for the connection does not include the following setting:

```
(SRVR = DEDICATED)
```

The above setting will force your clients to request for a dedicated server (see the next section titled "Requesting a Dedicated Server" for more information). You also need to configure Net8 clients to resolve names (Net8 aliases) by using the TNSNAMES, ONAMES, or HOSTNAME method. By default, a client will request a shared server. You can query the V$CIRCUIT view to confirm that a client is using MTS for the connection. One entry will be added to this view for every client connection. A sample of the output from V$CIRCUIT is shown below:

```
SQLWKS> SELECT CIRCUIT, SERVER FROM V$CIRCUIT;
CIRCUIT   SERVER
--------  --------
0D016E28  00
1 row selected.
```

The above query resulted in one row. This means that one client is using a shared server at this time. Note that you must use Net8 to use the MTS feature. Only clients connecting to the database using a Net8 connection can use MTS. MTS configuration does not apply to local database connections on Windows NT.

Requesting a Dedicated Server

As mentioned earlier, if MTS is configured on your database, the default connection for Net8 will use a shared server. Some database applications may issue queries continuously or may submit large transactions to the database. It is better to use a dedicated server for such applications. You can specifically request a dedicated server in the connection request. Modify the appropriate *alias* in the **tnsnames.ora** (or Oracle Names) using Net8 Assistant. Select the *service name* in the Navigator and configure the Advanced option (click on the Advanced button). Select the appropriate check box to request for a dedicated server as shown here:

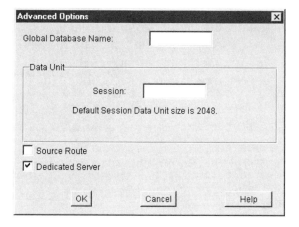

A sample TNSNAMES alias definition for dedicated server connections is provided below for your reference:

```
PROD.WORLD =
  (DESCRIPTION =
    (ADDRESS = (PROTOCOL = TCP)(HOST = aadkoli-lap.us.oracle.com)(PORT = 1521))
    (CONNECT_DATA = (SID = ORCL))
    (SRVR = DEDICATED)
  )
```

Again, use the V$CIRCUIT view to confirm that a shared server is not being used for a client requesting a dedicated server.

CAUTION
Avoid editing the **tnsnames.ora** *file manually.*
Use Net8 Assistant or Net8 Easy Config to make
necessary changes to this file.

Configuring Redundant Names Servers

If you are using Oracle Names for Net8 names resolution, you should create at least two separate Oracle Names Servers for redundancy. In this manner, if one node (or one of the region databases) is down, the other one is available to resolve Net8 names. Use Net8 Assistant to specify the hierarchy of names servers. Select the Profile tab in the Navigator and choose the option Preferred Oracle Names Servers. Click on the Add button to add the preferred servers in the order of preference as shown in Figure 7-3.

Our settings for preferred Names Servers added the following entries to the **sqlnet.ora** file:

```
NAMES.PREFERRED_SERVERS =
  (ADDRESS_LIST =
    (ADDRESS = (PROTOCOL = TCP)(HOST =
aadkoli-lap.us.oracle.com)(PORT = 1521))
    (ADDRESS = (PROTOCOL = TCP)(HOST =
rvelpuri-lap.us.oracle.com)(PORT = 1521))
  )
```

Using Hostnames for Net8 Resolution

If you are using a TCP/IP based network, you can use the hostnames from the TCP/IP configuration for Net8 name resolution. You need to ensure that

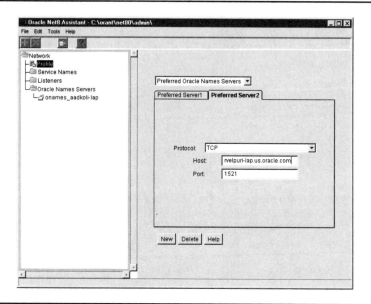

FIGURE 7-3. *Setting preferred Names Servers*

the hostnames are resolved with proper domain name services (DNS) or a **hosts** file. The **hosts** file on Windows NT is located in the **c:\winnt\ system32\drivers\etc** folder.

Use the following steps to configure Net8 hostname based resolution using Net8 Assistant:

1. Configure the profile.

   Expand the *profile* node in Net8 Assistant and ensure that the *hostname* method is listed in the naming methods.

2. Configure the database service.

   In the list of database services configured for the listener, ensure that the *global database name* is set to the hostname of the machine hosting the database.

No additional configuration is required on the clients. If you are using the hostname method for resolution, you do not need a **tnsnames.ora** file on the client. The sample files generated on our test machine are shown below for your reference:

```
# C:\ORANT\NET80\ADMIN\SQLNET.ORA Configuration
File:C:\orant\net80\admin\sqlnet.ora
# Generated by Oracle Net8 Assistant
SQLNET.EXPIRE_TIME = 0
SQLNET.ENCRYPTION_SERVER = requested
SQLNET.ENCRYPTION_CLIENT = requested
NAMES.DIRECTORY_PATH= (HOSTNAME)
# C:\ORANT\NET80\ADMIN\LISTENER.ORA Configuration
File:C:\orant\net80\admin\listener.ora
# Generated by Oracle Net8 Assistant
PASSWORDS_LISTENER= (oracle)
LISTENER =
  (ADDRESS = (PROTOCOL = TCP)(HOST = aadkoli-lap.us.oracle.com)
(PORT = 1521))
SID_LIST_LISTENER =
  (SID_LIST =
    (SID_DESC =
      (GLOBAL_DBNAME = aadkoli-lap.us.oracle.com)
      (ORACLE_HOME = c:\orant)
      (SID_NAME = ORCL)
    )
  )
```

Note that the *GLOBAL_DBNAME* parameter in the **listener.ora** is set to the hostname of our machine. Use the entire hostname as the Net8 service name during the connection request.

Restrictions with the Hostname Method

If you are using the hostname method, you must have TCP/IP configured on the clients and the server along with Net8 TCP/IP Protocol Adapter. The listener must be configured to *listen* on port 1521. Finally, the *GLOBAL_DBNAME* parameter must be set to the hostname. The IP (Internet protocol) address cannot be used as a substitute.

Advanced Networking Options

Net8 has an add-on option called the Advanced Networking Option (ANO) that allows you to protect your data while it is being transmitted across a network. This option must be licensed separately from Oracle Corporation and is not available with the basic Net8 installation. Using ANO, you can enable the checksumming and data encryption features on the server and the clients. Checksumming and encryption ensure that data is not compromised when traversing the network. Net8 supports many data encryption algorithms. You must ensure that a common encryption algorithm is available on the client and the server. Without this, the client will not be able to decipher the data received from the server. Net8 will provide appropriate error messages if a common encryption algorithm is not available between the client and the server.

All the settings for checksumming and data encryption are stored in the **sqlnet.ora** files on the server and the client. Net8 Assistant can be used to generate a **sqlnet.ora** file with the proper settings. There is a very small performance overhead for checksumming and encryption. On most networks, this overhead is very trivial and does not affect overall performance.

Installing ANO

You can use Oracle Installer to install ANO. Figure 7-4 shows the ANO component installed on our machine.

Enabling Checksumming

If you choose to enable checksumming, it must be enabled on the server as well as the client. You can use Net8 Assistant to enable checksumming. Select the Profile node and choose the Advanced Networking Options from the list box. Select the Integrity tab and select the check boxes for checksumming, as shown in Figure 7-5.

Ensure that you have made checksumming mandatory by selecting *required* in the list box provided and save the configuration.

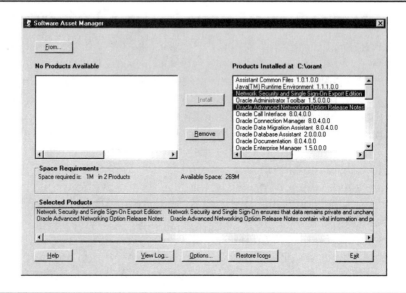

FIGURE 7-4. *Net8 Advanced Networking Option*

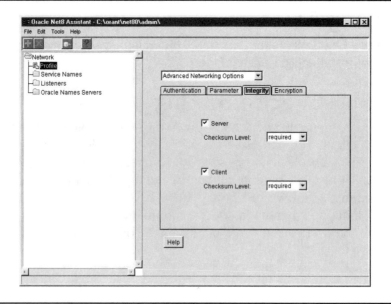

FIGURE 7-5. *Enabling Checksumming*

Enabling Encryption

Optionally, you can choose to encrypt data while it is traversing across the network. ANO provides a choice of encryption algorithms. Refer to the *Oracle Advanced Networking Option Administrator's Guide* for a listing of the available options for encryption algorithms. Net8 Assistant also can be used to configure encryption. Set options for the client and the server using the Encryption tab in the Advanced Networking Options, as shown in Figures 7-6 and 7-7.

Ensure that the server and the client have at least one common encryption algorithm. Note that we have chosen to use the DES40 encryption algorithm on both the client and the server.

You must also ensure that the client and the server have a matching encryption seed. We recommend that you confirm that checksumming and encryption are enabled using Net8 trace files. You must enable *Support* level tracing for Net8 to ensure that checksumming and encryption are

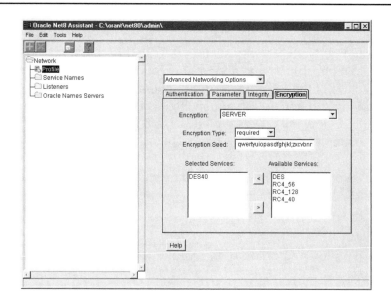

FIGURE 7-6. *Encryption settings for the server*

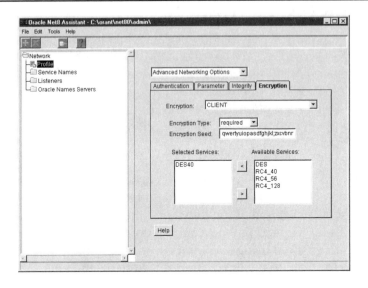

FIGURE 7-7. *Encryption settings for clients*

enabled (see the "Net8 Tracing" section later in this chapter). The trace file will indicate if checksumming and/or encryption is enabled. Figure 7-8 shows a section of the trace file from our client that confirms that checksumming and encryption are enabled on our installation.

We will see how data is encrypted in Net8 trace files with the following example.

Example: We disabled encryption and executed the following query with tracing enabled:

```
select user from dual;
```

Figure 7-9 shows a portion of the Net8 trace file that plainly shows the query we executed.

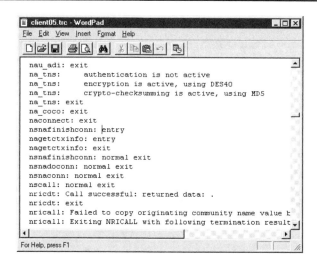

FIGURE 7-8. *Confirmation of ANO settings*

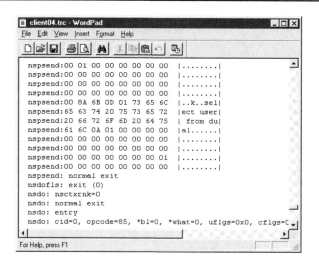

FIGURE 7-9. *Trace file showing text of the query*

Next, we enabled encryption and ran the same query. Figure 7-10 shows the same section of the trace file on our test installation. As you can see, the text of the query SELECT USER FROM DUAL is encrypted in this trace file.

A section of the **sqlnet.ora** file on our installation is shown below for your reference:

```
#sqlnet.authentication_services = (NONE)
SQLNET.ENCRYPTION_SERVER = requested
SQLNET.ENCRYPTION_CLIENT = requested
```

Authentication is also possible using authentication adapters like Kerberos and CyberSAFE. Refer to the *Oracle Advanced Networking Option Administrator's Guide* for more information on ANO.

Password Management

In Chapters 5 and 6, we have seen how users are created and how a user password can be set and reset using User Manager as well as by using SQL commands like CREATE USER and ALTER USER. Oracle8 has advanced features for password management that were not available on previous

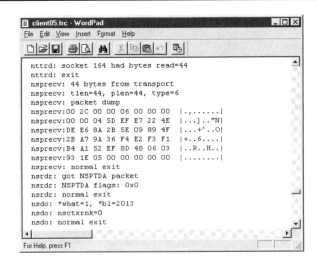

FIGURE 7-10. *Trace file showing encrypted query*

releases. New Oracle8 password features include aging and password expiration. DBAs can also control the complexity of a password by defining a *password verification function*. The advanced password features of Oracle8 are implemented using profiles. A profile in Oracle8 now includes the password resources listed in Table 7-1.

DBAs need to create named profiles with appropriate settings for the password resources described in Table 7-1. These profiles can then be assigned to users. We will demonstrate how password resources can be managed with an example.

Password Resource	Description
FAILED_LOGIN_ATTEMPTS	Number of failed login attempts before the account is locked.
PASSWORD_LIFE_TIME	Time after which the password expires.
PASSWORD_REUSE_TIME	Number of days before a password can be reused.
PASSWORD_REUSE_MAX	Number of password changes before a password can be reused.
PASSWORD_LOCK_TIME	Number of days for which an account will be locked after failed login attempts
PASSWORD_GRACE_TIME	Grace period after expiration of password during which a user can login after acknowledging a warning.
PASSWORD_VERIFY_FUNCTION	A PL/SQL script that allows sites to define the complexity of passwords. Certain passwords can also be disallowed.

TABLE 7-1. *Password Resources*

TIP
*Modify the DEFAULT profile and set password
resources so that these restrictions
automatically apply to all users created on the
database by default.*

Example: Ensure that Oracle accounts get locked after three failed attempts
and that passwords expire after 30 days automatically. Provide a grace time
of three days. Also, ensure that the usernames and common words like
"hello," "welcome," and "Oracle" are not used as passwords.

The solution is to create a profile with the required password restrictions
and assign this profile to users. In our example below, we will alter the
profile named *DEFAULT* and set the required password limits.

Step 1 Create a password verification function.

Copy the sample script **c:\orant\rdbms80\admin\utlpwdmg.sql** into a
new file. We will create a file named **c:\temp\ourpwd.sql**. Edit the script to
set the required password resources. Our modified script is shown below:

```
CREATE OR REPLACE FUNCTION verify_function
(username varchar2,
  password varchar2,
  old_password varchar2)
  RETURN boolean IS
   n boolean;
   m integer;
   differ integer;
   isdigit boolean;
   ischar  boolean;
   ispunct boolean;
   digitarray varchar2(20);
   punctarray varchar2(25);
   chararray varchar2(52);
BEGIN
   digitarray:= '0123456789';
   chararray:= 'abcdefghijklmnopqrstuvwxyzABCDEFGHIJKLMNOPQRSTUVWXYZ';
   punctarray:='!"#$%&()``*+,-/:;<=>?_';
   -- Check if the password is same as the username
   IF password = username THEN
     raise_application_error(-20001, 'Password same as user');
   END IF;
   -- Check for the minimum length of the password
   IF length(password) < 4 THEN
      raise_application_error(-20002, 'Password length less than 4');
```

```
END IF;
-- Check if the password is too simple. A dictionary of words may
-- be maintained and a check may be made so as not to allow the
-- words that are too simple for the password.
IF NLS_LOWER(password) IN ('welcome', 'oracle', 'hello') THEN
   raise_application_error(-20002, 'Password too simple');
END IF;
-- Check if the password contains at least one letter, one digit
-- and one punctuation mark.
-- 1. Check for the digit
isdigit:=FALSE;
m := length(password);
FOR i IN 1..10 LOOP
   FOR j IN 1..m LOOP
      IF substr(password,j,1) = substr(digitarray,i,1) THEN
         isdigit:=TRUE;
          GOTO findchar;
      END IF;
   END LOOP;
END LOOP;
IF isdigit = FALSE THEN
   raise_application_error(-20003, 'Password should contain \
   at least one digit, one character and one punctuation');
END IF;
-- 2. Check for the character
<<findchar>>
ischar:=FALSE;
FOR i IN 1..length(chararray) LOOP
   FOR j IN 1..m LOOP
      IF substr(password,j,1) = substr(chararray,i,1) THEN
         ischar:=TRUE;
          GOTO findpunct;
      END IF;
   END LOOP;
END LOOP;
IF ischar = FALSE THEN
   raise_application_error(-20003, 'Password should contain \
   at least one digit, one character and one punctuation');
END IF;
-- 3. Check for the punctuation
<<findpunct>>
ispunct:=FALSE;
FOR i IN 1..length(punctarray) LOOP
   FOR j IN 1..m LOOP
      IF substr(password,j,1) = substr(punctarray,i,1) THEN
         ispunct:=TRUE;
          GOTO endsearch;
      END IF;
   END LOOP;
END LOOP;
IF ispunct = FALSE THEN
```

```
            raise_application_error(-20003, 'Password should contain \
            at least one digit, one character and one punctuation');
        END IF;
        <<endsearch>>
        -- Check if the password differs from the previous password by at
        -- least 3 letters
        IF old_password = '' THEN
            raise_application_error(-20004, 'Old password is null');
        END IF;
        -- Everything is fine; return TRUE ;
        differ := length(old_password) - length(password);
        IF abs(differ) < 3 THEN
            IF length(password) < length(old_password) THEN
                m := length(password);
            ELSE
                m := length(old_password);
            END IF;
            differ := abs(differ);
            FOR i IN 1..m LOOP
                IF substr(password,i,1) != substr(old_password,i,1) THEN
                    differ := differ + 1;
                END IF;
            END LOOP;
            IF differ < 3 THEN
                raise_application_error(-20004, 'Password should differ \
                by at least 3 characters');
            END IF;
        END IF;
        -- Everything is fine; return TRUE ;
        RETURN(TRUE);
END;
/
-- This script alters the default parameters for Password Management
-- This means that all the users on the system have Password Management
-- enabled and set to the following values unless another profile is
-- created with parameter values set to different value or UNLIMITED
-- is created and assigned to the user.
ALTER PROFILE DEFAULT LIMIT
PASSWORD_LIFE_TIME 30
PASSWORD_GRACE_TIME 3
PASSWORD_REUSE_TIME 1800
PASSWORD_REUSE_MAX UNLIMITED
FAILED_LOGIN_ATTEMPTS 3
PASSWORD_VERIFY_FUNCTION verify_function;
```

Step 2   Run the script as the user *SYS*.

The script must be run as the user *SYS*. We will run the **ourpwd.sql** script
as shown below:

```
SVRMGR> connect sys/change_on_install
Connected.
SVRMGR> @c:\temp\ourpwd
Statement processed.
Statement processed.
```

Step 3   Test the new profile.
A test of the altered profile is shown below:

```
SVRMGR> connect system/manager
Connected.
SVRMGR> alter user scott identified by hello;
alter user scott identified by hello
*
ORA-28003: password verification for the specified password failed
ORA-20002: Password too simple
SVRMGR> connect scott/tigr
ORA-01017: invalid username/password; logon denied
SVRMGR> connect scott/tige
ORA-01017: invalid username/password; logon denied
SVRMGR> connect scott/tger
ORA-28000: the account is locked
```

DBAs can unlock an account using Security Manager or the ALTER USER command as shown below:

```
SVRMGR> connect system/manager
Connected.
SVRMGR> alter user scott account unlock;
Statement processed.
```

Altering Profiles with Security Manager

Security Manager can also be used to modify profiles, while password resources can be set using GUI. Figure 7-11 shows a sample screen of Security Manager that was used to provide the same settings for password resources as our example above.

Auditing

Windows NT allows for auditing at the operating system level. The NT Security log shows events that are related to security. The Oracle8 Server

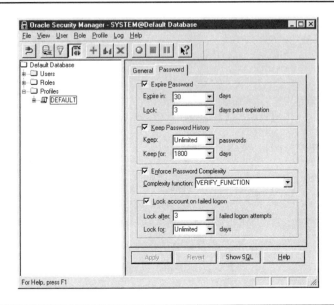

FIGURE 7-11. *Setting password resources*

also has an auditing feature that can be used to audit database access at the user and object levels.

Windows NT Auditing

Auditing can be enabled at a user or group level in Windows NT. The settings for auditing can be modified using User Manager. Select the user or group you are interested in, then select Policies | Audit to set the auditing options. The audit log can be viewed through Event Viewer. Figure 7-12 shows a sample entry in the Security log for an invalid login attempt at the operating system level.

Oracle8 Auditing

The Oracle8 Server allows for auditing like earlier versions of Oracle. There is also a feature that allows for the audit trail to be created on an operating system file rather than the table AUD$. Unfortunately, this feature does not work on Windows NT. If you attempt to set the AUDIT_FILE_DEST

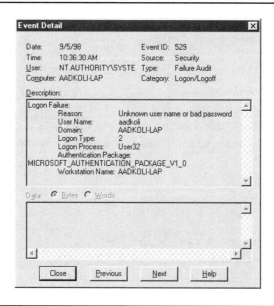

FIGURE 7-12. *Security event in Windows NT*

parameter in the INIT.ORA, you will see an error when you attempt to start up your database, as shown below:

```
LRM-00101: unknown parameter name 'audit_file_dest'
ORA-01078: failure in processing system parameters
```

On Windows NT, you must set up the database to write the audit trail to the AUD$ table by setting the following parameter in the INIT.ORA:

```
audit_trail = db
```

You must use the SQL command AUDIT to enable system- or object-level auditing. The audit trail is written to the AUD$ table. We have provided an example below:

```
SVRMGR> connect sys/change_on_install
Connected.
SVRMGR> audit connect by guest;
Statement processed.
```

```
SVRMGR> connect guest/guest
Connected.
SVRMGR> select user from dual;
USER
------------------------------
GUEST
1 row selected.
SVRMGR> connect sys/change_on_install
Connected.
SVRMGR> select userid,comment$text,logoff$time from aud$;
USERID    COMMENT$TEXT                         LOGOFF$TI
------    ---------------------------------    ------------
GUEST     Authenticated by: DATABASE           05-SEP-98
```

TIP

The AUD$ table resides in the SYSTEM tablespace by default. It can become difficult to manage the SYSTEM tablespace because of the fast growth of the AUD$ table. You should move the AUD$ table to some other tablespace using the CREATE TABLE AS command in SQL. We recommend that you create a separate tablespace to hold the AUD$ table to ease maintenance. We present a sample session to perform this task of moving the AUD$ table below:

```
SVRMGR> create tablespace aud_tb datafile
'c:\orant\database\aud.ora' size 2m;
Statement processed.
SVRMGR> create table aud_temp tablespace aud_tb as
    2> select * from aud$ where 1=2;
Statement processed.
SVRMGR> rename aud$ to aud$$;
Statement processed.
SVRMGR> rename aud_temp to aud$;
Statement processed.
SVRMGR> create index i_aud$ on aud$(sessionid,ses$tid)
tablespace aud_tb;
Statement processed.
```

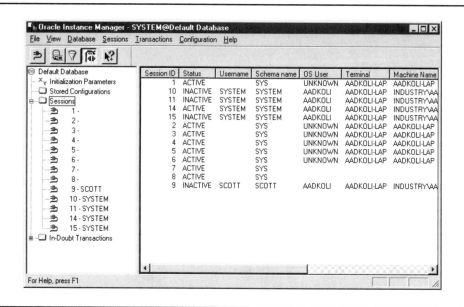

FIGURE 7-13.   *Managing sessions from Instance Manager*

Managing Sessions

Instance Manager can be used to manage sessions. Unwanted sessions
can also be terminated using Instance Manager. Select the Sessions node to
view current sessions on the database. Figure 7-13 shows a sample screen
on our installation.

   You can use the V$SESSION and V$PROCESS views in the data
dictionary to get the same information. Unwanted sessions can be
terminated with the ALTER SYSTEM KILL SESSION command.

Performance Tuning

Performance tuning at many sites is an iterative effort that can involve many
areas. We will restrict our discussion to Windows NT–specific features

related to tuning. Refer to *Oracle8 Tuning,* which provides in-depth information on server tuning.

Tuning Memory

The goal is to distribute fast access physical memory between various Oracle database structures. You should always tune memory after tuning your applications but before tuning physical input/output (I/O). Memory tuning must be done at the operating system level as well as the Oracle instance level. It is important to ensure that the operating system does not use virtual memory (swap file or page file) if at all possible. Use Windows NT Diagnostics to obtain information on memory usage. Click Start | Programs | Administrative Tools (Common) | Windows NT Diagnostics to get access to this utility. Click on the Memory tab to see a screen similar to the one shown in Figure 7-14.

Pay special attention to the Pagefile section at the bottom of the screen. You must try and ensure that this file is used minimally. This ensures that

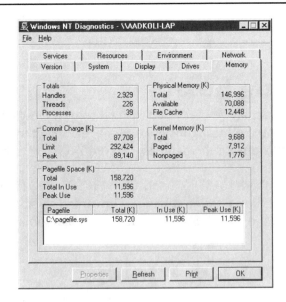

FIGURE 7-14. *History of physical memory usage on Windows NT*

you have sufficient physical memory for your applications. If you find that your pagefile is being used consistently at some size, you should consider adding physical memory to cover that size. Also consider using the PRE_PAGE_SGA parameter to ensure that all SGA pages are brought into memory. Set the parameter as shown below:

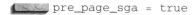
```
pre_page_sga = true
```

You can use Performance Monitor (PM) to track the pagefile. Select the Edit | Add to Chart option in PM and add the %Usage and %Usage Peak options to the chart for the Paging File object as shown here:

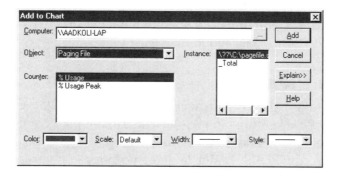

Also, keep track of the physical memory reported available by Windows NT Diagnostics. In Figure 7-14, you can see that about 70Mb of physical memory is reported as available for use. You can also track memory usage by choosing the Memory object in PM.

CPU Performance

It is unlikely that the CPU(s) will become a bottleneck for performance. However, you should track CPU performance in PM. Select the Processor object to view CPU usage statistics in PM.

Tuning Physical Input/Output

Physical I/O to disk can impact performance. Select the object Physical Disk in PM to view I/O statistics. At the very least, you should track disk writes and disk reads. The sum of these should be compared against the rating of your hard disk(s). Ensure that the hard disk and the disk controllers are not impacting performance.

If you have multiple disks, ensure that the pagefile is not created on the same disk as the Oracle database files. Use the Performance tab in the System applet under the Control Panel to set pagefile characteristics.

Oracle8 Performance Monitor

The Oracle8 Server on Windows NT is integrated with PM. Click Start | Programs | Oracle for Windows NT | Oracle8 Performance Monitor V8.0 to obtain Oracle-related statistics. When you launch Oracle8 Performance Monitor, Windows NT PM is launched with a workspace file named **c:\orant\dbs\oracle80.pmw** provided by Oracle Corporation. You can modify this file to suit your requirements.

Explain Plan

You can get information on the access path for a particular query by using the EXPLAIN PLAN command in SQL. The explain plan command is useful for application tuning and requires the creation of a table named PLAN_TABLE. The PLAN_TABLE table can be created by using the SQL script in the file **c:\orant\rdbms80\admin\utlxplan.sql**. Refer to the *Oracle8 SQL Reference* for information on the EXPLAIN PLAN command.

Instance Tuning Scripts

All the standard SQL scripts for instance tuning are available with Oracle8 on Windows NT. They reside in the folder **c:\orant\rdbms80\admin**. These include **utlestat.sql**, **utlbstat.sql**, **utlchain.sql**, **utldtree.sql**, and **utllockt.sql**.

Performance Pack for Oracle Enterprise Manager

Oracle8 Server maintains comprehensive information about the state of the database in the data dictionary. In the past, DBAs were expected to write SQL statements or use Monitor to view statistics. This required them to learn intricate details about the data dictionary and write complex queries which can be time-consuming. Performance Pack (PP) is a set of applications and tools provided by Oracle Corporation that allow DBAs to obtain real-time information on database performance graphically. In this section, we will introduce the applications and tools available with PP.

Installation of Performance Pack

Oracle Installer can be used to install PP. Install the product component named "Oracle Enterprise Manager Performance Pack" by using a custom installation process. PP needs to be licensed separately and is not available with the standard Oracle8 media. No additional configuration is required after installation.

Performance Tuning Applications

As mentioned earlier, PP consists of a set of tools and utilities that allow DBAs to monitor performance graphically. We will now introduce the applications included in the performance pack.

Oracle Performance Manager

Oracle Performance Manager (OPM) allows DBAs to monitor database performance in real-time. Table 7-2 lists the methods to launch OPM.

Method	Procedure
OEM Console	1. Use shortcut for Performance Manager from the Performance Pack Toolbar. 2. Select Tools-> Performance Pack -> Oracle Performance Manager.
Program Group	Click on Start	Programs	Oracle Enterprise Manager	Performance Manager.
Oracle Administrator Toolbar	Create a shortcut to **c:\orant\bin\vmm.exe**.
Command Line	Execute **c:\orant\bin\vmm.exe**.

TABLE 7-2. *Launching Oracle Performance Manager*

OPM provides a graphical view for a variety of statistics. All statistics are available in pre-defined charts that can be displayed by using the Display menu. Table 7-3 provides a summary of charts built into OPM.

Display Menu Item	Description	Charts Available
Contention	Provides statistics related to contention	Circuit, Dispatcher, Free List Hit% Latch, Lock, Queue, Redo Allocation Hit %, Rollback NoWait Hit %, and Shared Server.
Database Instance	Usage statistics for the instance	Process, Session, System Statistics, Table Access, Tablespace, Tablespace Free Space, # Users Active, # Users Logged On, # Users Waiting, # Users Waiting for Locks, and # Users Running.
I/O	Input/output activity on the database	File I/O Rate, File I/O Rate Details, Network I/O Rate, and System I/O Rate.
Load	Information on database activity	Buffer Gets Rate, Network Bytes Rate, Redo Statistics Rate, Sort Rows Rate, Table Scan Rows Rate, and Throughput Rate.
Memory	Memory usage for the instance	Buffer Cache Hit %, Data Dict Cache Hit %, Library Cache Hit %, Library Cache Details, SQL Area, Memory Allocated, Memory Sort Hit %, Parse Ratio, and Read Consistency Hit %.

TABLE 7-3. *Statistics Available with Oracle Performance Manager*

Display Menu Item	Description	Charts Available
Overview	An overview of performance statistics (see Figure 7-15 below)	A variety of statistics for all round database performance
Parallel Server	Statistics for Oracle Parallel Server	Statistics include total block pings, block pings by tablespace, block pings by instance, File I/O rate, File I/O rate by file and instance, Lock activity, Sessions, User information
User Defined	Any user defined charts and tables	DBAs created charts and tables using SQL statements.

TABLE 7-3.   *Statistics Available with Oracle Performance Manager* (continued)

As seen in Table 7-3, OPM provides a comprehensive view of database performance for DBAs. Figure 7-15 shows a graphical overview of the performance statistics for our starter database.

OPM also allows DBAs to customize the charts. For example, if you are interested in monitoring free space in a particular tablespace, you can write your own query on the DBA_FREE_SPACE view and include that in OPM statistics.

Oracle Lock Manager
Oracle Lock Manager (OLM) allows DBAs to monitor locks on the database. You can obtain information on current locks and also get a listing of the sessions that are blocking or waiting for locks. While OLM provides information on locking across the database, Oracle Top Sessions allows you to get information on a specific session.

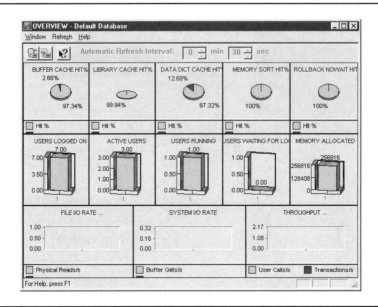

FIGURE 7-15. *Statistical overview of database performance*

Use a Oracle user with *SYSDBA* privileges to use OLM effectively.
Table 7-4 lists the methods that can be used to launch Lock Manager.

Method	Procedure
OEM Console	1. Use shortcut for Lock Manager from the Performance Pack Toolbar. 2. Select Tools-> Performance Pack -> Oracle Lock Manager.
Program Group	Click on Start	Programs	Oracle Enterprise Manager	Lock Manager.
Oracle Administrator Toolbar	Create a shortcut to **c:\orant\bin\vml.exe**.
Command Line	Execute **c:\orant\bin\vml.exe**.

TABLE 7-4. *Launching Oracle Lock Manager*

OLM allows you to view all locks acquired on the database or just the blocking or waiting locks. A sample screen from OLM is shown here:

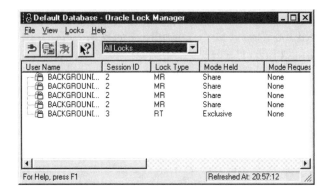

Oracle Top Sessions

While OLM allows you to view locks across the database, you can get complete session information using Oracle Top Sessions (OTS). The resources used by each session along with the activity can be viewed graphically using OTS. Furthermore, DBAs can choose to display information on the top *n* sessions which are using a resource of their choice or all the sessions. Table 7-5 provides information on launching OTS.

Method	Procedure
OEM Console	1. Use shortcut for Oracle Top Sessions from the Performance Pack Toolbar. 2. Select Tools-> Performance Pack -> Oracle TopSessions.
Program Group	Click on Start	Programs	Oracle Enterprise Manager	Top-Session Monitor.
Oracle Administrator Toolbar	Create a shortcut to **c:\orant\bin\vms.exe**.
Command Line	Execute **c:\orant\bin\vms.exe**.

TABLE 7-5. *Launching Oracle Top Sessions*

Figure 7-16 shows a screen that provides information on the top ten sessions on our test machine.

Again, you should use OTS with a user account that has *SYSDBA* privileges for maximum benefits. You should also create the PLAN_TABLE in the schema of the user *sys* by executing the script **c:\orant\rdbms80\ admin\utlxplan.sql** before using OTS.

Session details can be viewed and unwanted sessions can be killed using OTS.

Oracle Tablespace Manager

DBAs must closely monitor space usage on databases. The amount of space available in tablespaces and the usage of data files must be tracked regularly. Database fragmentation can impact performance and must be monitored. Oracle Tablespace Manager (OTM) allows DBAs to perform all necessary tasks with tablespaces. Table 7-6 provides information on the methods that can be used to launch OTS.

OTM interface is almost identical to Storage Manager, except that it provides a graphical view of the extents being used and also fragmentation. A tablespace analyzer is also included. Figure 7-17 shows a typical screen

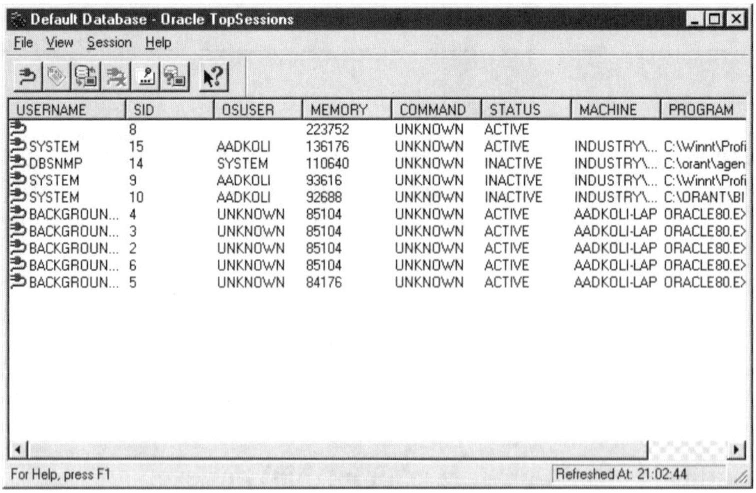

FIGURE 7-16. *Viewing session information using Oracle Top Sessions*

Method	Procedure
OEM Console	1. Use shortcut for Oracle Tablespace Manager from the Performance Pack Toolbar. 2. Select Tools-> Performance Pack -> Oracle Tablespace Manager.
Program Group	Click on Start | Programs | Oracle Enterprise Manager | Tablespace Manager.
Oracle Administrator Toolbar	Create a shortcut to **c:\orant\bin\vmt.exe**.
Command Line	Execute **c:\orant\bin\vmt.exe**.

TABLE 7-6.   *Launching Oracle Tablespace Manager*

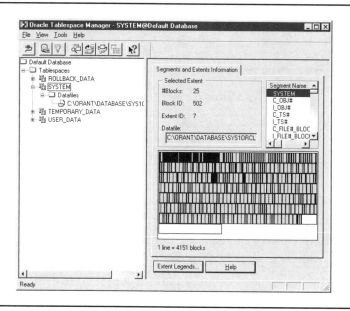

FIGURE 7-17.   *Obtaining tablespace information using Tablespace Manager*

from OTS that provides usage information on the *SYSTEM* tablespace on our starter database.

Oracle Trace

Oracle Trace is a utility that allows DBAs to capture database and Net8 traces. An API is also available for developers to pre-configure other products for Oracle Trace. A graphical interface called Trace Manager is also available. Table 7-7 provides a list of methods that can be used to launch Trace.

Oracle Trace requires a repository that can be created using Repository Manager. If a repository does not exist, you will see a dialog prompting you to create a repository within the user's schema. On Windows NT, you need to ensure that the Windows NT user launching Trace has been granted the right "logon as a batch job". Refer to the "Setting Preferred Credentials" section in Chapter 5 for further information on this topic. Oracle Trace can only use databases that have been discovered using OEM.

Oracle Trace allows you to pre-define events for a product that supports Oracle Trace API (Net8 and the database are supported as of now). Events are submitted in terms of *collections*. Once submitted, collections are submitted as jobs and can be tracked from the OEM console. Refer to Chapter 5 for more information on managing jobs through OEM.

Method	Procedure
OEM Console	1. Use shortcut for Oracle Trace from the Performance Pack Toolbar. 2. Select Tools-> Performance Pack -> Oracle Trace.
Program Group	Click on Start | Programs | Oracle Enterprise Manager | Trace.
Oracle Administrator Toolbar	Create a shortcut to **c:\orant\bin\epc.exe**.
Command Line	Execute **c:\orant\bin\epc.exe**.

TABLE 7-7. *Launching Oracle Trace*

Oracle Expert

Oracle Expert is a tool that can be used for database performance tuning. Oracle Expert uses historical information like trends to provide recommendations for database configuration. Poor performance is detected automatically and recommendations are provided. Oracle Expert can also help DBAs with *what-if* scenarios and allow them to learn about tuning. Table 7-8 provides information on launching Oracle Expert.

Oracle Expert has a wizard that will guide you through your tuning session. Information on the session can be saved as a named session. Data can be collected by repeated sampling of the database and then used to make recommendations. These recommendations can be accepted and even implemented from Oracle Expert directly. A dialog from the data collection process is shown here:

Method	Procedure
OEM Console	1. Use shortcut for Oracle Expert from the Performance Pack Toolbar. 2. Select Tools-> Performance Pack -> Oracle Expert.
Program Group	Click on Start	Programs	Oracle Enterprise Manager	Oracle Expert.
Oracle Administrator Toolbar	Create a shortcut to **c:\orant\bin\xpui.exe**.
Command Line	Execute **c:\orant\bin\xpui.exe**.

TABLE 7-8. *Launching Oracle Expert*

In the screen just shown, we have chosen to collect data every five minutes and compile statistics based on four samples. Information on the status of sampling can also be obtained from this dialog. You can also use Oracle Expert to analyze the instance.

Based on the data gathered, Oracle Expert will make recommendations for changes in your configuration. Figure 7-18 shows the list of changes recommended by Oracle Expert on our test database.

You can choose to accept the suggestions provided by Oracle Expert by clicking on the Implement tab. If you choose to do so, Oracle Expert will create an INIT.ORA file with the required changes.

Oracle8 Server Diagnostics

The Oracle8 Server provides some built-in diagnostic facilities. While DBAs can use this information to diagnose RDBMS-related issues, these diagnostics are more useful to developers and support analysts at Oracle Corporation. However, every DBA must be familiar with the utilities to

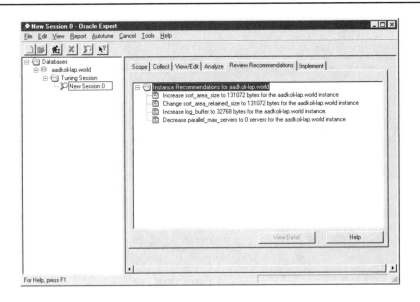

FIGURE 7-18. *Recommendations provided by Oracle Expert*

generate the required diagnostics. We will first look at the trace files
produced by the Oracle8 Server and then look at some diagnostic tools.

Oracle8 Server Trace Files

The Oracle8 Server for Windows NT maintains an alert file in the
\orant\rdbms80\trace folder. The name of the file has the format
<sid>alrt.log, where *sid* is the name of the database. For the starter database,
the file is named **orclalrt.log**. The file is commonly referred to as the
alert.log file in Oracle documentation. It is created automatically when
the database is created. A small section of this file is included here for
your reference:

```
Starting up ORACLE RDBMS Version: 8.0.4.0.0.
System parameters with non-default values:
  processes               = 59
  shared_pool_size        = 3500000
  control_files           = C:\orant\DATABASE\ctl1ORCL.ora
  db_block_buffers        = 200
  db_block_size           = 2048
  log_buffer              = 8192
  log_checkpoint_interval = 10000
  db_files                = 1024
  db_file_multiblock_read_count= 8
  sequence_cache_entries  = 10
  sequence_cache_hash_buckets= 10
  remote_login_passwordfile= SHARED
  global_names            = TRUE
  distributed_lock_timeout = 300
  distributed_transactions = 5
  mts_service             = ORCL
  mts_dispatchers         = (ADDRESS=(PARTIAL=YES)(PROTOCOL=tcp))
  (DIS=4)(SES=126)(CON=126)
(TIC=15)(POO=NO)(MUL=NO)(LIS=(address=(protocol=tcp)
(host=aadkoli-lap.us.oracle.com)(port=1521)))
  mts_servers             = 12
  mts_max_servers         = 12
  mts_max_dispatchers     = 4
  mts_listener_address    = (address=(protocol=tcp)
(host=aadkoli-lap.us.oracle.com)(port=1521))
  open_links              = 4
  audit_trail             = DB
  db_name                 = ORCL
```

```
    text_enable             = TRUE
    job_queue_processes     = 2
    job_queue_interval      = 10
    job_queue_keep_connections= FALSE
    parallel_max_servers    = 5
    background_dump_dest     = %RDBMS80%\trace
    user_dump_dest           = %RDBMS80%\trace
    max_dump_file_size       = 10240
Sat Sep 05 10:55:19 1998
PMON started with pid=2
Sat Sep 05 10:55:19 1998
DBW0 started with pid=3
Sat Sep 05 10:55:19 1998
LGWR started with pid=4
Sat Sep 05 10:55:20 1998
CKPT started with pid=5
Sat Sep 05 10:55:20 1998
SMON started with pid=6
Sat Sep 05 10:55:20 1998
RECO started with pid=7
Sat Sep 05 10:55:20 1998
SNP0 started with pid=8
Sat Sep 05 10:55:20 1998
starting up 12 shared server(s) ...
Sat Sep 05 10:55:20 1998
SNP1 started with pid=9
Sat Sep 05 10:55:21 1998
starting up 4 dispatcher(s) for network protocol
'(ADDRESS=(PARTIAL=YES)(PROTOCOL=tcp))'...
Sat Sep 05 10:55:22 1998
alter database  mount
Sat Sep 05 10:55:23 1998
Successful mount of redo thread 1.
Sat Sep 05 10:55:23 1998
Completed: alter database  mount
Sat Sep 05 10:55:23 1998
alter database open
Sat Sep 05 10:55:24 1998
Thread 1 opened at log sequence 24
  Current log# 4 seq# 24 mem# 0: C:\ORANT\DATABASE\LOG1ORCL.ORA
```

The **alert.log** file contains information on the INIT.ORA parameters with which the database was started. There are entries for each of the background processes that were started. Other information includes the thread that is being used by the instance and the log sequence number. If a tablespace or rollback segment is added or altered, information is recorded in this file. A timestamp is provided for each operation. A sample entry for a CREATE TABLESPACE operation is shown below:

```
create tablespace aud_tb datafile 'c:\orant\database\aud.ora' size 2m
Sat Sep 05 11:11:23 1998
```

Critical database errors are also logged in the **alert.log** file. You must routinely check the **alert.log** for such errors. You can configure Oracle Enterprise Manager to raise an alert via pager or e-mail when there is a critical error in the **alert.log** . Chapter 5 provides more information on this topic.

In addition to the **alert.log** file, a set of trace files is created for each background process. These files are created in the folder designated by the INIT.ORA parameter BACKGROUND_DUMP_DEST. The names of the files are of the format *<sid><process>.trc* on Windows NT. A listing of the trace files for the starter database from the **c:\orant\rdbms80\trace** folder is provided below:

```
C:\orant\RDBMS80\TRACE> dir orcl*.trc
  Volume in drive C is DRIVE_C
  Volume Serial Number is 3127-16CF
  Directory of C:\orant\RDBMS80\TRACE
09/05/98  10:55a                12,425 orclDBW0.TRC
09/05/98  10:55a                12,425 orclLGWR.TRC
09/05/98  10:55a                12,425 orclCKPT.TRC
09/05/98  10:55a                12,425 orclSMON.TRC
09/05/98  10:55a                12,425 orclRECO.TRC
09/05/98  11:49a                 5,425 orclPMON.TRC
09/05/98  10:55a                10,500 orclSNP0.TRC
09/05/98  10:55a                10,500 orclSNP1.TRC
08/31/98  09:17p                 1,750 orclARCH.TRC
```

Optionally, DBAs can get user trace files. User trace files must be enabled by setting the following INIT.ORA parameters:

```
sql_trace=true
user_dump_dest=%RDBMS80%\trace
```

User trace files on Windows NT have the format *oraxxxxx.trc* for their names and are created in the folder designated by USER_DUMP_DEST. A sampling of a user trace file is provided below:

```
Dump file C:\orant\RDBMS80\trace\ORA00219.TRC
Sat Sep 05 12:38:01 1998
ORACLE V8.0.4.0.0 - Production vsnsta=0 vsnsql=c vsnxtr=3
Windows NT V4.0, OS V5.101, CPU type 586
Oracle8 Enterprise Edition Release 8.0.4.0.0 - Production
With the Partitioning and Objects options
PL/SQL Release 8.0.4.0.0 - Production
Windows NT V4.0, OS V5.101, CPU type 586
Instance name: orcl
Redo thread mounted by this instance: 1
Oracle process number: 26
pid: db
Sat Sep 05 12:38:01 1998
*** SESSION ID:(9.12) 1998.09.05.12.38.01.350
====================
PARSING IN CURSOR #1 len=246 dep=0 uid=0 oct=42 lid=0 tim=0
hv=868647326 ad='bf6d4fc'
alter session set nls_language= 'AMERICAN' nls_territory=
'AMERICA' nls_currency= '$' nls_iso_currency= 'AMERICA'
nls_numeric_characters= '.,' nls_calendar= 'GREGORIAN'
nls_date_format= 'DD-MON-YY' nls_date_language= 'AMERICAN'
nls_sort= 'BINARY'
END OF STMT
```

Formatting Trace Files

The Oracle Server includes a utility named *TKPROF* that can be used to format user trace files. Execute **c:\orant\bin\tkprof80.exe** to access this utility on Windows NT. The usage is shown below for your reference, along with an example:

```
Usage: tkprof tracefile outputfile [explain= ] [table= ]
              [print= ] [insert= ] [sys= ] [sort= ]
  table=schema.tablename   Use 'schema.tablename' with 'explain=' option.
  explain=user/password    Connect to ORACLE and issue EXPLAIN PLAIN.
  print=integer    List only the first 'integer' SQL statements.
  aggregate=yes|no
  insert=filename  List SQL statements and data inside INSERT statements.
  sys=no           TKPROF does not list SQL statements run as user SYS.
  record=filename  Record non-recursive statements found in the trace file.
  sort=option      Set of zero or more of the following sort options:
```

```
   prscnt  number of times parse was called
   prscpu  cpu time parsing
   prsela  elapsed time parsing
   prsdsk  number of disk reads during parse
   prsqry  number of buffers for consistent read during parse
   prscu   number of buffers for current read during parse
   prsmis  number of misses in library cache during parse
   execnt  number of execute was called
   execpu  cpu time spent executing
   exeela  elapsed time executing
   exedsk  number of disk reads during execute
   exeqry  number of buffers for consistent read during execute
   execu   number of buffers for current read during execute
   exerow  number of rows processed during execute
   exemis  number of library cache misses during execute
   fchcnt  number of times fetch was called
   fchcpu  cpu time spent fetching
   fchela  elapsed time fetching
   fchdsk  number of disk reads during fetch
   fchqry  number of buffers for consistent read during fetch
   fchcu   number of buffers for current read during fetch
   fchrow  number of rows fetched
   userid  userid of user that parsed the cursor
C:\orant\RDBMS80\TRACE> tkprof80 ora00219.trc system.lis
TKPROF: Release 8.0.4.0.0 - Production on Sat Sep 5 12:49:35 1998
Copyright 1997 Oracle Corporation.  All rights reserved.
```

A portion of the formatted trace file output in the **system.lis** file created in our example is shown below:

```
TKPROF: Release 8.0.4.0.0 - Production on Sat Sep 5 12:49:35 1998
(c) Copyright 1997 Oracle Corporation.  All rights reserved.
Trace file: ora00219.trc
Sort options: default
********************************************************************
count    = number of times OCI procedure was executed
cpu      = cpu time in seconds executing
elapsed  = elapsed time in seconds executing
disk     = number of physical reads of buffers from disk
query    = number of buffers gotten for consistent read
current  = number of buffers gotten in current mode (usually for update)
rows     = number of rows processed by the fetch or execute call
**********************************************************************
alter session set nls_language= 'AMERICAN' nls_territory= 'AMERICA'
  nls_currency= '$' nls_iso_currency= 'AMERICA' nls_numeric_characters= '.,'
  nls_calendar= 'GREGORIAN' nls_date_format= 'DD-MON-YY' nls_date_language=
  'AMERICAN' nls_sort= 'BINARY'
call      count      cpu    elapsed       disk      query    current       rows
-------  ------  --------  ---------- ---------- ---------- ---------- ----------
Parse        3     0.00       0.00          0          0          0          0
```

```
Execute      3      0.00      0.00         0           0           0           0
Fetch        0      0.00      0.00         0           0           0           0
------- ------  --------  ----------  ----------  ----------  ----------  ----------
total        6      0.00      0.00         0           0           0           0
Misses in library cache during parse: 2
Optimizer goal: CHOOSE
Parsing user id: SYS
```

Trace Events

The Oracle8 Server also includes a feature that can be used to obtain diagnostic information based on an event. Events of interest can be tracked by adding parameters to the INIT.ORA or by using the ALTER SESSION command. This feature should always be used under the supervision of customer support representatives from Oracle Corporation. We are including an example here to help you with the usage.

Example: To set an event to obtain more information on the error "ORA-00604: error occurred at recursive SQL level num", add the following parameter to the INIT.ORA file:

```
event = "604 trace name errorstack forever"
```

Setting the above parameter would ensure that a dump of the error stack is provided every time a process encounters the ORA-604 error.

The same event can be set using the ALTER SESSION command, as shown below:

```
SVRMGR> alter session set events '604 trace name errorstack forever';
Statement processed.
```

Again, our goal is to help you save some time if and when it becomes necessary to enable trace events. You should not set trace events without the guidance of support analysts from Oracle Corporation.

Modifying the Starter Database

The database installed when you choose to perform a *typical* installation using the Oracle Installer is referred to as the starter database. The starter database has a name (or SID) of *ORCL* on Windows NT. While the starter database is fully functional and can be used right away, you should make a few modifications before using it in production. In this section, we will recommend some minimal modifications. We have also included examples based on our installation. We would like to point out that the changes we are proposing will need to be tailored further to satisfy the needs of your site.

Creating Starter Databases: Installer vs. Database Assistant

Before we begin, we would like to point out that there are some differences between the starter databases created with the Oracle Installer and the one created from Database Assistant. The starter database created during the installation is simply an image of a database on the Oracle media. The starter database created by Database Assistant has a different structure. The differences in the tablespace names are shown in Table 7-9.

In the following sections we have provided tips on modifications that you can make to the starter database before using it in production. We have used the starter database that was created during the installation in our discussion.

Change Passwords for Built-in Users

The first step should be to change passwords for the built-in users provided by Oracle Corporation. Use Security Manager to change the passwords of

Description	Tablespace in Starter Database Created by Oracle Installer	Tablespace in Starter Database Created by Database Assistant
For system objects	SYSTEM	SYSTEM
For rollback segments	ROLLBACK_DATA	RBS
For user objects	USER_DATA	USR
For temporary segments	TEMPORARY_DATA	TEMPORARY
For indexes	N/A	IDX

TABLE 7-9. *Tablespaces in Starter Database*

the users created on the starter database. At the very minimum, change the passwords for the users *SYS* and *SYSTEM*.

The password for the user *internal* should also be protected as this user has SYSDBA privileges. You can use the **oradim80** utility to reset the password for the user *internal*. We would like to remind you that this user is expected to be de-supported in version 8.1.

If required, you could create additional DBA-level users at this time. You should also create password files and set up external authentication based on the Windows NT operating system at this time.

Create Repositories

If you are planning to use Oracle Enterprise Manager (OEM), you should create the necessary repository. Decide on the owner of the repository and create the repository under this user's schema. You should not use the user *SYS* as the repository owner. If you are using OEM, ensure that the *preferred credentials* are set correctly. Chapter 5 provides information on this topic.

Mirror Control Files

The starter database on Windows NT has only one control file. For a production database, you must mirror the control files. Oracle Corporation recommends that you keep at least three copies of your control files on separate volumes (or even better, on separate physical hard disks) for redundancy. We will now walk through the process of mirroring control files.

Step 1   Shut Down the Database.
Shut down the database in *normal* or *immediate* mode using Instance Manager or Server Manager.

Step 2   Mirror the Control Files.
Use NT Explorer or the **copy** command to mirror the control files to the required locations. We will create one additional copy of the control file to the logical drive **d:** as shown below:

```
C:\orant\DATABASE> copy ctl1orcl.ora d:\orant\ctl2orcl.ora
          1 file(s) copied.
```

Note that the copy of the control file is named **ctl2orcl.ora** and it has been placed in the **d:\orant** folder.

Step 3 Edit the Parameter File.

Edit the parameter file and add the new control files created in step 2. Modify the **c:\orant\database\initorcl.ora** and ensure that the CONTROL_FILES parameter is set appropriately. The original and new settings for this parameter for our example are shown below:

```
control_files = C:\orant\DATABASE\ctl1ORCL.ora          - ORIGINAL SETTING
control_files = C:\orant\DATABASE\ctl1ORCL.ora, D:\orant\ctl2orcl.ora
                                                         - MODIFIED SETTING
```

Step 4 Start Up the Database.

Use Instance Manager or Server Manager to start up the database.

Tune the System Global Area

The Oracle database uses data structures in an area of memory called the System Global Area (SGA) to manage the database. The SGA impacts performance directly. Tune the SGA based on your needs by modifying appropriate INIT.ORA parameters (refer to the *Oracle8 Tuning* and *Oracle8 Reference* manuals for more information). We have provided a list of parameters that you should take into consideration for your site below:

```
db_block_buffers
shared_pool_size
log_checkpoint_interval
processes
log_buffer
audit_trail
max_dump_file_size
log_archive_start
log_archive_dest
log_archive_format
rollback_segments
remote_login_passwordfile
sql_trace
user_dump_dest
background_dump_dest
sort_area_size
sort_area_retained_size
```

If you are planning to use MTS, add the required parameters. We included a section on MTS earlier in this chapter.

NOTE
*The INIT.ORA for the starter database created
by Database Assistant is also slightly different
from the one created by Oracle Installer.*

Mirror Log Files

You should plan on mirroring online redo log files. This will help you in
performing complete recovery. The starter database provides four online
redo log groups, but they are not mirrored. We will step through the
process below.

Step 1   Mount the Database in Restricted Mode.
   Shut down the database in *normal* or *immediate* mode if it is running.
Mount the database in *restricted* mode:

```
SVRMGR> startup restrict mount
ORACLE instance started.
Total System Global Area        11705004 bytes
Fixed Size                         47788 bytes
Variable Size                   11173888 bytes
Database Buffers                  409600 bytes
Redo Buffers                       73728 bytes
Database mounted.
```

Step 2   Archive Log Files.
   If the database is in *archivelog* mode, archive the log files. Use Instance
Manager or the ARCHIVE LOG LIST command to determine this
information. We will use the SQL command as shown below:

```
SVRMGR> archive log list
Database log mode             Archive Mode
Automatic archival            Enabled
Archive destination           C:\orant\RDBMS80\
Oldest online log sequence    9
Next log sequence to archive  12
Current log sequence          12
```

   Since the database is in *archivelog* mode, we will archive the online
redo log files. If your database is not in *archivelog* mode, skip this step. If

there are no log files to be archived, you will get a message similar to the one shown below. Ignore this message.

```
SVRMGR> archive log all;
ORA-00271: there are no logs that need archiving
```

Step 3 Add the Log Members to All Four Groups.

You can now add log members to the log groups using the ALTER DATABASE command. Again, for redundancy, you should create log members on separate hard disks. For the starter database, you can only add one log member for each group as the maximum is set to 2 (the *maxlogmembers* clause in CREATE DATABASE).

```
SVRMGR> alter database add logfile member 'd:\orant\log1orcl.ora' to group 4;
Statement processed.
SVRMGR> alter database add logfile member 'd:\orant\log2orcl.ora' to group 3;
Statement processed.
SVRMGR> alter database add logfile member 'd:\orant\log3orcl.ora' to group 2;
Statement processed.
SVRMGR> alter database add logfile member 'd:\orant\log4orcl.ora' to group 1;
Statement processed.
```

Step 4 Open the Database.

Use Instance Manager or Server Manager to open the database.

Modify the Default Profile

The DEFAULT profile is automatically assigned to all users created on the database. You should customize the DEFAULT profile to your needs. Use Security Manager or the ALTER PROFILE command to modify the profile to suit your requirements. We have provided an example in the section titled "Password Management" earlier in this chapter.

Add and/or Modify Tablespaces

The starter database is provided with four tablespaces. You should add new tablespaces and/or modify existing ones to suit your needs. The default tablespaces have *maxextents* set to 121. You should consider changing this to *unlimited*. Storage Manager can be used to set this property for a tablespace. At the very least, you should set this property for the tablespace *SYSTEM*. Figure 7-19 shows a sample screen for the tablespace *SYSTEM*.

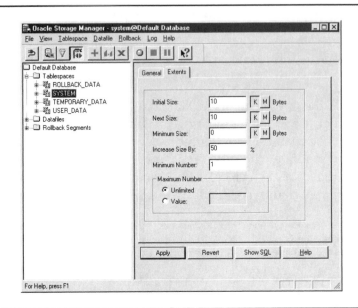

FIGURE 7-19. *Setting unlimited extents for a tablespace*

Add or Modify Datafiles

The starter database creates one datafile for each of the four tablespaces. Table 7-10 shows the datafiles created on the starter database along with their tablespace and sizes.

Datafile	Tablespace	Size (Mb)
c:\orant\database\sys1orcl.ora	SYSTEM	60
c:\orant\database\usr1orcl.ora	USER_DATA	8
c:\orant\database\tmp1orcl.ora	TEMPORARY_DATA	2
c:\orant\database\rbs1orcl.ora	ROLLBACK_DATA	10

TABLE 7-10. *Datafiles Created on the Starter Database*

Add new datafiles to tablespace if required. Also modify the *Auto Extension* property if required. Autoextension is enabled for all datafiles on the starter database.

Add or Modify Rollback Segments

The starter database is created with 18 rollback segments named *RB1* through *RB16*, *SYSTEM*, and *RB_TEMP*. Add, drop, or modify the rollback segments to suit your requirements. Note that you cannot drop the *SYSTEM* rollback segment.

Duplex Archived Log Files

In a production database, it is important to ensure that the archived log files are not lost at any time. Full recovery is not possible if the archived log files are not available. Use the parameter LOG_ARCHIVE_DUPLEX_DEST to duplex the archived log files. Again, you should set this parameter to a different disk drive, as shown below:

```
log_archive_duplex_dest=d:\orant
```

The default destination for archived log files for the starter database is **c:\orant\database\archive**.

Recovery Manager

You should consider using Recovery Manager (RMAN) for database backups at your site. If you have multiple databases, you should use RMAN with a recovery catalog. Recovery is much easier with the recovery catalog. We have discussed RMAN in Chapters 5 and 6. You should also refer to the on-line documentation by pointing your browser to the file **c:\orant\doc\database.804\a55928\ch5.htm**.

Creating Multiple Databases on the Same Machine

The Windows NT operating system can support multiple Oracle8 databases (instances) simultaneously. Separate services are created for each instance and can be managed separately. You can add multiple database services to the Net8 listener configuration by using Net8 Assistant. A sample **listener.ora** file for two database services on the same machine is shown below:

```
# C:\ORANT\NET80\ADMIN\LISTENER.ORA Configuration
File:C:\orant\net80\admin\listener.ora
# Generated by Oracle Net8 Assistant
PASSWORDS_LISTENER= (oracle)
LISTENER =
  (ADDRESS_LIST =
    (ADDRESS = (PROTOCOL = IPC)(KEY = oracle.world))
    (ADDRESS = (PROTOCOL = IPC)(KEY = ORCL))
    (ADDRESS = (PROTOCOL = IPC)(KEY = EXTPROC0))
    (ADDRESS = (PROTOCOL = NMP)(SERVER = AADKOLI-LAP)(PIPE = ORAPIPE))
    (ADDRESS = (PROTOCOL = TCP)(HOST = aadkoli-lap)(PORT = 1521))
    (ADDRESS = (PROTOCOL = TCP)(HOST = aadkoli-lap)(PORT = 1526))
    (ADDRESS = (PROTOCOL = TCP)(HOST = 127.0.0.1)(PORT = 1521))
    (ADDRESS = (PROTOCOL = IPC)(KEY = ORC0))
  )
SID_LIST_LISTENER =
  (SID_LIST =
    (SID_DESC =
      (SID_NAME = extproc)
      (PROGRAM = extproc)
    )
    (SID_DESC =
      (GLOBAL_DBNAME = aadkoli-lap)
      (SID_NAME = ORCL)
    )
    (SID_DESC =
      (GLOBAL_DBNAME = Oracle8)
      (SID_NAME = ORC0)
    )
  )
```

Note that the two SIDs (*ORCL* and *ORC0*) are listed separately in the list of SIDs for the listener. The listener is also configured to *listen* for new connections on two TCP/IP ports (1521 and 1526 in this example). Both databases can be accessed via any port. Alternatively, you could create a separate listener for each instance.

TIP
Set the environment variable ORACLE_SID to designate your default database.

Net8 Tracing

DBAs are frequently required to diagnose issues in a client/server environment. Additional diagnostic information to solve issues related to connectivity, security, and performance can be obtained from Net8 trace files. We must caution you that Net8 trace files are complex, and you will not be able to decipher all the information provided in a trace file. However, this information can be useful to support analysts and developers at Oracle Corporation and help them resolve customer issues.

Listener Tracing

Listener trace files can provide diagnostic information on Net8 listener. Three levels of tracing are defined: 1) user, 2) administrator, and 3) support. The information recorded in the trace files varies based on the level of tracing requested. User-level provides minimal information while support-level provides detailed information that can be used by Oracle support analysts. You can use the Net8 Assistant to enable listener tracing. Select the listener for which you want trace information and select General Parameters from the list box. Choose the Logging & Tracing tab and set the parameters for tracing as shown in Figure 7-20.

Be sure to save the network configuration and restart the Net8 listener after modifying the listener parameters. The trace setting for the listener is recorded in the **listener.ora** file. A typical entry is shown below:

```
TRACE_LEVEL_LISTENER = SUPPORT
```

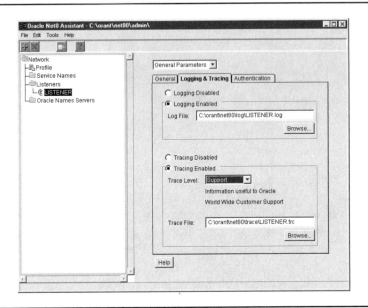

FIGURE 7-20. *Setting up listener tracing*

You can also control listener tracing by using the **trace** command in the *Listener Control* utility. The **status** command in the utility can also provide the current status of tracing. We provide a sample listing below for these features:

```
LSNRCTL> help trace
trace OFF | USER | ADMIN [<listener_name>] : set tracing to the specified level
LSNRCTL> trace off
Connecting to (ADDRESS=(PROTOCOL=TCP)(HOST=aadkoli-lap.us.oracle.com)(PORT=1521)
)
The command completed successfully
LSNRCTL> trace admin
Connecting to (ADDRESS=(PROTOCOL=TCP)(HOST=aadkoli-lap.us.oracle.com)(PORT=1521)
)
Opened trace file: C:\orant\NET80\trace\listener.trc
The command completed successfully
LSNRCTL> status
Connecting to (ADDRESS=(PROTOCOL=TCP)(HOST=aadkoli-lap.us.oracle.com)(PORT=1521)
)
STATUS of the LISTENER
-----------------------
Alias                   LISTENER
Version                 TNSLSNR80 for 32-bit Windows: Version 8.0.4.0.0 - Prod
uction
```

```
Start Date                04-SEP-98 14:24:54
Uptime                    0 days 0 hr. 6 min. 4 sec
Trace Level               support
Security                  ON
SNMP                      OFF
Listener Parameter File   C:\orant\NET80\admin\listener.ora
Listener Log File         C:\orant\NET80\log\listener.log
Listener Trace File       C:\orant\NET80\trace\listener.trc
Services Summary...
   EXTPROC                   has 1 service handler(s)
   ORCL           has 1 service handler(s)
The command completed successfully
```

You can use the **set** command in the *Listener Control* utility to configure the listener. We have provided some examples below:

```
LSNRCTL> help set
The following operations are available after set
An asterisk (*) denotes a modifier or extended command:
password            rawmode              trc_file
trc_directory       trc_level            log_file
log_directory       log_status           current_listener
connect_timeout     startup_waittime     use_plugandplay
save_config_on_stop
LSNRCTL> set trc_directory
Parameter Value: c:\temp
Connecting to
(ADDRESS=(PROTOCOL=TCP)(HOST=aadkoli-lap.us.oracle.com)(PORT=1521)
)
LISTENER parameter "trc_directory" set to c:\temp
The command completed successfully
LSNRCTL> show trc_directory
Connecting to
(ADDRESS=(PROTOCOL=TCP)(HOST=aadkoli-lap.us.oracle.com)(PORT=1521)
)
LISTENER parameter "trc_directory" set to c:\temp
The command completed successfully
```

Net8 Client and Server Tracing

Net8 also provides the facility for obtaining trace information separately on the server and the client. The settings are provided in the **sqlnet.ora** file. Net8 Assistant can be used to set tracing parameters for the client and server. Select the Profile node and choose to set the General parameters. Use the Tracing tab to set trace parameters and the Logging tab to set parameters for a log file. Figure 7-21 shows a sample screen from our installation.

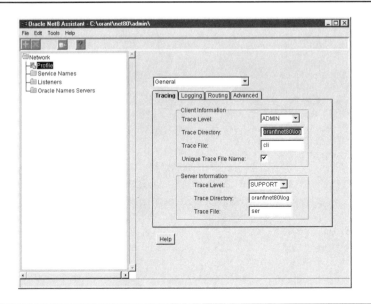

FIGURE 7-21. *Net8 client and server tracing*

Optionally, you can generate a unique trace file for each client. Again, three levels of tracing are defined: 1) user, 2) admin, and 3) support. The information recorded in the trace files varies depending on the level of tracing enabled. A section of the **sqlnet.ora** on our installation is provided below for your reference:

```
# Generated by Oracle Net8 Assistant
TRACE_DIRECTORY_CLIENT = c:\orant\net80\log
TRACE_UNIQUE_CLIENT = on
NAME.DEFAULT_ZONE = world
NAMES.DEFAULT_DOMAIN = world
TRACE_DIRECTORY_SERVER = c:\orant\net80\log
USE_DEDICATED_SERVER = on
TRACE_FILE_CLIENT = cli
TRACE_FILE_SERVER = ser
TRACE_LEVEL_CLIENT = ADMIN
TRACE_LEVEL_SERVER = SUPPORT
SQLNET.EXPIRE_TIME = 0
```

We would like to remind you that Net8 trace files are more useful to Oracle support analysts than to the average DBA.

Using Oracle 16-bit Applications Under Windows NT

Occasionally, some sites require running 16-bit Windows applications (MS-Windows 3.1) under Windows NT. You can use such applications against Oracle8; however, you will not be able to use Oracle8 features from such applications.

In order to use 16-bit applications, install SQL*Net Server version 2.x for Windows NT along with the necessary protocol adapters. The SQL*Net version 2.x service on Windows NT is named *OracleTNSListener*. Make sure that this service is started. Next, configure the SQL*Net version 2.x server by modifying the configuration files in the **c:\orant\network\admin** folder.

Install the 16-bit application(s) in a separate folder along with SQL*Net version 2.x for MS-Windows 3.1 (the default folder is **c:\orawin**) along with the necessary protocol adapters. Create the configuration files for SQL*Net for Windows 3.1 in the **c:\orawin\network\admin** folder. You will now be able to run 16-bit applications against Oracle8 Server.

CAUTION
*Ensure that the Net8 listener and the SQL*Net version 2.x listener are configured to use different ports, if you are using TCP/IP.*

Table 7-11 provides the compatibility matrix for 16-bit and 32-bit applications under Windows NT.

Scheduling Jobs Using Windows NT Scheduler

In Chapters 5 and 6, we have seen how Recovery Manager (RMAN) can be used to schedule backups. In this section, we will see cold backups can be scheduled using Windows NT Scheduler.

Tools	Windows NT Version 3.5x	Windows NT Version 4.x
Oracle 16-bit tools	Yes	No
Oracle 16-bit tools with 16-bit SQL*Net	Yes	No
SQL*Net 16-bit version 2.0 or higher	Yes	No
SQL*Net 32-bit version 2.2	Yes	No
SQL*Net 32-bit version 2.3.2 or higher	Yes	Yes
Oracle 32-bit tools	Yes	Yes
Oracle 32-bit tools with 16-bit SQL*Net	No	No
Oracle 32-bit tools with 32-bit SQL*Net	Yes	Yes
Oracle 16-bit tools with Net8	No	No
Oracle 32-bit tools with Net8	Yes	Yes

TABLE 7-11. *Oracle 16-bit and 32-bit Compatibility Matrix on Windows NT*

Step 1   Create a SQL script to shut down the database.
Create a file named **shutdown.sql** that contains the following:

```
connect internal/<password>
shutdown immediate
startup restrict
shutdown normal
exit
```

Step 2   Create a SQL script to start up the database.
Create a file named **startup.sql** which contains the following commands:

```
connect internal/<password>
startup
exit
```

Step 3   Create a batch file for the backup job.

Create a batch file named **orabak.bat** (or a command file with extension **.cmd**) that contains the following:

```
c:\orant\bin\svrmgr30.exe @shutdown.sql
backup c:\orant\database\*.* <target for backup>
c:\orant\bin\svrmgr30.exe @startup.sql
```

Step 4   Schedule the batch file for execution.

Schedule the batch file created in step 3 for execution at the desired time using the Windows NT Scheduler as shown below:

```
C:\ > at 02:00 c:\temp\orabak.bat
Added a new job with job ID = 0
Ensure that you have provided the full path to the batch file.  You can verify
if the job has been scheduled by using the at command as shown below:
C:\> at
Status ID   Day                    Time            Command Line
-------------------------------------------------------------------------------
        0   Tomorrow               02:00 AM        c:\temp\orabak.bat
```

We are using the **backup** command in Windows NT to create the backup. You could use an alternative command like **copy** to copy the files.

TIP
Provide complete path information to all the files in your scripts.

The Windows NT Scheduler (the **at** command) writes to the System log if there are any errors. Use Event Viewer to view the System log and ensure that there are no errors from your backup job.

CHAPTER
8

Database Upgrades and Migration

n the previous chapters, we covered a variety of topics that should be of interest to DBAs on Windows NT. In Chapter 3, we listed upgrades and migration as two of the major responsibilities of Oracle DBAs. In fact, upgrades and migration are so important that we felt that an entire chapter was warranted to cover these areas. We have discussed various issues related to upgrades and migration using case studies. We recommend that you browse all the case studies before you design your upgrade or migration strategy. This will allow you to adapt a method that works best for your site.

Migration vs. Upgrade

An upgrade involves a change of software from one minor release to the next. All Oracle software has a version number of the format A.B.C.D, where 'A' designates a major revision change (such as Oracle7 to Oracle8) and the remaining three digits represent enhancements, bug fixes, and porting changes. An upgrade is a change of the version of software involving the last three digits. An upgrade usually does not require any changes in existing applications and is a relatively simple process. A typical example of an upgrade is a change from Oracle8 Server version 8.0.3.0 to 8.0.4.0.

A migration is a change in the major version number (i.e., the first digit). A migration requires detailed planning and is a longer process as compared to an upgrade. A typical migration is a change from Oracle7 to Oracle8. Some Oracle documentation also uses the term migration when data is migrated from another platform (a change in port or operating system), or even a non-Oracle database. An example of a migration involving a port change is the migration of an Oracle database from UNIX to Windows NT. An example of a migration from a non-Oracle database is the migration of an MS Access database (an **.mdb** file) to an Oracle database.

As with the rest of this book, we will keep our focus on Windows NT as we cover upgrade and migration issues in this chapter. Again, we have looked at GUI-based as well as command-line interface (CLI)-based solutions. We will look at a typical upgrade from Oracle8 version 8.0.3 to 8.0.4 as well as a migration from Oracle7 to Oracle8. We have also covered migration options from other platforms using Export/Import and COPY in this chapter. At the end of the chapter, we have listed the options available for migration from non-Oracle databases.

Database Upgrades

As we mentioned at the beginning of this chapter, an upgrade involves a change in software to take benefit of enhancements or bug fixes. An upgrade does not involve a change in the first digit of the version number. For the purposes of our discussion, we will use an upgrade from Oracle8 Server version 8.0.3.0 to version 8.0.4.0 as an example.

An upgrade is best handled by using Database Migration Assistant (DMA) on Windows NT. There are two possibilities when such an upgrade is performed from version 8.0.3 to 8.0.4: 1) an upgrade performed while maintaining the existing directory structure, and 2) an upgrade performed while creating a new directory structure. We will look at both procedures in further detail.

NOTE
Windows NT uses the terms "folders" and "subfolders" to describe directories and subdirectories. We will use the terms interchangeably in this chapter.

Performing an Upgrade While Retaining Existing Structure

An upgrade with no changes in the directory structure is usually a trivial procedure. The procedure consists of four major steps:

1. Back up the existing database.

2. Upgrade the software.

3. Run upgrade scripts.

4. Test the upgrade.

If the results from the testing indicate that the upgrade had an adverse effect on some applications, you should be able to backtrack to the previous version.

One of the major pros of performing an upgrade into the same directory is that no additional space is required on the hard disk to maintain a second directory structure for the Oracle installation. Additional space is only required on a disk (or a tape) for the backup. If the upgrade fails, you simply need to restore the backup to maintain the status quo. A major pitfall in this kind of upgrade is that the downtime can be unnecessarily high. All users and applications will not be able to use the database during such an upgrade. If your site can afford some downtime (evenings or weekends), you should use this method since it is the simplest.

We will now illustrate an upgrade from Oracle8 version 8.0.3 to 8.0.4 into the same directory.

GUI Approach Using Oracle Enterprise Manager

You can use Oracle Enterprise Manager (OEM) or DMA to perform the upgrade using GUI. We will describe the procedure using OEM tools in this section and use DMA in the next section. If you do not have access to DMA, you can use the GUI-based procedure described below to perform an upgrade.

Step 1   Shut down the database.

The first step is to perform a normal shutdown of the database. A shutdown with the *IMMEDIATE* or the *ABORT* option will not work. You must also ensure that no datafiles or tablespaces are offline before you shut down the database. The sample session provided below lists the required steps:

Connect to the database as a privileged user with Instance Manager (IM) and shut down the database with the *IMMEDIATE* option. Mount the database again by using IM. Select Sessions | Restrict to ensure that no unprivileged users or applications can connect to the database. Open the database at this point in time.

Start Storage Manager (SM) and connect to the database as a privileged user such as *internal* with the *SYSDBA* role. Click on the Tablespaces node in the Navigator to get a listing of all the tablespaces belonging to the database. Note the names and the status of each tablespace. Ensure that all tablespaces are online. If there are any tablespaces listed as offline, bring them online using SM.

Expand the Datafiles node and get a listing of all the datafiles belonging to the database along with their status. Ensure that the status of all datafiles is either online or system. Again, use SM to bring datafiles online, if necessary.

Back in IM, select the node Initialization Parameters and choose the Instance Specific tab. Note the setting for the CONTROL_FILES parameter.

Using SQL Worksheet, connect to the database as a privileged user such as *internal* using the *SYSDBA* role. Use the following query to determine the online redo log groups and their members:

```
select group#, member from v$logfile;
```

Close the SQL Worksheet and Storage Manager sessions. Shut down the database from Instance Manager using the *NORMAL* option.

NOTE
We have assumed that the database to be migrated is not a part of a distributed system. If so, you must also ensure that there are no "in-doubt" transactions using IM.

Step 2   Create a backup.

Create a backup of all the files necessary to restore your system. If you have sufficient disk space (or space on a tape), create a backup of the entire Oracle directory structure (**c:\orant**), including all subdirectories. Ensure that you have included all the datafiles, log files, control files, and the parameter file for the database in the backup. If you do not have sufficient space to hold all this data, create a backup of just the datafiles, log files, control files, and the parameter file. If required, you can restore the Oracle software (version 8.0.3 in our example) using the distribution media.

Step 3   Back up the configuration files.

Create a backup of configuration files for Net8 and applications on your site. The Net8 configuration files are in the **c:\orant\net80\admin** folder. This is just a precautionary measure since the Oracle Installer will not typically overwrite the Net8 configuration files during the upgrade.

Step 4   Install the software upgrade.

Use Oracle Installer to install the software upgrade. In our example, install Oracle8 Server version 8.0.4 into the same folder as version 8.0.3. Oracle

Installer will overwrite a majority of the files. During the installation, choose the option that does not install a starter database (the radio button None). The version 8.0.4 software will be installed and the existing database will be preserved. New items will also be added to the Oracle program groups.

Step 5   Open the database in restricted mode.
   View the installation log file to confirm that the installation in Step 4 completed normally. Open the database in restricted mode using IM.

Step 6   Update the catalog.
   Connect as the user *internal* or the user *sys* and execute the **c:\orant\ rdbms80\admin\cat8004.sql** script. This script will upgrade your database catalog to version 8.0.4.0.

Step 7   Test the upgrade.
   Run the required tests to ensure that all the applications are functioning normally. Ensure that there are no invalid objects in the database by using the following query:

```
select * from all_objects where status='INVALID';
```

Step 8   Create a backup.
   Create a backup of the upgraded database. This is to ensure that you do not have to perform the upgrade procedure in case of a database failure that requires restoration from a backup.

Step 9   Open the database and track performance.
   Open the database for normal use. Keep a close watch on the performance and files such as the alert log for any abnormal behavior.

GUI Approach Using Database Migration Assistant

Database Migration Assistant (DMA) can also be used to perform upgrades. We will not discuss this procedure here as we have included a full section on DMA in the section titled "Performing an Upgrade into a New Directory Structure" later in this chapter. If you have DMA, this is a preferred method to OEM tools discussed in the previous section.

CLI Approach

We will use Server Manager (SVRMGR) to illustrate the procedure of a database upgrade from version 8.0.3 to 8.0.4 while retaining the Oracle directory structure.

Step 1   Shut down the database.

   Again the first step is to perform a normal shutdown of the database. A shutdown with the *IMMEDIATE* or the *ABORT* option will not work. You must also ensure that no datafiles or tablespaces are offline before you shut down the database. We provide a listing of a sample session below to perform a normal shutdown, along with the intermediate steps:

```
SVRMGR> connect internal/oracle
Connected.
SVRMGR> shutdown immediate
Database closed.
Database dismounted.
ORACLE instance shut down.
SVRMGR> startup restrict
ORACLE instance started.
Total System Global Area          8137388 bytes
Fixed Size                          47788 bytes
Variable Size                     7606272 bytes
Database Buffers                   409600 bytes
Redo Buffers                        73728 bytes
Database mounted.
Database opened.
SVRMGR> select tablespace_name,status from dba_tablespaces
     2> where status != 'ONLINE';
TABLESPACE_NAME                     STATUS
------------------------------ ---------
0 rows selected.
SVRMGR> select file_name,status from dba_data_files
     2> where status != 'AVAILABLE';
FILE_NAME STATUS
----------
 -------
0 rows selected.
```

   If any records are returned for the above queries to determine offline tablespaces or datafiles, you must bring them online before you perform the upgrade. You can use the ALTER TABLESPACE and ALTER DATABASE commands for this purpose, as shown below:

```
SVRMGR> alter tablespace temporary_data online;
Statement processed.
SVRMGR> alter database datafile 'c:\ora734\database\tmp1orcl.ora' online
```

Next, we will obtain a listing of all the datafiles and online redo log groups, along with log members and the control files, to ensure that the backup we create in the next step includes all the files belonging to this database.

```
SVRMGR> select file_name from dba_data_files;
FILE_NAME
--------------------------------------------
C:\ORA804\DATABASE\USR1ORCL.ORA
C:\ORA804\DATABASE\RBS1ORCL.ORA
C:\ORA804\DATABASE\TMP1ORCL.ORA
C:\ORA804\DATABASE\SYS1ORCL.ORA
4 rows selected.
SVRMGR> select group#, member from v$logfile;
GROUP#     MEMBER
---------- ---------------------------------
         1 C:\ORA804\DATABASE\LOG2ORCL.ORA
         2 C:\ORA804\DATABASE\LOG1ORCL.ORA
2 rows selected.
SVRMGR> select value from v$parameter where name like 'control_files';
VALUE
---------------------------------
C:\ORA804\DATABASE\ctl1orcl.ora
1 row selected.
```

Shut down the database using the *NORMAL* option. This is now possible as the database was opened in restricted mode and there should be no user sessions.

```
SVRMGR> shutdown
Database closed.
Database dismounted.
ORACLE instance shut down.
```

Again, we are assuming that the database is not part of a distributed system and that there are no in-doubt transactions.

Step 2   Create a backup.

Create a backup of all the files necessary to restore your system. If you have sufficient disk space (or space on a tape), create a backup of the entire Oracle directory structure (**c:\orant**), including all subdirectories. Ensure that you have included all the datafiles, log files, control files, and the parameter file for the database in the backup. If you do not have sufficient space to hold all this data, create a backup of just the datafiles, log files, control files, and the parameter file. You can always restore the Oracle software (version 8.0.3 in our example) using the distribution media.

Step 3   Back up the configuration files.

Create a backup of the configuration files for Net8 and applications on your site. The Net8 configuration files are in the **c:\orant\net80\admin** folder. The Oracle Installer will not overwrite the Net8 configuration files during the upgrade in most cases. However, this is just a precautionary measure.

Step 4   Install the software upgrade.

Use Oracle Installer to install the software upgrade. In our example, install Oracle8 Server version 8.0.4 into the same folder as version 8.0.3. Oracle Installer will overwrite a majority of the files. During the installation, choose the option that does not install a starter database (the radio button None). The version 8.0.4 software will be installed and the existing database will be preserved.

Step 5   Open the database in restricted mode.

View the installation log file to confirm that the installation in Step 4 completed normally. Open the database in restricted mode using Server Manager, as shown below:

```
SVRMGR> startup restrict
ORACLE instance started.
Total System Global Area        8137388 bytes
Fixed Size                        47788 bytes
Variable Size                   7606272 bytes
Database Buffers                 409600 bytes
Redo Buffers                      73728 bytes
Database mounted.
Database opened.
```

Step 6   Update the catalog.

Connect as the user *internal* or the user *sys* and execute the **c:\orant\ rdbms80\admin\cat8004.sql** script. This script will upgrade your database catalog to version 8.0.4.0. This script will run for 20 to 30 minutes, depending on your hardware.

```
SVRMGR> @c:\ora804\rdbms80\admin\cat8004.sql
DROP INDEX system.repcat$_repprop_dblink_how
*
ORA-01418: specified index does not exist
  ON system.repcat$_repprop (dblink, how, recipient_key)
         *
ORA-00942: table or view does not exist
ALTER TABLE system.repcat$_generated
*
ORA-00942: table or view does not exist
   CHECK (reason in (0, 1, 2, 3, 4, 5, 6, 7, 9, 10))
. . .
. . .
Statement processed.
Statement processed.
Statement processed.
0 rows processed.
4 rows processed.
Statement processed.
```

Step 7   Test the upgrade, create a backup, and monitor performance.

Test the upgrade for any abnormal behavior. Create a backup before opening the database to users. Monitor performance closely to ensure that the upgrade does not adversely affect any applications.

Performing an Upgrade into a New Directory Structure

There are many ways to perform the upgrade if you are installing the version 8.0.4 software into a new directory. The procedures for upgrade described in the previous section titled "Performing an Upgrade while Retaining Existing Structure" can also be adapted to perform an upgrade into a new directory structure. However, we will illustrate two new methods using DMA. DMA can also be used to upgrade into the existing Oracle directory. We would like to remind you that DMA is the preferred method.

Upgrading While Installing the New Version

If you are planning to install the new 8.0.4 version of the software into a new directory structure, the upgrade can be performed during the installation. We will step through the process here for your benefit.

Step 1 Shut down the database and create a back up.

Use the procedure described in the previous section to shut down the database in *normal* mode and create a full backup. As an alternative, you can create the backup using DMA itself as part of the procedure. The DMA Wizard will present you with an opportunity to do so.

Step 2   Upgrade software with Oracle Installer.

Use Oracle Installer to install the new 8.0.4 version into a new directory structure. During the installation process, Oracle Installer will detect the existing database automatically. You will be provided an option to use DMA to upgrade the database. If you elect to do so, DMA will take you through the procedure using a wizard. We will not describe the wizard here as we have detailed the wizard in the next section titled "Manual Upgrade using Database Migration Assistant". However, we will point out a couple of oddities.

During the installation, you will see a dialog box that provides a list of products that cannot be installed in more than one Oracle folder on the Windows NT machine. In other words, the same product cannot be installed under separate Oracle homes. The Oracle8 ODBC driver and the Oracle Migration Assistant for Microsoft Access are two such products. If you want to make these products available in the new Oracle directory structure, you must deinstall them from the old Oracle home before you perform the upgrade.

Another point to note is that Net8 Listener will not be started automatically for the upgraded version. This is to ensure that there are no conflicts (such as TCP/IP ports) between the configuration of the existing Net8 listener and the new one.

NOTE

You can run SQL*Net 2.x listener and Net8 listener simultaneously on the same machine. However, ensure that there are no conflicts between the listeners. If you are using TCP/IP, ensure that the two listeners are using different ports.

Separate program groups are automatically created by the Oracle Installer during this installation process. You can merge the existing and newly created program groups using Windows NT Explorer.

Step 3   Perform tests and create a backup of the new version.

After the upgrade, perform the necessary tests to ensure that there is no adverse effect and create a full backup.

If you wish to undo the changes of the database upgrade, refer to the section titled "Undoing an Upgrade" later in this chapter.

Manual Upgrade Using Database Migration Assistant

As we have seen in the previous section, Oracle Installer will automatically detect any existing databases and provide you with an opportunity to use DMA to perform the upgrade. If you choose to not do so, you can use the manual procedure described in this section to perform the upgrade.

NOTE
A good reason to not perform the upgrade during installation is to minimize downtime. You can ensure that the new version of the software is installed properly while the older version of the database is in use.

In any case, if you have chosen to not perform the database upgrade during the installation, you can use DMA as described here. We will use a sample installation that has Oracle8 Server version 8.0.3 installed in a directory named **c:\ora803,** with the new 8.0.4 version installed in the **c:\ora804** folder. Furthermore, the Oracle homes are named ORACLE_803 and ORACLE_804.

Start DMA and follow instructions provided by the wizard. Select the database that you want to migrate from the list detected by the wizard, as shown in Figure 8-1.

You will need to provide the password for the user *internal* as well as the location of the parameter file for the version 8.0.3 database. Next, you will

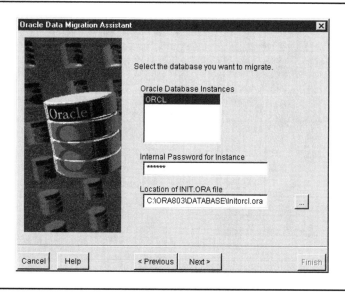

FIGURE 8-1. *Selecting a database for upgrade*

see an option where you can choose to move your database into a new location, as shown in Figure 8-2. Select this option since we want to move the database from the **c:\ora803\database** folder to **c:\ora804\database**.

DMA can create a backup of your existing database. You should select this option if you have not done so before starting this procedure. A sample screen with this option selected is shown in Figure 8-3.

DMA will provide you with a progress report during the upgrade. The procedure will take over 20 minutes for the starter database on version 8.0.3. A dialog box will confirm the end of the upgrade, followed by a screen that provides reports on the procedure. Figure 8-4 shows a sample of the screen from which you can view the reports.

The log files for DMA are created in the **c:\ora804\jre11\classes\dbmig** folder and are named **orclsummary.log** and **orclcat8004.log**. An option to backtrack to the original database is also provided. This is the button labeled Restore Backup Database, seen in Figure 8-4.

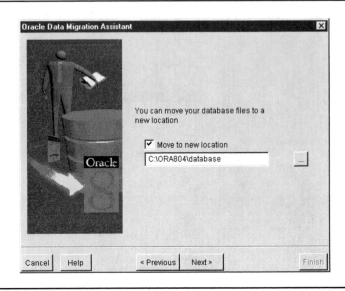

FIGURE 8-2. *Moving a database to a new location*

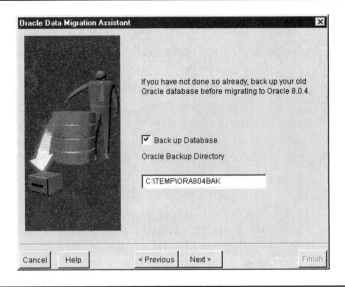

FIGURE 8-3. *Creating a backup during upgrade*

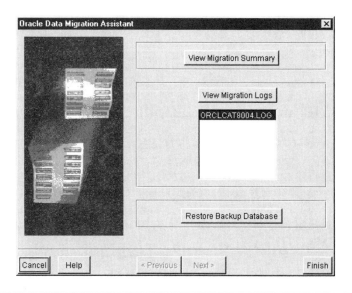

FIGURE 8-4. *Viewing logs and summary*

NOTE
*During the upgrade, the size of the datafiles may increase due to Auto-extension. Ensure that you have sufficient disk space to allow for such extension. If the Auto-extension feature is not enabled for the system datafile and the datafiles holding the rollback segments, the upgrade may fail if you do not have about 20Mb available in these tablespaces. We have provided a directory listing of our original 8.0.3 database and a listing for the 8.0.4 database after the upgrade. Notice the changed sizes of the system datafiles **sys1orcl.ora** and **rbs1orcl.ora**, the datafiles containing the rollback segments since Auto-extension was enabled on our database:*

```
C:\> dir c:\ora803\database\*.ora
  Volume in drive C is DRIVE_C
  Volume Serial Number is 3127-16CF
```

```
        Directory of c:\ora803\database
07/01/97   11:49a                   6,921  INITORCL.ORA
09/10/98   10:13a              20,973,568  SYS1ORCL.ORA
09/10/98   10:13a               3,147,776  USR1ORCL.ORA
09/10/98   10:13a               5,244,928  RBS1ORCL.ORA
09/10/98   10:13a               2,099,200  TMP1ORCL.ORA
09/10/98   10:13a                 205,312  LOG2ORCL.ORA
09/10/98   10:13a                 205,312  LOG1ORCL.ORA
09/10/98   10:13a               2,500,608  CTL1ORCL.ORA
C:\> dir c:\ora804\database\*.ora
 Volume in drive C is DRIVE_C
 Volume Serial Number is 3127-16CF
 Directory of c:\ora804\database
09/10/98   11:03a              31,459,328  SYS1ORCL.ORA
09/10/98   10:24a               3,147,776  USR1ORCL.ORA
09/10/98   11:03a              15,730,688  RBS1ORCL.ORA
09/10/98   10:24a               2,099,200  TMP1ORCL.ORA
09/10/98   11:03a                 205,312  LOG2ORCL.ORA
09/10/98   11:03a                 205,312  LOG1ORCL.ORA
09/10/98   10:23a                   6,973  INITORCL.ORA   for 8.0.4
09/10/98   10:24a               2,500,608  CTL1ORCL.ORA
```

After the database upgrade procedure is complete, ensure that the INIT.ORA file for the upgraded database has the proper compatibility parameter as shown below:

```
compatible = 8.0.4.0.0
```

All the features of the new version will not be available if this parameter is not set.

Undoing the Upgrade

If you want to undo the upgrade from 8.0.3 to 8.0.4, you can use the backup created by DMA. Click the Restore Backup Database button in DMA (see Figure 8-4) or use the batch file named **orclback.bat** that was created by DMA. The batch file will reside in the same folder that was used for the backup, **c:\temp\ora804bak**, in our example. You can run this batch program to undo the database upgrade. A sample run of this batch file is shown below:

```
C:\temp\ORA804BAK> orclback
C:\temp\ORA804BAK>rem
 -- Run this script to Restore Oracle Database Instance ORCL
C:\temp\ORA804BAK>oradim80 -delete -sid ORCL
C:\temp\ORA804BAK>ocopy80 C:\TEMP\ORA804BAK\Initorcl.ora
C:\ORA803\DATABASE\Init
orcl.ora
C:\ORA803\DATABASE\INITORCL.ORA
C:\temp\ORA804BAK>ocopy80 C:\TEMP\ORA804BAK\SYS1ORCL.ORA
C:\ORA803\DATABASE\SYS1
ORCL.ORA
C:\ORA803\DATABASE\SYS1ORCL.ORA
C:\temp\ORA804BAK>ocopy80 C:\TEMP\ORA804BAK\USR1ORCL.ORA
C:\ORA803\DATABASE\USR1
ORCL.ORA
C:\ORA803\DATABASE\USR1ORCL.ORA
C:\temp\ORA804BAK>ocopy80 C:\TEMP\ORA804BAK\RBS1ORCL.ORA
C:\ORA803\DATABASE\RBS1
ORCL.ORA
C:\ORA803\DATABASE\RBS1ORCL.ORA
C:\temp\ORA804BAK>ocopy80 C:\TEMP\ORA804BAK\TMP1ORCL.ORA
C:\ORA803\DATABASE\TMP1
ORCL.ORA
C:\ORA803\DATABASE\TMP1ORCL.ORA
C:\temp\ORA804BAK>ocopy80 C:\TEMP\ORA804BAK\LOG2ORCL.ORA
C:\ORA803\DATABASE\LOG2
ORCL.ORA
C:\ORA803\DATABASE\LOG2ORCL.ORA
C:\temp\ORA804BAK>ocopy80 C:\TEMP\ORA804BAK\LOG1ORCL.ORA
C:\ORA803\DATABASE\LOG1
ORCL.ORA
C:\ORA803\DATABASE\LOG1ORCL.ORA
C:\temp\ORA804BAK>ocopy80 C:\TEMP\ORA804BAK\CTL1ORCL.ORA
C:\ORA803\DATABASE\CTL1
ORCL.ORA
C:\ORA803\DATABASE\CTL1ORCL.ORA
C:\temp\ORA804BAK>oradim80 -new -sid ORCL -intpwd oracle -starttype srvc
-startmode auto -pfile C:\ORA803\DATABASE\Initorcl.ora
```

Manual Upgrade by Moving the Database Files to a New Location

Sometimes DBAs do not have access to OEM or DMA. In this case, a manual procedure can be used to upgrade from one version to another. This involves moving the database files to a new location and updating the control file with the changes. This procedure can be safely used for minor version upgrades (changes in the third or fourth digit of the version number) since a rebuild of the database is not required. We will illustrate this process with the use of the **c:\ora803** and **c:\ora804** folders from test installation.

Step 1   Create a backup of 8.0.3 database.

Use Windows NT Explorer or the **copy** command to create a backup of the database. Again, this is a cold backup and you must ensure that the database was shut down in *NORMAL* mode, and that there were no tablespaces and datafiles offline before shutting down the database.

Step 2   Copy the database files to the new location.

Query the data dictionary or use Storage Manager to obtain a listing of all the datafiles, online redo log groups, and control files for the 8.0.3 database. Copy the database files and the parameter file (INIT.ORA) to the new location for the 8.0.4 database:

```
C:\temp\ORA804BAK> copy *.ora c:\ora804\database
INITORCL.ORA
SYS1ORCL.ORA
USR1ORCL.ORA
RBS1ORCL.ORA
TMP1ORCL.ORA
LOG2ORCL.ORA
LOG1ORCL.ORA
CTL1ORCL.ORA
        8 file(s) copied.
```

Step 3   Modify the parameter file to point to the new control file.

Edit the INIT.ORA file to be used for the 8.0.4 database and modify the CONTROL_FILES parameter to point to the new location, as shown below:

```
control_files = C:\ORA804\DATABASE\ctl1orcl.ora
```

If you do not do this, you will continue to use the database files from the old location since the old control file has pointers to these files.

Step 4   Rename files for 8.0.3 database.

We will rename the database files belonging to the old 8.0.3 database just to avoid a situation where these files are used by mistake:

```
C:\ORA803\DATABASE>ren *.ora *.bak
```

Step 5   Mount the 8.0.4 database.

Mount the database using Server Manager. Note that the database cannot be opened because database files have been moved to a new location and the control file is yet to be updated:

```
SVRMGR> connect internal/oracle
Connected.
SVRMGR> startup nomount pfile=c:\ora804\database\initorcl.ora
ORACLE instance started.
Total System Global Area       8137388 bytes
Fixed Size                       47788 bytes
Variable Size                  7606272 bytes
Database Buffers                409600 bytes
Redo Buffers                     73728 bytes
SVRMGR> alter database mount;
Statement processed.
```

Step 6   Rename all the datafiles and log files.

In this step, we will update the control file with the new locations for the datafiles and the online redo log files (or log groups). The ALTER DATABASE RENAME command can be used to accomplish this, as shown below:

```
SVRMGR> alter database rename file 'c:\ora803\database\sys1orcl.ora' to
     2> 'c:\ora804\database\sys1orcl.ora';
Statement processed.
SVRMGR> alter database rename file 'c:\ora803\database\usr1orcl.ora' to
     2> 'c:\ora804\database\usr1orcl.ora';
Statement processed.
SVRMGR> alter database rename file 'c:\ora803\database\rbs1orcl.ora' to
     2> 'c:\ora804\database\rbs1orcl.ora';
Statement processed.
SVRMGR> alter database rename file 'c:\ora803\database\tmp1orcl.ora' to
     2> 'c:\ora804\database\tmp1orcl.ora';
Statement processed.
SVRMGR> alter database rename file 'c:\ora803\database\log1orcl.ora' to
     2> 'c:\ora804\database\log1orcl.ora';
Statement processed.
SVRMGR> alter database rename file 'c:\ora803\database\log2orcl.ora' to
     2> 'c:\ora804\database\log2orcl.ora';
Statement processed.
SVRMGR> alter database open;
Statement processed.
```

Step 7 Upgrade the database catalog.

Open the database in restricted mode and run a script to upgrade the database catalog to 8.0.4, as shown below:

```
SVRMGR> shutdown
Database closed.
Database dismounted.
ORACLE instance shut down.
SVRMGR> startup restrict pfile=c:\ora804\database\initorcl.ora
ORACLE instance started.
Total System Global Area          8137388 bytes
Fixed Size                          47788 bytes
Variable Size                     7606272 bytes
Database Buffers                   409600 bytes
Redo Buffers                        73728 bytes
Database mounted.
Database opened.
SVRMGR> @c:\ora804\rdbms80\admin\cat8004.sql
DROP INDEX system.repcat$_repprop_dblink_how
*
ORA-01418: specified index does not exist
  ON system.repcat$_repprop (dblink, how, recipient_key)
            *
ORA-00942: table or view does not exist
ALTER TABLE system.repcat$_generated
*
ORA-00942: table or view does not exist
    CHECK (reason in (0, 1, 2, 3, 4, 5, 6, 7, 9, 10))
. . .
. . .
Statement processed.
Statement processed.
Statement processed.
0 rows processed.
4 rows processed.
Statement processed.
```

The catalog upgrade should take 10 to 20 minutes.

Step 8 Create a backup, perform tests, and open the database.

Create a backup of the 8.0.4 database and perform the necessary tests to ensure that the applications are functioning properly. Monitor the performance and the **alert.log** file for any abnormal behavior. Open the database for normal use if everything looks normal.

Note that you must ensure that all the packages are available for use when you perform an upgrade. Use the following query to ensure that there are no objects that are 'invalid':

```
SELECT * FROM ALL_OBJECTS WHERE STATUS = 'INVALID';
```

If any packages are reported as 'invalid', use the ALTER PACKAGE command to recompile the package body or the package using the statements shown below:

```
ALTER PACKAGE <name> COMPILE PACKAGE;
ALTER PACKAGE <name> COMPILE BODY;
```

Migration on Windows NT

A migration involves a major version change, as in Oracle7 to Oracle8. Special precautions should be taken to ensure that the migration is performed with minimal downtime. Adequate backups must be created to ensure that you can abort the migration and get back to a point where the existing (older) version works normally. We will look at the migration options available on Windows NT in this section.

NOTE
Some Oracle documentation and text books also use the term "migration" to port a database from one operating system to another. We will also look at this process later in this chapter.

In all our discussions relating to migration, we will use a sample configuration that consists of an Oracle7 Server version 7.3.4 installed in the folder **c:\ora734**. We will use Oracle8 Server Enterprise Edition version 8.0.4 in our migration.

We begin with the migration options using Database Migration Assistant (DMA) and the Migration utility. These are the preferred methods to migrate an Oracle7 database on Windows NT to Oracle8. You can use Export/Import and the COPY methods, but these are much slower and are typically used while migrating from Oracle7 on other platforms to Oracle8 on Windows NT. We will cover these methods later in this chapter.

Performing a Migration While Retaining Existing Structure

The easiest migration process is to install Oracle8 Server in the same directory as the existing Oracle7 installation. Use this method if you want to use a single ORACLE_HOME on your machine. You should also use this method if you are planning to keep the existing Oracle7 installation intact for a while after installing Oracle8 Server. If you are planning to delete the Oracle7 installation after the migration to Oracle8 is complete, we recommend that you install Oracle8 Server into a different folder. This will allow you to save some disk space since you can clean up the Oracle7 installation.

NOTE
You must have Oracle7 version 7.1.3.3 or higher to migrate in one step to Oracle8 Server. If you have an older version of Oracle7 Server (including Oracle version 6.x), upgrade to a version of Oracle7 higher than 7.1.3 and then migrate to Oracle8.

BEFORE YOU BEGIN THE MIGRATION Create a full backup of your Oracle7 database. You must perform a normal shutdown after ensuring that there are no offline tablespaces or datafiles. You will also be given an opportunity to create a backup of your database if you are using DMA for the migration.

Also ensure that SQL*Net version 2.x Server is installed with the Oracle7 database as this will be required during the migration. You must ensure that the Oracle service for Oracle7 is available.

Performing the Migration During Installation

Use Oracle Installer from the Oracle8 Server media to install version 8.0.4 of the software. Choose to install Oracle8 software into the same Oracle home (the folder **c:\ora734** in our example). The Oracle8 installation will not overwrite any files from the Oracle7 installation as the file and folder names are completely unique in the two versions. Oracle Installer will automatically detect the Oracle7 Server and you should see a dialog box similar to the one shown here:

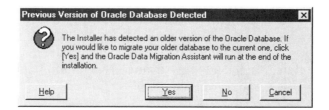

Database Migration Assistant (DMA) can automatically migrate your Oracle7 database to Oracle8 version 8.0.4. Select Yes if you want to use DMA for the migration. At the end of the installation of Oracle8 Enterprise Edition, the DMA Wizard will guide you through the migration. If you want to manually migrate your Oracle7 database at a later point in time, or if you want to create a fresh database using Oracle8, select No at this time. We will discuss these procedures in the later sections.

The migration procedure will give you an opportunity to move your database to a new directory. Do not select this option because we want the Oracle8 database to be created in the same folder(s) as the Oracle7 database. Optionally, you can also create a backup during the migration. DMA automatically upgrades the database catalog.

We have not provided details on the DMA Wizard here because the "Manual Migration Using Database Migration Assistant" section later in this chapter provides complete details.

You should create another backup soon after the migration is completed successfully. This will ensure that you can restore your database in Oracle8 directly, if necessary.

Manual Migration Using Database Migration Assistant

The Oracle8 Enterprise Edition provides a GUI utility called Database Migration Assistant that can be used to manually migrate from Oracle7 to Oracle8. In order to use this, you must have not used DMA to perform the migration during the installation of Oracle8 software (during automatic detection, as shown in the previous illustration).

Start DMA from the Oracle8 program group. The wizard will guide you through the migration. You will be provided a screen with a list of the databases detected on the machine, as shown in Figure 8-5.

You will need to provide the password for the user *internal* as well as the location of the INIT.ORA file for the Oracle7 database.

Next, you will be provided an opportunity to change the location of the database. Since we are not changing the location of the database, do not select this option. If you want to change the name of the database (from *ORCL* to something else), click the Advanced Migration Parameters button to provide the new name, as shown here:

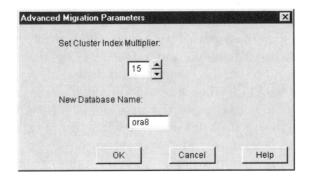

You will then be given an opportunity to create a backup of the database. If you choose to create a backup, provide a directory location after ensuring that there is sufficient disk space for the backup. Click on the Finish button to begin the migration. At the end of the procedure, you will be given an opportunity to view the logs created during the migration. The logs are available in the **c:\ora734\jre11\classes\dbmig** folder. If you chose to create a backup during the procedure, a batch file named **orclback.bat** was created for you. This batch file can be used to revert to the Oracle7 installation.

Manual Migration Using Database Migration Utility

Oracle8 Server also includes a Migration utility that can be used to migrate from Oracle7 to Oracle8 using CLI. The executable on Windows NT is named **mig80.exe**. In this section, we will see how this utility can be used to perform a migration from Oracle7 to Oracle8. Again, we will use our test installation of Oracle7 version 7.3.4 installed in the **c:\ora734** folder and migrate the database to Oracle8 version 8.0.4.

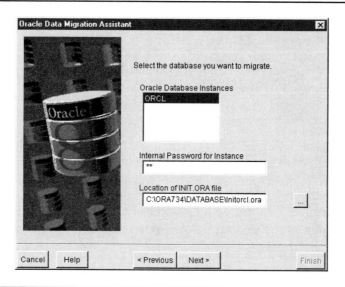

FIGURE 8-5. *Choosing database for migration*

NOTE
*While most of these tasks can be accomplished
using Oracle Enterprise Manager, we will use
CLI throughout this example.*

We recommend that you use only one session to complete all these tasks. Opening multiple sessions with privileged user accounts can adversely impact this procedure.

Step 1 Shut down the Oracle7 database.
You must shut down the database using the *NORMAL* option. If you shut down the database using the *IMMEDIATE* or the *ABORT* option, start up the database in restricted mode and shut down again as shown below:

```
SVRMGR> connect internal/oracle
Connected.
SVRMGR> shutdown immediate
Database closed.
Database dismounted.
ORACLE instance shut down.
```

```
SVRMGR> startup restrict
ORACLE instance started.
Total System Global Area          8137388 bytes
Fixed Size                          47788 bytes
Variable Size                     7606272 bytes
Database Buffers                   409600 bytes
Redo Buffers                        73728 bytes
Database mounted.
Database opened.
```

Step 2   Ensure that no tablespaces and datafiles are offline.

You must ensure that all tablespaces and datafiles that you are concerned with are online before the migration. Tablespaces and datafiles that are not online will not be migrated to Oracle8. Use queries similar to the ones shown in the session below to determine the status of the tablespaces and datafiles:

```
SVRMGR> select tablespace_name,status from dba_tablespaces
2> where status != 'ONLINE';
TABLESPACE_NAME                    STATUS
------------------------------     ---------
0 rows selected.
SVRMGR> select file_name,status from dba_data_files
    2> where status != 'AVAILABLE';
FILE_NAME                                      STATUS
----------------------------------------       -------
0 rows selected.
```

If any records are returned for the above queries and there are tablespaces or datafiles determined to be offline, you must bring them online before you perform the upgrade. You can use the ALTER TABLESPACE and ALTER DATABASE commands for this purpose, as shown below:

```
SVRMGR> alter tablespace temporary_data online;
Statement processed.
SVRMGR> alter database datafile 'c:\ora734\database\tmp1orcl.ora' online
```

Replace the above commands with the names of your tablespaces and datafiles.

Step 3 Obtain a listing of all files related to the database.

Next, we will obtain a listing of all the datafiles and online redo log groups, along with log members and the control files, to ensure that the backup we create in the next step includes all the files belonging to this database. You can use queries similar to the ones shown below:

```
SVRMGR> select file_name from dba_data_files;
FILE_NAME
---------------------------------------------------
C:\ORA734\DATABASE\USR1ORCL.ORA
C:\ORA734\DATABASE\RBS1ORCL.ORA
C:\ORA734\DATABASE\TMP1ORCL.ORA
C:\ORA734\DATABASE\SYS1ORCL.ORA
4 rows selected.
SVRMGR> select group#,member from V$logfile;
GROUP#     MEMBER
---------- ---------------------------------------
         2 C:\ORA734\DATABASE\LOG3ORCL.ORA
         2 C:\ORA734\DATABASE\LOG4ORCL.ORA
         1 C:\ORA734\DATABASE\LOG1ORCL.ORA
         1 C:\ORA734\DATABASE\LOG2ORCL.ORA
4 rows selected.
SVRMGR> select value from v$parameter where name like 'control_files';
VALUE
--------------------------------------------------------------------
C:\ORA734\DATABASE\ctl1orcl.ora, C:\ORA734\DATABASE\ctl2orcl.ora
1 row selected.
```

Step 4 Shut down the database.

Shut down the database using the *NORMAL* option. This should be possible because there are no user sessions since we started the database in restricted mode.

```
SVRMGR> shutdown
Database closed.
Database dismounted.
ORACLE instance shut down.
```

We are assuming that the database is not part of a distributed system and that there are no in-doubt transactions.

Step 5   Create a backup.

Create a backup of all the files necessary to restore your system. If you have sufficient disk space (or space on a tape), create a backup of the entire Oracle directory structure (**c:\ora734**), including all subdirectories. Ensure that you have included all the datafiles, log files, control files, and the parameter file for the database in the backup. If you do not have sufficient space to hold all this data, create a backup of just the datafiles, log files, control files, and the parameter file. You can restore the Oracle software (version 7.3.4 in our example) using the distribution media.

Step 6   Back up configuration files.

Create a backup of configuration files for SQL*Net and applications on your site. The SQL*Net configuration files are in the **c:\ora734\network\ admin** folder. The Oracle Installer will not overwrite the SQL*Net configuration files during the upgrade. This is just a precautionary measure.

Step 7   Install the new version of the software.

Use Oracle Installer to install the new software version. In our example, install Oracle8 Server version 8.0.4 into the folder **c:\ora734**. The installer should detect the existing Oracle7 database and will recommend that you perform the migration using DMA. Ignore this option as we are using **mig80.exe**. During the installation, also choose the option that does not install a starter database (the radio button None). The version 8.0.4 software will be installed and we can use the Migration utility to migrate the Oracle7 database.

Step 8   Ensure that the Oracle7 database is shut down.

Ensure that the Oracle7 is not running. The Migration utility expects to find the database shut down. It will start up the database automatically when required.

Step 9   Start the Oracle service.

Start the Oracle service using the Services applet or from the command line as shown below:

```
C:\ORA734\BIN> net start oracleserviceorcl
The OracleServiceORCL service is starting.
The OracleServiceORCL service was started successfully.
```

Note that *orcl* is the SID of our database. Replace this with the name of your database, if necessary. Also ensure that the ORACLE_SID environment variable is set to the name of the database that you wish to migrate, as shown below:

```
C:\ORA734\BIN> set oracle_sid=orcl
```

Step 10   Run the Migration utility.

Use the Migration utility to perform the migration. You will need to provide the location of the parameter file for the Oracle7 database (this is not required if both Oracle7 and Oracle8 are installed in the same directory). You will need the password for the user *internal* to complete this procedure.

Execute **mig80.exe** to start the utility. A help option is also available, as seen below:

```
C:\ORA804\BIN> mig80 help=yes
ORACLE7 to ORACLE8 Migration Utility Release 8.0.4.0.0 - Production
command line arguments:
 PFILE              - use alternate init.ora
 SPOOL              - spool output to file
 CHECK_ONLY         - estimate V8 catalog space requirement ONLY (default=FALSE)
 NO_SPACE_CHECK     - do not execute the space check (default=FALSE)
 DBNAME             - current database name (db_name in init.ora)
 NEW_DBNAME         - new database name (max. 8 characters)
 MULTIPLIER         - seg$/uet$ cluster index size increase factor (default=15)
 NLS_NCHAR          - specify the nchar characterset value
```

The Migration utility needs to fit the catalogs for Oracle7 and Oracle8 into the SYSTEM tablespace during the migration. You should ensure that the SYSTEM tablespace has sufficient room before starting the migration. You can do so by using the *CHECK_ONLY* option as shown below:

```
C:\> mig80 pfile=c:\ora734\database\initorcl.ora spool=c:\temp\mig.txt
check_only=true
estimated space requirement for V8 version of V7 catalog objects is 4534 blocks
estimated space requirement for new V8 catalog objects is 395 blocks
estimated space requirement for total V8 catalog is 5001 blocks
free space found in system tablespace is 973 blocks
insufficient space for new dictionaries, 10242048 bytes needed, 1992704 found
) v8 catalog space requirement:  10242048
free space found:  1992704
```

As seen in the above output, about 10Mb (10,242,048 bytes to be precise) of additional space is required in the SYSTEM tablespace to hold the new dictionaries. Add space by starting the database and adding a new datafile to the SYSTEM space using Storage Manager or the ALTER TABLESPACE command shown below:

```
alter tablespace system add datafile <file name> size <number>;
```

During the migration process, the rollback segments also expand considerably. Ensure that the tablespace containing your rollback segments has at least 20Mb of free space. You can use a query similar to the one shown below to determine the free space in your tablespace containing rollback segments:

```
select sum(bytes) from dba_free_space where tablespace_name
='ROLLBACK_DATA';
```

We will run the Migration utility and choose to retain the database name, as shown below:

```
C:\> mig80 pfile=c:\ora734\database\initorcl.ora spool=c:\temp\mig.txt
starting up database ...
ORACLE7 password:
mounting database ...
opening  database ...
#^ connect (internal)
drop table grant_mig_priv$;
create table grant_mig_priv$ (
  name   varchar2("M_IDEN"),
  owner varchar2("M_IDEN"),
  grantorname    varchar2("M_IDEN"),          /* grantor user number */
  granteename    varchar2("M_IDEN"),          /* grantee user number */
  privilege#   number not null,            /* table privilege number */
  sequence#    number not null,             /* unique grant sequence */
  parent       rowid,                                    /* parent */
  option$      number,                /* null = none, 1 = grant option */
  col#         number);    /* null = table level, column id if column grant */
. . .
. . .
update ts$ set inc# = (select inc# from sys.ts$ where name = 'SYSTEM')
where name = 'SYSTEM';
#^ connect (internal)
shutting down database ...
```

The above procedure should run for 20 to 30 minutes, depending on the speed of your machine. Use the *new_dbname* parameter when you issue the above command if you wish to change the name of your database.

Step 11 Shut down and delete the Oracle7 service.

Use the Services applet or the **net stop** command to shut down the Oracle services. Use **oradim73.exe** to delete the Oracle7 service, as shown below:

```
C:\> oradim73 -delete -sid orcl
```

NOTE
*The name of the **oradimxx.exe** program is version dependent. Replace **xx** with the version of Oracle7 that you have installed—for example, **oradim72.exe** on version 7.2 and **oradim71.exe** for version 7.1.*

Step 12 Check the parameter file for Oracle8.

Modify any INIT.ORA parameters you want at this time. For example, if you have chosen to install new options and cartridges in Oracle8, you will need to increase the size of the shared pool. Also, ensure that the compatibility is set for the new Oracle8 database, as shown below:

```
compatible = 8.0.4.0.0
```

Step 13 Create new Oracle8 services.

Use **oradim80** to create new Oracle services:

```
C:\> oradim80 -new -startmode auto -pfile c:\ora734\database\inito
rcl.ora -sid orcl -intpwd aa -starttype srvc
```

Use the Services applet under the Control Panel to ensure that the service was created. You will need to start the Oracle8 service at this time.

Step 14 Start the instance and convert the database.

Start the Oracle8 instance and convert the database as shown below. Note that we are using Server Manager 3.0 in this step.

CAUTION
*Do not mount or open the database at this time
or it could get corrupted.*

```
C:\> svrmgr30
Oracle Server Manager Release 3.0.4.0.0 - Production
(c) Copyright 1997, Oracle Corporation.  All Rights Reserved.
Oracle8 Enterprise Edition Release 8.0.4.0.0 - Production
PL/SQL Release 8.0.4.0.0 - Production
SVRMGR> connect internal/oracle
Connected.
SVRMGR> startup nomount
ORACLE instance started.
Total System Global Area         7727788 bytes
Fixed Size                         47788 bytes
Variable Size                    7196672 bytes
Database Buffers                  409600 bytes
Redo Buffers                       73728 bytes
SVRMGR> alter database convert;
Statement processed.
```

You must open the database with the *RESETLOGS* option as shown below:

```
SVRMGR> alter database open resetlogs;
Statement processed.
```

Step 15   Run scripts to upgrade catalog.
   A few scripts must be run in order to upgrade the catalog. At the minimum, run the two scripts mentioned below:

```
SVRMGR> @c:\ora734\rdbms80\admin\cat8000.sql
SVRMGR> @c:\ora734\dbs\pupbld.sql
```

The **cat8000.sql** script will run for over 30 minutes. If you are using advanced replication, you must also run **catrep8m.sql** at this time. Similarly, run **catparr.sql** for the Parallel Server.

Step 16   Check for invalid objects.
   Query the ALL_OBJECTS view to get a listing of invalid objects on the newly created database. You can use the following query:

```
select object_name,object_type from all_objects where status='INVALID';
```

Fix any issues with invalid objects. You can use the ALTER PACKAGE command to recompile any packages or package bodies that are not valid.

Step 17   Shut down the database and create a backup.

Shut down the newly created version 8.0.4 database in normal mode. Do not use the *immediate* or *abort* option at this time. It is important that the database be shut down normally to preserve integrity and consistency. Schedule a full backup using your preferred method. A backup is highly recommended since we have opened the database with the *resetlogs* option.

Step 18   Delete the Oracle7 installation.

Remove the Oracle7 services using **oradim73.exe** and deinstall the Oracle7 software using Oracle Installer.

Performing a Migration into a New Directory Structure

If you are planning to remove your Oracle7 installation after a successful migration to Oracle8, you should install Oracle8 into a new directory structure (or Oracle home). This will allow you to remove the Oracle7 directory structure completely and save some disk space. All the migration methods discussed in the previous section can be adapted to create a new directory structure for the Oracle8 Server. We will review the options briefly.

Migration During Installation

Use Oracle Installer to install Oracle8 Server into a new Oracle home. The installer will detect the existing Oracle7 database and give you an opportunity to migrate the database to the new Oracle home. This is the easiest method to use if you have access to DMA. Ensure that you select the option to move the database to a new location as shown in Figure 8-6. You should also select the option to create a backup of the Oracle7 database.

Manual Migration with Database Migration Assistant

Install Oracle8 into the new Oracle home. Do not use DMA to migrate the Oracle7 database during installation. Also, do not create a starter database during this installation. Start DMA and follow the instructions provided by the wizard to perform the migration. Again, ensure that you select the option to move the database to a new location, as shown in Figure 8-6.

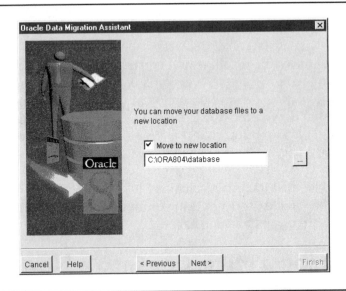

FIGURE 8-6. *Moving a database to a new location*

Manual Migration Using the Migration Utility

Install Oracle8 Server into the new directory structure and follow
instructions for a manual upgrade into the same directory, as detailed
previously in this chapter. Once the Oracle8 database is created in the same
directory structure, you can move it to a new location using the steps below:

Step 1 Copy the database files to the new location.

Query the data dictionary or use Storage Manager to obtain a listing of
all the datafiles, online redo log groups, and control files for the 7.3.4
database. Copy the database files and the parameter file (INIT.ORA) to the
new location for the 8.0.4 database:

```
C:\ora734\database> copy *.ora c:\ora804\database
INITORCL.ORA
SYS1ORCL.ORA
USR1ORCL.ORA
RBS1ORCL.ORA
TMP1ORCL.ORA
LOG2ORCL.ORA
```

```
LOG1ORCL.ORA
CTL1ORCL.ORA
        8 file(s) copied.
```

Step 2 Modify the parameter file to point to the new control file.

Edit the INIT.ORA file to be used for the 8.0.4 database and modify the CONTROL_FILES parameter to point to the new location, as shown below:

```
control_files = C:\ORA804\DATABASE\ctl1orcl.ora
```

Step 3 Rename files for 7.3.4 database.

We will rename the database files belonging to the old 7.3.4 database just to avoid a situation where these files are used by mistake in the following steps:

```
C:\ORA734\DATABASE>ren *.ora *.bak
```

Step 4 Mount the 8.0.4 database.

Mount the database using Server Manager. Note that the database cannot be opened as database files have been moved to a new location.

```
SVRMGR> connect internal/oracle
Connected.
SVRMGR> startup nomount pfile=c:\ora804\database\initorcl.ora
ORACLE instance started.
Total System Global Area        8137388 bytes
Fixed Size                        47788 bytes
Variable Size                   7606272 bytes
Database Buffers                 409600 bytes
Redo Buffers                      73728 bytes
```

Step 5 Rename all the datafiles and log files.

In this step, we have to update the control file with the new locations for the datafiles and the online redo log files (or log groups). The ALTER DATABASE RENAME command can be used to accomplish this, as shown below:

```
SVRMGR> alter database rename file 'c:\ora734\database\sys1orcl.ora' to
2> 'c:\ora804\database\sys1orcl.ora';
Statement processed.
SVRMGR> alter database rename file 'c:\ora734\database\usr1orcl.ora' to
    2> 'c:\ora804\database\usr1orcl.ora';
Statement processed.
```

```
SVRMGR> alter database rename file 'c:\ora734\database\rbs1orcl.ora' to
    2> 'c:\ora804\database\rbs1orcl.ora';
Statement processed.
SVRMGR> alter database rename file 'c:\ora734\database\tmp1orcl.ora' to
    2> 'c:\ora804\database\tmp1orcl.ora';
Statement processed.
SVRMGR> alter database rename file 'c:\ora734\database\log1orcl.ora' to
    2> 'c:\ora804\database\log1orcl.ora';
Statement processed.
SVRMGR> alter database rename file 'c:\ora734\database\log2orcl.ora' to
    2> 'c:\ora804\database\log2orcl.ora';
Statement processed.
SVRMGR> alter database open;
Statement processed.
```

Step 6   Create a backup after testing.

As always, perform the necessary tests to ensure normal behavior and schedule a backup.

Using Export/Import for Migration

We have detailed the use of Database Migration Assistant and the Migration utility on Windows NT in the previous sections. While these are the preferred methods for migration, the Export/Import utilities can also be used for the migration. You must create a full database export of the Oracle7 database using Data Manager or the Export utility of Oracle7. The export file must then be imported into an Oracle8 database. Ensure that appropriate SQL*Net and Net8 configurations are available to access the Oracle7 and Oracle8 databases. We have listed the steps involved in this method below.

Step 1   Shut down the database and take a full backup.

Shut down the Oracle7 database in the normal mode and create a full backup. Again, ensure that there are no tablespaces or datafiles offline. If you are using a distributed database, ensure that there are no in-doubt transactions.

Step 2   Open the database and create an export file.

Open the Oracle7 database in restricted mode and use the Export utility or Data Manager to perform a full database export:

```
C:\> exp73 userid=system/manager file=c:\temp\ora7.dmp log=c:\temp\exp.log full=y
```

It is not necessary to open the database in restricted mode as the Export utility will create a consistent export file. However, opening the database in restricted mode ensures that no changes are left behind in the Oracle7 database when you migrate to Oracle8.

Step 3   Install Oracle8 software and create a database.

Use Oracle Installer to install Oracle8 software and create a starter database.

Step 4   Precreate required tablespaces and users.

If you want to maintain the same structure as your Oracle7 database, you can skip this step. If you want to change the structure of the database, use the Oracle8 Import utility or Data Manager to list the contents of the export file, as shown below:

```
C:\> imp80 userid=system/manager file=c:\temp\ora7.dmp
full=yes show=yes log=c:\temp\ora7.log
```

View the contents of the export file and precreate the tablespaces and users with new definitions, as required. You can use the CREATE TABLESPACE and the CREATE USER commands or OEM tools to create tablespaces and users.

Step 5   Perform the import.

Use the Import utility or Data Manager to perform the import, as shown below:

```
C:\> imp80 userid=system/manager file=c:\temp\export\ora7.dmp
full=yes ignore=yes log=c:\temp\imp.log
```

View the log file for any errors and ensure that the import was successful.

Create a backup after the necessary testing. Optionally, delete the Oracle7 installation using Oracle Installer.

Migration Using the COPY Command

You can use the COPY command of SQL*Plus to re-create tables in Oracle7 in Oracle8. Use Oracle Installer to install the Oracle8 software and create a database. Ensure that appropriate versions of SQL*Net and Net8 software are installed. Use SQL*Plus to issue the necessary COPY commands to re-create the tables required.

Refer to Chapter 7 of the *SQL*Plus User's Guide and Reference* for details on the COPY command. View the file **c:\orant\doc\sqlplus.804\ a53717\ch7.htm** to access online documentation.

Migration from Other Platforms to Windows NT

Many sites are migrating their Oracle Server from other platforms to Windows NT. You can use the Export/Import utilities to migrate an Oracle7 database from any platform to Windows NT. The SQL*Plus COPY command can also be used with appropriate SQL*Net and Net8 software for connecting to the source and target databases.

Migration to Windows NT Using Export/Import

The process of migrating an Oracle7 database on any platform to Windows NT is almost identical to the process of migrating from Oracle7 to Oracle8 using Export/Import on Windows NT. We will provide the salient steps below:

Step 1   Shut down the database, take a full backup, and create the export file.

Shut down the database in the normal mode and create a full backup. Again, ensure that there are no tablespaces or datafiles offline. If you are using a distributed database, ensure that there are no in-doubt transactions.

Step 2   Copy the export file to the Windows NT machine.

Transfer the export file from the source operating system to Windows NT using utilities like **ftp** across the network. You must transfer the file in binary mode for proper results.

Step 3 Open the database and create an export file.

Open the Oracle7 database in restricted mode and use the Export utility or Data Manager to perform a full database export on the source operating system:

```
C:\> exp73 userid=system/manager file=/ora/data/ora7.dmp log=/tmp/exp.log full=y
```

Step 3 Install Oracle8 software on Windows NT and create a database.

Use Oracle Installer to install Oracle8 software and create a starter database on the Windows NT machine.

Step 4 Precreate required tablespaces and users.

It is likely that the path names of the datafiles for the tablespaces in the export file are different. List the contents of the control file using the Import utility on Windows NT, as shown below:

```
C:\> imp80 userid=system/manager file=c:\temp\ora7.dmp
full=yes show=yes log=c:\temp\ora7.log
```

View the contents of the export file and precreate the tablespaces and users with new definitions, as required.

NOTE
The path names to files on other operating systems are likely to be different since operating systems use different conventions. For example, the UNIX operating system uses '/' whereas Windows NT uses '\'.

A sample of an export file from UNIX is shown below:

```
"CREATE TABLESPACE "TEST" DATAFILE  '/home/test/dbf/test1TEST.dbf' SIZE 1024"
"0     , '/home/test/dbf/testTEST.dbf' SIZE 1048576      DEFAULT STORAGE ("
"INITIAL 10240 NEXT 10240 MINEXTENTS 1 MAXEXTENTS 121 PCTINCREASE 50) ONLINE"
" PERMANENT"
"CREATE TABLESPACE "RBS" DATAFILE  '/home/test/dbf/rbsdata.dbf' SIZE 1048576"
"0     , '/home/test/dbf/rbsTEST.dbf' SIZE 8388608      DEFAULT STORAGE ("
"INITIAL 131072 NEXT 131072 MINEXTENTS 2 MAXEXTENTS 121 PCTINCREASE 0) ONLINE"
" PERMANENT"
```

We recommend that you create a SQL script by using text from the export file to precreate the necessary tablespace with your path names.

Step 5   Perform the import.

Use the Import utility or Data Manager to perform the import, as shown below:

```
C:\> imp80 userid=system/manager file=c:\temp\export\ora7.dmp
full=yes ignore=yes log=c:\temp\imp.log
```

View the log file for any errors and ensure that the import was successful. As always, perform the necessary tests and create a backup.

Similarly, to migrate an Oracle database from Novell Netware to Windows NT, use the Export NLM (network loadable module) on Netware to create an export file, copy it to Windows NT, and then import it into the Windows NT database.

Migrating a Database Without Change in Version

The term *migration* is also used when speaking about migrating a database from one operating system to another (a porting change) without any change in the database version. If you have Net8 configured on the source and target machines, you can use Import and Export on either the source or the target machine to complete the migration. We have provided an example below.

Example: Migrate an Oracle8 version 8.0.3 database from Novell Netware to Windows NT on Oracle8 version 8.0.3.

We will assume that Net8 is configured on both the Novell Netware as well as the Windows NT box.

Solution 1:   Use Export and Import NLMs on the Netware machine:

1. Load Export NLM on the Netware console and take a full database export.

2. Create a starter database on Windows NT.

3. Use the *SHOW=YES* option to get a dump of the export file. Create a SQL script from the dump to precreate the tablespaces and users on

the Windows NT database. This is to avoid problems with naming convention for the datafiles.

4. Load Import NLM on the Netware console; then import the export file that was created in step 1 into the Windows NT database that was created in step 2. Use Net8 to connect to the remote Windows NT machine.

Solution 2:   Use the Export and Import utilities (or Data Manager) on Windows NT:

1. Use the Export utility on Windows NT to take a full database export of the database on the Netware box.

2. Create a starter database on Windows NT.

3. Use the *SHOW=YES* option to get a dump of the export file. Create a SQL script from the dump to precreate the tablespaces and users on the Windows NT database. This is to avoid problems with naming convention for the datafiles.

4. Use the Import utility on Windows NT to import the export file that was created in step 1 into the Windows NT database that was created in step 2.

Migrating from Other Platforms Using COPY

The SQL*Plus COPY command uses the SQL layer to copy data from the source table to the destination table and works perfectly across platforms. You must install the necessary SQL*Net and Net8 software and configure service names or aliases that can be used in the COPY command, as shown in the example below:

```
COPY FROM scott/tiger@ora7 TO scott/tiger CREATE emp USING select * from emp;
```

In the above example, *ora7* is a SQL*Net alias to an Oracle7 database on a Sun Solaris machine and we are creating a SCOTT.EMP table in the default Windows NT database named *ORCL*.

Choosing the Best Method for Migration

We have seen that there are several options available to migrate from one version of Oracle to another. It can be difficult to choose the best method. We will provide some guidelines in this section.

1. If you are migrating from Oracle7 version 7.1.3.3 or higher and you have access to Database Migration Assistant (DMA), this is the best method. If you do not have access to DMA, use the Migration utility. DMA and the Migration utility are the quickest methods since they modify the headers of existing datafiles to work with the new version.

2. If you are migrating from a different platform, use the Export/Import utilities.

3. If you need to migrate particular schemas from Oracle7 to Oracle8, also consider using the Export/Import utilities. Create a starter database in Oracle8 and import only the schemas of interest into this starter database.

4. Use the COPY method to migrate small portions of your database. If you have a situation where you have a few tables in Oracle7 that need to be migrated to Oracle8, it is easier to create a new database in Oracle8 and use the COPY command to re-create the tables in Oracle8.

5. If you are planning to run one version of Oracle7 and/or one version of Oracle8 in parallel, install both versions into one Oracle home. However, if you are moving entirely to Oracle8, install Oracle8 in a separate folder. This will allow you to completely clean up the Oracle7 installation.

Migrating from Non-Oracle Databases

The integration of several operating systems and databases can prove to very challenging, and many sites spend several hundreds and thousands of dollars to build and manage heterogeneous systems. In this section, we will provide a glimpse of migration from non-Oracle databases to Oracle8 Server.

Migration from Microsoft Access

Migration from Microsoft Access to Oracle8 is perhaps one of the easiest migrations to accomplish. Use Oracle Migration Assistant for MS Access to perform the migration. We have included a section on the utility as well as an example in Chapter 5. You can migrate several **.mdb** files into a single Oracle8 database.

Migration from DB2

Oracle8 Server provides seamless access to DB2 databases via SQL*Net and database links. DB2 databases can be integrated into a system along with Oracle8 databases. However, if you wish to migrate the data, you can use SQL to re-create any objects from DB2 into an Oracle8 database. Another option is to use SQL or any other utility to dump DB2 data onto flat files and use Data Manager or SQL*Loader to load data in these files into an Oracle database.

Migration from ODBC-Compliant Databases

Open database connectivity (ODBC) technology allows tools to access a variety of databases. If you have installed the appropriate ODBC driver for a database, you can access the data via ODBC. SQL commands can be issued to these databases to copy over data into an Oracle database using statements such as CREATE TABLE..SELECT AS. Almost every database vendor provides a method to dump data to files. Data Manager or SQL*Loader can be used to load data from these files into an Oracle8 database.

Oracle8 Enterprise Edition on Windows NT has a product named Oracle Objects for OLE. You can write applications using Visual Basic and C/C++ to extract data from non-Oracle databases. Object linking and embedding (OLE) can be convenient in situations where the target database supports OLE. Visual FoxPro and Microsoft Excel are good examples of such products.

Third-Party Tools

Many third-party tools are available to migrate non-Oracle data into an Oracle database. We recommend that you search the Internet for tools that will work in your situation. We found two sites that discuss data migration tools. You can visit *http://www.adbtech.com* and investigate a tool named Data Mapper or *http://www.scribesoft.com* for a tool named KitchenSync.

Refer to the file **c:\orant\doc\database.804\a55928\ch7.htm** in your online documentation for more information on migration.

CHAPTER
9

Windows NT for UNIX and Novell Netware Users

e have covered all major aspects of database administration on Windows NT in the previous chapters. As the popularity of Windows NT grows, some sites are considering migration from other platforms to Windows NT. Some sites have already migrated from platforms such as UNIX and Novell Netware, or have decided to make future investments in Windows NT. This chapter is dedicated to Oracle DBAs experienced with UNIX and Novell Netware. The goal is to get Oracle DBAs on these platforms jump-started on Windows NT. We have included quick references to commands for GUI as well as CLI in a tabular format. These tables are designed to provide instant information that will allow experienced DBAs to perform familiar tasks on Windows NT with minimal effort. UNIX and Netware-savvy DBAs can benefit by keeping these tables handy. We would like to point out one detail before we begin; like other operating systems, there are many methods to perform tasks on Windows NT. The methods that we list in this chapter are *our* preferred methods to perform a task. These methods should be viewed as a starting point from which you can develop your own list of preferred methods.

We have also provided references to useful links in Oracle documentation for Windows NT–specific information. These links have been tested on our installation of *Oracle8 Server Enterprise Edition* version 8.0.4.

Directory Structure for Oracle8

Windows NT uses the term *folder* for directories. The default installation of Oracle8 on Windows NT installs all Oracle software (server, tools, networking, and applications) in the **\orant** folder. Use Windows NT Explorer or the **tree** command to view the structure. To obtain a listing of the **\orant** folder and redirect the output to a file, use the command shown below:

```
C:\> tree c:\orant > orant.lis
```

Table 9-1 lists some key folders used by Oracle8 on Windows NT. We have used **c:\orant** as our base folder (ORACLE_HOME).

Folder Name	Contents
c:\orant\bin	Executables for Oracle software as files with extensions of **.exe** or **.dll** Tip: Include this folder in the PATH.
c:\orant\core40	Server message files
c:\orant\dbs	Message files for toolkit and some SQL Plus–related SQL scripts
c:\orant\doc	HTML-based online documentation. Start with **index.htm**
c:\orant\database	Datafiles, log files, control files, and the parameter file by default
c:\orant\database\archive	Archived log destination
c:\orant\rdbms80\trace	Trace files for background process and **alert.log** file
c:\orant\rdbms80\admin	SQL scripts to create the database catalog, system packages, and other sample scripts
c:\orant\net80	Net8 product folder
c:\orant\net80\admin	Net8 configuration files
c:\orant\sysman\ifiles	Default location for parameter files (OEM)
c:\ornat\sysman\scripts	Subfolders for SQL and TCL scripts (OEM)

TABLE 9-1.   *Key Oracle Folders on Windows NT*

Depending on the product(s) installed, you will see a variety of product folders in addition to those mentioned above. For information on Oracle folders, point your browser to the **c:\orant\doc\database.804\ a55928\apa.htm** file on your installation. Table 9-2 provides a listing of some key Oracle files on Windows NT.

Name of File	Description
c:\orant\database\initorcl.ora	Parameter file for starter (seed) database named *ORCL* on Windows NT. Tip: The naming convention used for parameter files on Windows NT is **init<sid>.ora**. The folder **c:\orant\database** is used as a default location.
setup.exe	Executable to launch the installation for any Oracle product from CD-ROM media. This file is located in the *root* directory on the media.
c:\orant\bin\orainst.exe	Executable to launch Oracle Installer from the hard disk. Tip: Click Start | Programs | Oracle for Windows NT | Oracle Installer to launch the installer.
c:\orant\orainst\nt.rgs	Product registration file; view this file to get a listing of Oracle products installed on Window NT machines.
c:\orant\rdbms80\trace\ orclALRT.LOG	**alert.log** for default database named *ORCL*. The naming convention for **alert.log** on Windows NT is **<sid>alrt.log**.
c:\orant\doc\index.htm	Start page for non-Java Oracle documentation.
c:\orant\doc\welcome.htm	Start page for Java based Oracle documentation.

TABLE 9-2. *Key Files on Oracle8 for Windows NT*

Environment Variables

On Windows NT, environment variables such as PATH are set using the System applet under the Control Panel. Click Start | Settings | Control Panel and start the System applet. Choose the Environment tab to set variables like PATH, TEMP, and CLASSPATH.

CAUTION

An environment variable set at the command prompt is not available system-wide and only applies to that particular window.

To view current settings, click Start | Programs | Administrative Tools (Common) | Windows NT Diagnostics and click on the Environment tab. You could also use the **echo** command to view the setting for a variable, as shown in the example below:

```
C:\> echo %PATH%
C:\orant\bin;C:\WINNT\system32;C:\WINNT;C:\ORANT\ows\3.0\bin;C:\ORAWIN\BIN;
```

Oracle products use Windows NT registry extensively. Launch Registry Editor by executing **regedit.exe** and select *HKEY_LOCAL_MACHINE->SOFTWARE->ORACLE* to view entries for Oracle products. Variables required by development tools such as Designer 2000 and Developer 2000 are set here.

View the file **c:\orant\doc\database.804\a55928\apc.htm** for more information on this subject.

ORACLE_HOME and ORACLE_SID

These variables are set in Windows NT registry. Use **regedit.exe** to edit the registry. Select *HKEY_LOCAL_MACHINE->SOFTWARE->ORACLE* to view ORACLE_HOME and ORACLE_SID.

The default setting for ORACLE_HOME is the folder **c:\orant** and the default SID is *ORCL*. You can click Start | Programs | Oracle For Windows

NT | Oracle Home Selector to select a particular ORACLE_HOME.
Alternatively, execute **c:\orant\bin\ohsel.exe**. This command only works if
you have multiple Oracle homes.

INIT.ORA Parameters

The *Oracle8 Reference* provides complete details on INIT.ORA parameters
for Oracle databases. View the file
c:\orant\doc\database.804\a55928\apb.htm for Windows NT–specific
details on INIT.ORA parameters.

Oracle Background Processes

Oracle on Windows NT uses similar background processes to those used on
UNIX. However, Oracle is implemented as a combination of services. To
view Oracle services, you can use NT Task Manager. Select the Processes
tab to view **oracle80.exe**. You can also verify if all the background
processes were started successfully by using Event Viewer. Start Event
Viewer and select Log | Application to view application events. A record of
Oracle background processes will be available in the application log. Here
is a sample application log entry for the PMON process:

```
Initializing PGA for process PMON in instance orcl.
```

Error Messages

The Oracle documentation includes generic Oracle error messages. View
the file **c:\orant\doc\database.804\a55928\apd.htm** for information on
Windows NT–specific messages. This file also provides examples of
redirecting error messages to a file using Windows NT operators.
Operating-system-related errors have the format *OSD-xxxxx*. Error messages
in the range ORA 9200–ORA 9500 are also operating system errors.

Freeing Memory

Occasionally, Oracle is unable to free memory back to the Operating
system. This is similar to a situation where shared memory or semaphores

cannot be freed on UNIX. In such situations, DBAs use the **ipcrm** command to free shared memory and semaphores. If you want to unload memory used by Oracle on Windows NT, use Task Manager to kill **oracle80.exe** or shut down the *OracleServiceORCL* service.

Administering Domains and Users

Windows NT Server provides GUI tools to administer domains and domain users. Primary and secondary domain servers can be established. Domain administrators can perform system administration tasks across the network. There is also a command named **net** (also available on Windows NT Workstation) that allows you to manage domains, users, and resources on the network. Type **net /?** for usage information, as shown below:

```
C:\> net /?
The syntax of this command is:
NET [ ACCOUNTS | COMPUTER | CONFIG | CONTINUE | FILE | GROUP | HELP |
     HELPMSG | LOCALGROUP | NAME | PAUSE | PRINT | SEND | SESSION |
     SHARE | START | STATISTICS | STOP | TIME | USE | USER | VIEW ]
```

To get help on a particular command, type **net help <command>**. To get help on the *Send* option, use the following:

```
C:\> net help send
The syntax of this command is:
NET SEND {name | * | /DOMAIN[:name] | /USERS} message
Sends messages to other users, computers, or messaging names
on the network. The Messenger service must be running to receive messages.
You can send a message only to an name that is active on the network.
If the message is sent to a username, that user must be logged on
and running the Messenger service to receive the message.
You can send a message only to an name that is active on the network.
If the message is sent to a username, that user must be logged on
and running the Messenger service to receive the message.
name                    Is the username, computername, or messaging name
                        to send the message to. If the name is a
                        computername that contains blank characters,
                        enclose the alias in quotation marks (" ").
*                       Sends the message to all the names in your group.
/DOMAIN[:name]          Sends the message to all the names in the
                        workstation domain. If name is specified, the
                        message is sent to all the names in the specified
```

```
                          domain or workgroup.
/USERS                    Sends the message to all users connected to
                          the server.
message                   Is text to be sent as a message.
NET HELP command | MORE displays Help one screen at a time.
```

Database Startup and Shutdown

The easiest method to shut down a database is to stop the Oracle services *OracleServiceORCL* and *OracleStartORCL*. To shut down all instances on a Windows NT machine, it is sufficient to shut down *OracleServiceORCL*. The services for other instances will be shut down after providing a warning to the user.

The preferred GUI method is to use Instance Manager. Chapter 5 provides information on Instance Manager.

In character mode, use Server Manager to issue commands for database shutdown and startup. Start Server Manager by executing **c:\orant\bin\svrmgr30.exe**. Refer to Chapter 6 for more information on this subject.

Managing Net8 and Web Listeners

The Listener Control Utility and Names Control Utility for Net8 management are also available on Windows NT. They can be accessed by executing **lsnrctl80.exe** and **namesctl80.exe**, respectively.

An easier way to manage the Net8 Listener and the Names Servers is to use the Services applet to manage the services *OracleTNSListener80* and *OracleNamesService80*.

Similarly, the Web Application Server listeners can also be controlled uses the Services applet or the **owsctl** utility.

Resource Requirements

The CD-ROM insert provided with the media will list specific resource requirements for the product. We have also included information on sizing and choosing hardware in Chapter 1. However, you can use the following information as a guideline for minimum requirements:

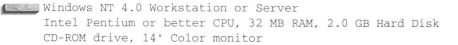
```
Windows NT 4.0 Workstation or Server
Intel Pentium or better CPU, 32 MB RAM, 2.0 GB Hard Disk
CD-ROM drive, 14" Color monitor
```

Performing Tasks: Windows NT vs. UNIX

The UNIX operating system is rich in features and provides several commands and utilities that cover almost all the needs for users. One of the many attractions to UNIX for diehard fans is that everything in UNIX is based on a *file*. While Windows NT has a large set of commands and utilities, it does not have all the UNIX commands. Windows NT also stresses providing a GUI to its commands and utilities. In Table 9-3, we will present a set of Windows NT commands and utilities and their UNIX counterparts. The table is ordered alphabetically on the UNIX commands. We remind you that the NT equivalents are close matches and do not provide the exact functionality as their UNIX counterparts.

Table 9-4 lists common system maintenance utilities on Windows NT along with their UNIX equivalents.

UNIX Command/Utility	Windows NT GUI[1]	Windows NT CLI[2]
adb	N/A[3]	N/A[3]
ar	N/A[3]	N/A[3]
at	N/A	at
atq	N/A	at
bc	Calculator	calc
cat	N/A	type
cc	N/A[1]	N/A[1]
cd	Navigator in NT Explorer	cd

TABLE 9-3.   *UNIX Command Equivalents in Windows NT*

UNIX Command/Utility	Windows NT GUI[1]	Windows NT CLI[2]
chgrp	User 77Manager	N/A
chmod	Set file properties using NT Explorer	attrib
chpass	User Manager	N/A
clear	N/A	cls
cmp	N/A	comp
compress	Select volume in My Computer or Explorer and set file properties	compact[4]
cp	Edit menu in NT Explorer	copy
csh[5]	Command prompt	cmd or command
date	NT Taskbar	date /t or date
dc	Calculator	calc
df	1. Select disk in My Computer or Explorer and set file properties. 2. Select volume in Explorer and look up status bar	dir (see the last line of output)
diff	N/A	comp or fc
du	File properties in Explorer	dir /s
echo	N/A	echo
ed	N/A	edlin
emacs	Notepad or Wordpad	notepad, write, or edit
find	Find	find
finger	N/A	finger
ftp	N/A	ftp

TABLE 9-3. *UNIX Command Equivalents in Windows NT* (continued)

UNIX Command/Utility	Windows NT GUI[1]	Windows NT CLI[2]
gdb	N/A[3]	N/A[3]
grep	Use Advanced option in Find	findstr
groups	User Manager	N/A
gzip	N/A	compact
hostname	Network applet under Control Panel	Not supported
install	Add/remove programs in Control Panel	setup
kill	Server applet under Control Panel	net session
locate	Find	find
lock	CTRL-ALT-DEL and select Lock Workstation	N/A
lpq	Click Start	Settings	Printer	lpq
lpr	N/A	lpr
ls	Use NT Explorer	dir
man	Click Start	Help	help
mkdir	Use NT Explorer	mkdir or md
more	N/A	more
mv	Use NT Explorer	move or rename
netstat	N/A	netstat
passwd	User Manager	net user
ping	N/A	ping
popd	N/A	popd
pushd	N/A	pushd

TABLE 9-3. *UNIX Command Equivalents in Windows NT* (continued)

UNIX Command/Utility	Windows NT GUI[1]	Windows NT CLI[2]
ps	Task Manager	N/A
pwd	Title bar in NT Explorer	cd
rm	NT Explorer	del or erase
rm –r	NT Explorer	del /s
rmdir	NT Explorer	rmdir or rd
sh[5]	Command prompt	cmd or command
sort	N/A	sort
telnet	N/A	telnet
time	Taskbar	time /t or time
users	Server applet under Control Panel	N/A
vi	Notepad or Wordpad	notepad, write, or edit

[1]Click on Start | Programs to access necessary program groups.
[2]Click on Start | Run or execute from command prompt.
[3]Install a development tool or programming environment to get these tools. The **debug** command is to debug MS-DOS programs only.
[4]For NTFS only.
[5]Windows NT does not have shells, but has a command interpreter. However, third-party shells are available and can be loaded with the **shell** command.

TABLE 9-3.   *UNIX Command Equivalents in Windows NT* (continued)

Additional Windows NT Commands and Utilities

While Windows NT supports GUI, it has some features and commands that are geared for CLI. Some of these commands are specific to the PC domain

Maintenance Task/Command/ Operation	Windows NT GUI	Windows NT CLI
intro	Help	**help**
adduser	User Manager	**net user**
arp	N/A	**arp**
cron	N/A	**at**
disklabel	File properties in NT Explorer	**label**
dump	Windows NT Backup	**backup**
format	Disk Administrator	**format**
fsck	Built-in tool in NT Explorer	**chkdsk**
ifconfig	Network applet under Control Panel	**ipconfig**
iostat	Performance Monitor	N/A
mount_nfs	Set sharing property in NT Explorer	**net share**
shutdown	Click Start	Shutdown	
traceroute	N/A	**tracert**
vmstat	Performance Monitor	N/A

TABLE 9-4. *UNIX System Commands in Windows NT*

and are not available in other operating systems. In Table 9-5, we list some useful commands and utilities on Windows NT.

Oracle8 on Windows NT for Novell Netware Users

Like UNIX based sites, some Novell Netware sites have made a move to migrate to Windows NT. This section is designed for experienced Oracle DBAs on Novell Netware 4.x and 5.x who have added responsibilities of

Task	Command	Usage/Example
append	Enables programs to open datafiles in appended directories as if these files were in the current directory	**Append c:\orant\sysman\scripts** will ensure that the files in **c:\orant\sysman\scripts** appear to be available in the current directory.
assoc	Associate a file extension with a file type	**assoc .ora=txtfile** will ensure that you can open a file with a **.ora** extension by using the START command. Example: **start initorcl.ora** will open the file in a text editor.
call	Call one batch file from another without stopping the calling batch file	**call** <batch filename>
cls	Clear screen	**cls**
color	Sets color attributes for foreground and background for the console window	**color 02** gives a green color; every color is represented by a two-digit number.
convert	Convert FAT to NTFS; use Disk Administrator instead	**convert c: /FS:NTFS**
diskcomp	Compare contents of two floppy disks	**diskcomp a: b:**
diskcopy	Copy contents of one floppy to another	**diskcopy a: a:** copies from one floppy to another on the same drive. Follow instructions on the screen.

TABLE 9-5. *Useful Windows NT Commands*

Task	Command	Usage/Example
mem	Programs in MS-DOS subsystem	**mem/c**
replace	Replaces files in the destination directory with files in the source directory that have the same name	**replace c:\temp\test* c:** replaces all files named **test*** in **c:** from **c:\temp**.
subst	Associate a path with a logical drive letter	**subst f: c:\temp** Now you can refer to **c:\temp** as **f:**.
title	Sets title for command window	**title Oracle Console**
vol	Disk label and serial number	**vol c:** Volume in drive C is DRIVE_C. Volume Serial Number is 3127-16CF.
xcopy	Copies files and folders including subfolders	**xcopy c:\my_data*.* /s**

TABLE 9-5. *Useful Windows NT Commands* (continued)

administering Oracle8 Server on Windows NT. We have seen the directory structure for Oracle8 on Windows NT, common system and database administration tasks, and some key commands earlier in this chapter. We will now provide a quick comparison between Oracle8 Server on Novell Netware and Windows NT.

NOTE

At the time this book went into publication, Oracle8 Server version 8.0.3 was shipping on Netware while Oracle8 Server version 8.0.4 was shipping on Windows NT. This is the reason the Oracle home on Netware is named **oranw803***.*

Oracle DBA Tools on Windows NT

Unlike Novell Netware, all DBA tasks ranging from installation to tuning can be performed on the Windows NT console. It is not necessary to perform some tasks from the server console and others from a DOS based client like Netware. While CLI methods are also available to perform all tasks, Oracle8 on Windows NT takes advantage of the simple GUI provided by the operating system. All management tools are available in GUI form with wizards. Oracle Enterprise Manager (OEM) can be used to perform almost all administrative tasks. The OEM performance pack allows DBAs to also view performance metrics graphically.

Specifically, Oracle8 Server on Novell Netware includes network loadable modules (NLMs) for Server Manager, Export, Import, SQL*Loader, Recovery Manager, Oracle Password utility, Net8 Easy Configuration utility, and SQL*Plus. All other tools and utilities have to be used on a client (Windows 3.1, Windows 95, or Windows NT). Oracle8 Server on Windows NT includes all tools. A client is not required for any administration as all tasks can be performed on the Windows NT console.

Key Comparisons in Oracle8 on Netware and Windows NT

Oracle8 Server on Windows NT is designed very similar to Novell Netware; however, there are also some key differences. Table 9-6 provides a quick comparison for the benefit of Novell administrators.

Description	On Novell Netware	On Windows NT
Default Oracle home	**oranw803**	**orant**
Name of starter database	oracle	oracle
SID of starter database	*ORCL*	*ORCL*
Loading Oracle Software	**:oraload**	Loaded on demand when service is started

TABLE 9-6. *Comparison Between Novell Netware and Windows NT Administration*

Description	On Novell Netware	On Windows NT
Unloading Oracle Software	**:oraunld**	Controlled by Windows NT based on virtual memory requirements
Starting up an Oracle8 database	**:orastart**	Service applet under Control Panel **oradim80.exe strtorcl.cmd**
Shutting down an Oracle8 database	**:orashut** or **stopdb.sql**	Service applet under Control Panel **oradim80.exe orashut.bat**
Starting up a database automatically with the system startup	Add **orastart** to **autoexec.ncf** file	Set Oracle service for automatic start up using Services applet or **oradim80.exe**
Starting Server Manager	**:load svrmgr30**	Execute **svrmgr30.exe**
Parameter file for the starter database	**oranw803\ database\ initorcl.ora**	**\orant\database\initorcl.ora**
Control file for the starter database	**oranw803\ database\ ctl1orcl.ora**	**\orant\database\ctl1orcl.ora**
Data files for starter database	**sys1orcl.ora**, **usr1orcl.ora**, **rbs1orcl.ora**, **tmp1orcl.ora**	same
Number of log groups for the starter database	2	4

TABLE 9-6.   *Comparison Between Novell Netware and Windows NT Administration* (continued)

Description	On Novell Netware	On Windows NT
Log members for the starter database	**log1orcl.ora** and **log2orcl.ora**	**log1orcl.ora**, **log2orcl.ora**, **log3orcl.ora**, and **log4orcl.ora**
Users in the starter database	*sys, system, scott, demo, ctxsys,* and *dbsnmp*	*sys, system, scott, demo, ordsys, mdsys,* and *dbsnmp*
Tablespaces in the starter database	SYSTEM, USER_DATA, TEMPORARY_DATA, and ROLLBACK_DATA	Same
Listener control utility	**:load lsnctl80**	Execute **lsnrctl80.exe**
Oracle Names control utility	**:load namctl80**	Execute **namesctl80.exe**
Loading the Net8 listener	**:load tnslsnr**	Automatically loaded when listener is started
Starting listener	1. **:load tnslsn80** <lsnr> 2. LSNRCTL> **start**	1. Use Services Applet 2. LSNRCTL>**start**
Starting intelligent agent	LSNRCTL>**db msnmp_start**	1. Use Services Applet to start *OracleAgent80* 2. LSNRCTL>**dbmsnmp_start**

TABLE 9-6.   *Comparison Between Novell Netware and Windows NT Administration* (continued)

Description	On Novell Netware	On Windows NT
Stopping intelligent agent	LSNRCTL>**db msnmp_stop**	1. LSNRCTL>**dbmsnmp_stop** 2. Use Services Applet to stop *OracleAgent80*
Location of trace files	**oranw803\ rdbms80\ trace**	**\orant\rdbms80\trace**
Alert log file	**oranw803\ rdbms80\ orclalrt.log**	**\orant\rdbms80\trace\ orclalrt.log**
Invoking the Oracle Installer	**:load install** (version 4) **:nwconfig** (version 5)	1. Execute **setup.exe** or **orainst.exe** from media 2. Click Start | Programs | Oracle for Windows NT | Oracle Installer
Net8 easy configuration utility	**:easycfg**	1. Click Start | Programs | Oracle for Windows NT | Oracle Net8 Easy Config 2. Execute **n8sw.exe**
Net8 configuration file	**oranw803\ net80\ admin**	**\orant\net80\admin**
Configuration file specifying language, territory, character set, Oracle home, etc.	**config.ora** file	Windows NT registry; use **regedit.exe** to view and modify. There is no **config.ora** on Windows NT

TABLE 9-6.   *Comparison Between Novell Netware and Windows NT Administration* (continued)

Description	On Novell Netware	On Windows NT
Using operating system to map users, groups, and organizational units to Oracle users and groups	Novell Directory Services (NDS) along with INIT.ORA parameters like OS_ROLES, REMOTE_OS_ AUTHENT, and OS_AUTHENT _PREFIX	Windows NT users and groups defined using User Manager along with INIT.ORA parameters OS_ROLES, REMOTE_OS_AUTHENT, and OS_AUTHENT_PREFIX
Exporting data	1. **:load export** for CLI 2. **:load nwexport** for menu driven interface	1. Execute **exp80.exe** for CLI 2. Use Data Manager for GUI
Importing data	1. **:load imp80** for CLI 2. **:load nwimp80** for menu driven interface	1. Execute **imp80.exe** for CLI 2. Use Data Manager for GUI

TABLE 9-6. *Comparison Between Novell Netware and Windows NT Administration* (continued)

APPENDIX

A

Frequently Asked Questions

e round off this book by presenting answers to some frequently asked questions (FAQs) to Oracle Corporation's support staff. The FAQ is presented in a question-answer format for easy reading.

Q. How much memory and hard disk space do I need to run Oracle8 Server on Windows NT?

A. Oracle8 Server needs a minimum of 48Mb of RAM and 200Mb of hard disk space. Other add-ons, including cartridges, Partitioning option, and Objects option, require more resources. Refer to the insert provided with the CD-ROM media for complete information on resource requirements.

Q. Can I use Windows NT 4.0 Workstation to run an Oracle8 Server, or do I need Windows NT 4.0 Server?

A. Oracle8 Server runs on both Windows NT 4.0 Workstation and Server. The only exception is the Oracle Parallel Server option, which requires the NT 4.0 Server.

Q. Can I use FAT file system with Oracle8 Server?

A. Yes, you can use FAT file system with Oracle8 Server.

Q. Can I use my Oracle 16-bit MS-Windows 3.1 applications on Windows NT?

A. Yes, 16-bit applications can be used against Oracle8 Server. Refer to Chapter 7 for compatibility information.

Q. Can I use SQL*Net 2.x to connect to Oracle8 Server?

A. Yes, you can use SQL*Net 2.x on the client and the server to connect to Oracle8 Server with Oracle7 applications. Oracle8 applications will need Net8 on the client and the server to connect to Oracle8. For example, Developer/2000 version 1.x applications can connect to Oracle8 Server using SQL*Net 2.3.

Q. Can I use Oracle7 applications against Oracle8?

A. Yes, you can. However, you must use SQL*Net to connect to Oracle8. In addition, only the Oracle7 features will be available to you. In other words, the Oracle8 Server will behave like an Oracle7 Server in this situation.

Q. I have just received media for Oracle8 Server and there is no documentation. Where do I begin?

A. Begin with the instructions in the insert included with the CD-ROM media. Sufficient instructions for installation are available in this insert. Also refer to the *Getting Started* documentation provided with the product.

Q. What is the difference between **setup.exe** and **orainst.exe** on the product media? Which one do I use for my installation?

A. You can use either of these executables to invoke the installer. They both launch Oracle Installer.

Q. Can I install Oracle8 Server on Windows NT 3.51?

A. No, Oracle8 Server requires Windows NT 4.0.

Q. Does Windows NT support multiple Oracle8 databases on one machine?

A. Yes, you can create as many databases as your resources will permit on Windows NT. Each database must have a unique name (SID).

Q. Is the Advanced Replication option available on Windows NT?

A. Yes, Oracle8 Server on Windows NT supports Advanced Replication.

Q. What network protocols must I install to use client/server applications on Windows NT?

A. Oracle8 Server supports TCP/IP, IPX/SPX, Named Pipes, and LU6.2 protocols. You can use any of these in your environment to run client/server applications against Oracle8 Server.

Q. Do I need to create a Net8 listener for every database on Windows NT?

A. No, one Net8 listener can support multiple Oracle8 database services.

Q. Can I configure multiple Net8 listeners on Windows NT?

A. Yes, you can configure multiple Net8 listeners on Windows NT. You must ensure that there are no conflicts in the configuration. For example, the name of the listener and the TCP port information must be unique for each listener.

Q. Does Oracle8 Server require a file system or can I use raw partitions?

A. Oracle8 Server on Windows NT can use raw partitions. The Oracle Parallel Server option requires raw partitions.

Q. I am confused. Should I use NT Backup Manager or Oracle Recovery Manager for my backups?

A. If you have a large and mission-critical database, or you have multiple databases on your site, you should use Oracle Recovery Manager (RMAN) along with a recovery catalog. If you have a small database (like Personal Oracle8), you should use NT Backup Manager and NT Recovery Manager, as they are easy to use.

Q. I schedule a weekly backup of our Windows NT Server. Is this not a sufficient Oracle database backup?

A. That depends on your requirements. If a weekly backup of your database is sufficient for your needs, then you should include the database in the weekly backup of your machine. However, you must ensure that the database is shut down before the backup to ensure consistency and integrity.

Q. Where are the environment settings for Oracle8 Server on Windows NT? How do I modify them?

A. All the settings besides the path are made in the Windows NT registry. Use **regedit.exe** to invoke Registry Editor. Select the key *HKEY_LOCAL_ MACHINE->SOFTWARE->ORACLE* to view/modify the settings for Oracle8 Server. Refer to the file **c:\orant\doc\database.804\a55928\apc.htm** for online documentation on this topic.

Q. I was told that Developer 2000 is not supported on Windows NT 4.0. Is this true?

A. You can run Developer 2000 version 1.3.2 or higher on Windows NT 4.0.

Q. I have been using Oracle Workgroup Server. Has Oracle Corporation stopped making this product? I do not see version 8.0 of Oracle Workgroup Server in the list of products. How come?

A. Oracle Workgroup Server has been renamed in Oracle8. Use the Oracle8 Server (Standard Edition) or Oracle8 Server Enterprise Edition for Windows NT.

Q. I forgot the password that I provided for the Oracle8 database during installation. I cannot start up the database now. Do I have to reinstall the product?

A. No, you can use **oradim80.exe** to reset the password for the user *internal*. Refer to Chapter 5 for more information on this procedure.

Q.   Does Oracle8 Server support extended filenames or am I restricted to the 8.3 filenaming convention?

A.   You can use extended filenames with Oracle8 Server on Windows NT.

Q.   Previous versions of Oracle Server required that all products be installed in one Oracle home. Is this still a restriction?

A.   No, Oracle8 allows you to install Oracle products in multiple directory structures or Oracle homes. Use Oracle Home Selector in the Oracle for Windows NT program group to switch between Oracle homes.

Q.   Is external authentication supported on Windows NT?

A.   Yes, you can use external authentication on Windows NT. Refer to Chapter 5 for more information on this topic.

Q.   What are the Oracle8 limits on Windows NT?

A.   Point your browser to the file **C:\orant\doc\database.804\ a55928\apb.htm** for the Windows NT–specific limits.

Q.   Where are Windows NT–specific errors documented? I do not see anything in my documentation on these errors.

A.   Windows NT–specific errors are in the range OSD 4000–OSD 4999. They are documented in the *Oracle8 Getting Started* manual. Refer to the file **C:\orant\doc\database.804\a55928\apd.htm** for online documentation of these errors.

Q.   I heard that the SERIALIZABLE parameter is no longer valid in Oracle8. Is this true?

A.   Yes, this parameter is obsolete in Oracle8. The default behavior of Oracle8 is similar to that when the SERIALIZABLE parameter is set to FALSE. Use the SET TRANSACTION ISOLATION LEVEL SERIALIZABLE command if you want to change the behavior.

Q.   Is the Parallel Server option available on Windows NT?

A.   Yes, but you must acquire and license Oracle Parallel Server separately from Oracle Corporation on Windows NT.

Q.   I hear that Oracle8 for Windows NT provided a variety of GUI tools for performance tuning. I do not see them on my installation. How do I install these?

A.   You must license Oracle Enterprise Manager Performance Pack from Oracle Corporation separately to get these tools. Refer to Chapter 7 for more details.

Q.   I have always used the Export and Import utilities for upgrades. Is this method desupported on Oracle8?

A.   No, Export and Import can still be used for upgrades. However, this is a slow method of migration. Database Migration Assistant or the Migration utility **mig80.exe** are recommended methods for migration to Oracle8. Refer to Chapter 8 for information on migration.

Q.   Can SQL*Net and Net8 coexist on Windows NT?

A.   Yes, they can. You must ensure that there are no conflicts in the configuration. For example, you must configure SQL*Net and Ne8 listeners on different ports for TCP/IP-based networks.

Q.   Can Oracle7 and Oracle8 coexist on Windows NT?

A.   Yes, they can. You can install Oracle8 in the same directory as Oracle7 or in a separate directory. There are no issues since the filenames for Oracle7 and Oracle8 are different.

Q.   Can I install multiple versions of Oracle8 in the same directory?

A.   No, you cannot. You must install Oracle8 versions in separate directories (or Oracle homes). Use Oracle Home Selector to select an Oracle home.

Q.   I think there is room for improvement in Oracle documentation. Where do I send my suggestions and comments?

A.   Oracle Corporation is striving to improve its documentation set. Your suggestions and comments will be welcomed. Use the online survey to send your comments and suggestions. Point your browser to the file **c:\orant\ doc\survey.htm** in the online documentation.

Index

Get Your **FREE** Subscription to Oracle Magazine

Stay informed and increase your productivity with every issue of *Oracle Magazine*. Inside each FREE, bimonthly issue you'll get:

- Up-to-date information on Oracle Data Server, Oracle Applications, Network Computing Architecture, and tools
- Third-party news and announcements
- Technical articles on Oracle products and operating environments
- Software tuning tips
- Oracle customer application stories

Three easy ways to subscribe:

1 MAIL Cut out this page, complete the questionnaire on the back, and mail it to: *Oracle Magazine,* P.O. Box 1263, Skokie, IL 60076-8263.

2 FAX Cut out this page, complete the questionnaire on the back, and fax it to **+ 847.647.9735.**

3 WEB Visit our Web site at **www.oramag.com.** You'll find a subscription form there, plus much more!

If there are other Oracle users at your location who would like to receive their own subscription to *Oracle Magazine,* please photocopy the form and pass it along.

You must answer all eight questions below.

1 What is the primary business activity of your firm at this location?
(circle only one)
- 01 Agriculture, Mining, Natural Resources
- 02 Architecture, Construction
- 03 Communications
- 04 Consulting, Training
- 05 Consumer Packaged Goods
- 06 Data Processing
- 07 Education
- 08 Engineering
- 09 Financial Services
- 10 Government—Federal, Local, State, Other
- 11 Government—Military
- 12 Health Care
- 13 Manufacturing—Aerospace, Defense
- 14 Manufacturing—Computer Hardware
- 15 Manufacturing—Noncomputer Products
- 16 Real Estate, Insurance
- 17 Research & Development
- 18 Human Resources
- 19 Retailing, Wholesaling, Distribution
- 20 Software Development
- 21 Systems Integration, VAR, VAD, OEM
- 22 Transportation
- 23 Utilities (Electric, Gas, Sanitation)
- 24 Other Business and Services _____

2 Which of the following best describes your job function? *(circle only one)*
CORPORATE MANAGEMENT/STAFF
- 01 Executive Management (President, Chair, CEO, CFO, Owner, Partner, Principal)
- 02 Finance/Administrative Management (VP/Director/Manager/Controller, Purchasing, Administration)
- 03 Sales/Marketing Management (VP/Director/Manager)
- 04 Computer Systems/Operations Management (CIO/VP/Director/Manager MIS, Operations)
- 05 Other Finance/Administration Staff
- 06 Other Sales/Marketing Staff

IS/IT Staff
- 07 Systems Development/Programming Management
- 08 Systems Development/Programming Staff
- 09 Consulting
- 10 DBA/Systems Administrator
- 11 Education/Training
- 12 Engineering/R&D/Science Management
- 13 Engineering/R&D/Science Staff
- 14 Technical Support Director/Manager
- 15 Webmaster/Internet Specialist
- 16 Other Technical Management/Staff

3 What is your current primary operating platform? *(circle all that apply)*
- 01 DEC UNIX
- 02 DEC VAX VMS
- 03 Java
- 04 HP UNIX
- 05 IBM AIX
- 06 IBM UNIX
- 07 Macintosh
- 08 MPE-ix
- 09 MS-DOS
- 10 MVS
- 11 NetWare
- 12 Network Computing
- 13 OpenVMS
- 14 SCO UNIX
- 15 Sun Solaris/SunOS
- 16 SVR4
- 17 Ultrix
- 18 UnixWare
- 19 VM
- 20 Windows
- 21 Windows NT
- 22 Other _____
- 23 Other UNIX _____

4 Do you evaluate, specify, recommend, or authorize the purchase of any of the following? *(circle all that apply)*
- 01 Hardware
- 02 Software
- 03 Application Development Tools
- 04 Database Products
- 05 Internet or Intranet Products

5 In your job, do you use or plan to purchase any of the following products or services?
(check all that apply)

SOFTWARE	Use	Plan to buy
01 Business Graphics	☐	☐
02 CAD/CAE/CAM	☐	☐
03 CASE	☐	☐
04 CIM	☐	☐
05 Communications	☐	☐
06 Database Management	☐	☐
07 File Management	☐	☐
08 Finance	☐	☐
09 Java	☐	☐
10 Materials Resource Planning	☐	☐
11 Multimedia Authoring	☐	☐
12 Networking	☐	☐
13 Office Automation	☐	☐
14 Order Entry/Inventory Control	☐	☐
15 Programming	☐	☐
16 Project Management	☐	☐
17 Scientific and Engineering	☐	☐
18 Spreadsheets	☐	☐
19 Systems Management	☐	☐
20 Workflow	☐	☐
HARDWARE		
21 Macintosh	☐	☐
22 Mainframe	☐	☐
23 Massively Parallel Processing	☐	☐
24 Minicomputer	☐	☐
25 PC	☐	☐
26 Network Computer	☐	☐
27 Supercomputer	☐	☐
28 Symmetric Multiprocessing	☐	☐
29 Workstation	☐	☐
PERIPHERALS		
30 Bridges/Routers/Hubs/Gateways	☐	☐
31 CD-ROM Drives	☐	☐
32 Disk Drives/Subsystems	☐	☐
33 Modems	☐	☐
34 Tape Drives/Subsystems	☐	☐
35 Video Boards/Multimedia	☐	☐
SERVICES		
36 Computer-Based Training	☐	☐
37 Consulting	☐	☐
38 Education/Training	☐	☐
39 Maintenance	☐	☐
40 Online Database Services	☐	☐
41 Support	☐	☐
42 **None of the above**	☐	☐

6 What Oracle products are in use at your site? *(circle all that apply)*
SERVER/SOFTWARE
- 01 Oracle8
- 02 Oracle7
- 03 Oracle Application Server
- 04 Oracle Data Mart Suites
- 05 Oracle Internet Commerce Server
- 06 Oracle InterOffice
- 07 Oracle Lite
- 08 Oracle Payment Server
- 09 Oracle Rdb
- 10 Oracle Security Server
- 11 Oracle Video Server
- 12 Oracle Workgroup Server

TOOLS
- 13 Designer/2000
- 14 Developer/2000 (Forms, Reports, Graphics)
- 15 Oracle OLAP Tools
- 16 Oracle Power Object

ORACLE APPLICATIONS
- 17 Oracle Automotive
- 18 Oracle Energy
- 19 Oracle Consumer Packaged Goods
- 20 Oracle Financials
- 21 Oracle Human Resources
- 22 Oracle Manufacturing
- 23 Oracle Projects
- 24 Oracle Sales Force Automation
- 25 Oracle Supply Chain Management
- 26 Other _____
- 27 **None of the above**

7 What other database products are in use at your site? *(circle all that apply)*
- 01 Access
- 02 BAAN
- 03 dbase
- 04 Gupta
- 05 IBM DB2
- 06 Informix
- 07 Ingres
- 08 Microsoft Access
- 09 Microsoft SQL Server
- 10 Peoplesoft
- 11 Progress
- 12 SAP
- 13 Sybase
- 14 VSAM
- 15 None of the above

8 During the next 12 months, how much you anticipate your organization will spend on computer hardware, software, peripherals, and services for your location? *(circle only one)*
- 01 Less than $10,000
- 02 $10,000 to $49,999
- 03 $50,000 to $99,999
- 04 $100,000 to $499,999
- 05 $500,000 to $999,999
- 06 $1,000,000 and over